THE RISE AND FALL OF HORATIO BOTTOMLEY

The Rise and Fall of Horatio Bottomley

The Biography of a Swindler

ALAN HYMAN

CASSELL · LONDON

CASSELL & COMPANY LTD
35 RED LION SQUARE, LONDON WC1R 4SJ
Sydney, Auckland
Toronto, Johannesburg

First published 1972

I.S.B.N. 0 304 29023 8

Printed in Great Britain by
The Camelot Press Ltd, London and Southampton
F.1271

FOR

NOREEN

Contents

PART III. THE LOST OPPORTUNITY

PART IV. THE ROAD TO RUIN

Illustrations

Foreword

I am just old enough to remember the First World War. At that time my Uncle Sydney, who was a variety agent, had a picturesque William IV office in St Martin's Place; my father sometimes brought me to see him there and he used to take us out to lunch in the West End. I fancy it was on a day in 1915, in which case I was five, that as my father and I were being transported to Uncle Sydney's office we came to a full stop because the roads were all blocked round Trafalgar Square. My father explained to me that a wonderful man by the name of Horatio Bottomley was speaking in the Square and that he always attracted crowds like this one. Bottomley seemed to be some kind of superman who cheered up the British public and mesmerized men to go and join the Army.

The next time Bottomley appeared on my horizon was in 1921; his name was in every newspaper because he had been accused by one Bigland of swindling thousands of poor people who had trusted him and bought his Victory Bonds. I was shocked to read this—it seemed completely out of character after his heroic role in the war—and when my father came home from the City I asked him the meaning of it.

'Horatio Bottomley is the biggest crook in England,' he informed me in his forthright way. 'But he's much too clever for Bigland—people have been trying to show him up for years and they got nowhere! We all know about Bottomley in the City, but he's as cunning as a wagonload of monkeys!'

'But what about his wonderful speeches in the war?' I asked.

'That's nothing to do with it—he's always had the gift of

the gab. You mark my words—they'll *never* get him!' declared my father.

However, my father proved to be wrong, and ever since Horatio Bottomley was found guilty at the Old Bailey of defrauding the public with his Victory Bonds I have been curious to know what made him tick.

His extraordinary career might have been invented by a Hollywood script-writer. Educated at a Victorian orphanage, he rose to become the best lay lawyer in the land and the most widely read journalist in Britain. He edited *John Bull* and made the paper a household name; he was a prominent M.P. who had 'the ideal House of Commons manner'; he was so popular during the First World War that Lloyd George was the only man who could match his appeal to the masses. Few men of humble origins have attained such heights in this century, but once he fell the public lost confidence in him and his spell was broken. When Bottomley came out of prison he was old, tired and ill and his life ended in abject failure.

I was surprised to find there were comparatively few books about him. The most valuable for source material was *The Real Horatio Bottomley*, by Henry Houston, who had been his political secretary. Houston based his book on a series of newspaper articles and had it 'ghosted' for him by a journalist; he made little attempt to tell a coherent story. However, he did a great deal of research on Bottomley's life, in the course of which he claimed to have travelled two thousand miles up and down Britain. The only serious biography of Bottomley, written by Julian Symons, was most perceptive and well worth reading, yet one felt instinctively that he had not said the last word about Horatio and might have treated his life in a different way. *Bottomley's Book* (1909) was quite informative, although brimming over with self-praise, while Reuben Bigland's brief volume about Bottomley gave me an insight into the mind of the semi-literate jack-of-all-trades from Birmingham who brought 'England's greatest hypocrite' to justice by his dogged persistence.

Finally, I discovered a rare book with the engaging title *The Gentle Art of Exploiting Gullibility*, written by a legal man who signed himself 'Tenax'. A witty and penetrating account of Bottomley's criminal activities, it exposed his rackets as a company promoter, threw fresh light on his Bond Clubs and debunked his unscrupulous methods when defending his cases in court. It transpired that 'Tenax' was the *nom-de-plume* of Edward Bell, a solicitor who played a vital part in the downfall of Horatio Bottomley. Having read *The Gentle Art of Exploiting Gullibility*, I was convinced that the best way of tackling a new biography of Bottomley was to narrate his life in chronological order as far as possible and to describe in some detail his crooked deals and his principal law cases.

Edward Bell's remarkable book was brought to my notice by Cyril Baylis, a retired solicitor who had been a partner in his firm, Carter and Bell. I owe an enormous debt to Cyril Baylis for giving me much information about Bottomley's life from 1912 onwards, and being good enough to advise me on all aspects of Bottomley's encounters with the law. During years of practice Baylis came into contact with most of the legal luminaries whom Bottomley encountered, including the late Lord Birkenhead, Sir Arthur Comyns Carr and Sir Travers Humphreys, and has supplied me with valuable information about the judges and counsel in Bottomley's principal cases. He also provided two of the photographs.

I recently went to Birmingham, partly to find out more about Sir Josiah Mason's orphanage where Bottomley was sent at the age of nine. It has been pulled down to make way for housing, but I got in touch with Mr E. B. Twemlow, secretary of Mason's Trust, whom I would like to thank for giving me details about the original orphan school and lending me some unique illustrative material. I also had a talk about Reuben Bigland with Mrs May Bigland, the widow of his nephew. She told me that Bigland was by no means a model citizen: he loved backing horses and never believed in hard work. All his nephews were in the building trade and he used to tell them, 'You boys'll never make any money—you're too honest!'

After visiting Birmingham I received letters from Mr Searle and Mr Freaks for which I am most grateful. Mr Searle, who had been at the orphanage, remembered Bottomley visiting them after he had made good in the 'University of Life'. Mr Freaks had been a rating when Bottomley came to see the Grand Fleet in 1917 and boosted the Navy's morale.

Anyone who delves into the career of Horatio Bottomley has to spend a lot of time looking up newspaper files. I am grateful for the generous help given to me by Mr Tom Kelly and Mr Prior of the *Daily Mail* Library and also for the splendid co-operation I have received from Mr Geoff Adams, Chief

Librarian of the *Birmingham Post and Mail*. And a special word of thanks is due to the indefatigable staff of the British Museum's Reading Room and to the staff of their Newspaper Library at Colindale.

I am grateful to the many people who have made suggestions to me for the book or have helped me with their memories of Horatio Bottomley. I single out my old friend, R. J. Minney, whom I consulted in the early stages of this project. R.J. wrote an excellent biography of Julius Elias (Viscount Southwood), a key figure in Bottomley's career, and he encouraged me to press on with this book, for which I thank him most warmly.

I am also grateful to David Tribe, author of a new biography of Charles Bradlaugh, for an interesting discussion on the possibility that Bradlaugh may have been the natural father of Horatio Bottomley, and for his help in checking the proofs of the early chapters.

I am indebted to Miss Margery Vosper—whose father, Dr Percy Vosper, attended Bottomley in the 1920s—for giving me a vivid account of life at The Dicker, Bottomley's country mansion.

Finally, I should also like to thank Lt.-Col. Jack Lotinga and Mr Basil Bradlaugh Bonner who kindly supplied me with photographs and personal information.

Steyning, Sussex
November 1971

ALAN HYMAN

Acknowledgements

As well as individuals mentioned in the Foreword, I am grateful to the following for permission to quote from copyright material: His Honour Judge Humphreys and Hodder & Stoughton, Ltd, for *Criminal Days*, by Sir Travers Humphreys; Mr Cyril Baylis for *The Gentle Art of Exploiting Gullibility*, by 'Tenax'; the Hamlyn Publishing Group, Ltd, for *Horatio Bottomley*, by Raymond Blathways; Hutchinson, Ltd, for *Leaves from my Unwritten Diary*, by Sir Harry Preston; Guy Deghy and Richards Press, Ltd, for *Paradise in the Strand*; Hurst & Blackett, Ltd, for *The Real Horatio Bottomley*, by Henry Houston; Curtis Brown, Ltd, and William Heinemann, Ltd, for *Secrets of a Showman*, by Sir Charles Cochran; Beverley Nichols, Curtis Brown, Ltd, and Doubleday & Co., Inc., for *25*; R. J. Minney and the Hamlyn Publishing Group, Ltd, for *Viscount Southwood*; and John Long, Ltd, for *The Wall is Strong*, by Gerald Clayton.

I

A PROMISING OUTSIDER

1 An Orphan's Lot

I know Charles Bradlaugh was my father. My mother was a very beautiful woman. She died when I was four.

HORATIO BOTTOMLEY, to James Douglas, *Sunday Express*, 1920

On Sundays Hyde Park was a regular meeting-place of the mid-Victorians. Hundreds of Londoners with their wives and families used to congregate there in a holiday mood, for Sunday was the only free day of the week for the working classes. The crowds cheered as the military bands marched past in their bright red uniforms and there were murmurs of appreciation as the immaculately attired riders cantered past down Rotten Row. But their favourite entertainment was watching the aristocrats and the plutocrats driving out in gorgeously equipped carriages: the women noticed every little detail about the clothes of the people in the carriages, whilst each turn-out was discussed when the families returned home to the London suburbs or to the humbler abodes east of Aldgate Pump.

An area opposite the Marble Arch was reserved for the open-air speakers who always found an audience ready to listen to them. A much larger crowd than usual assembled there on Sunday 24 June 1855 because it was a special occasion: James Bligh was speaking in protest against a new Bill, just introduced into Parliament by Lord Robert Grosvenor, which would make a vital difference to their lives if it ever became law. Known as the New Sunday Bill or the Sunday Trading Bill, it proposed to make it illegal for small traders to open on Sunday in various parts of London, such as Petticoat Lane and Leather Lane, with fines of up to £2 for offenders.* This ill-judged Bill ignored the fact that Sunday was the only day of the week when the poorer families were free to shop for clothes and shoes in the street markets.

James Bligh had a handbill beside him with a slogan proclaiming: *This is a tyrannical attack on the liberty of the people.*

Bligh was very careful to use moderate language in his attack on the New Sunday Bill, and yet the audience were in such wholehearted sympathy with him that they applauded every sentence. Suddenly two senior policemen appeared on the scene—Sir Richard Mayne, the Commissioner of Police, and a Superintendent—and brushed their way through the crowd. They ordered Bligh to stop speaking immediately or he would be arrested. He calmly obeyed and picked up his soap-box. The two policemen departed with the boos of the crowd ringing in their ears.

This high-handed action put the crowd in a bad mood. They moved forward in a body to the carriageway and, standing as close as they could possibly get to the aristocrats and the wealthy commoners cruising by in their carriages, glared at them angrily. Some of the crowd began to jeer at them.

'I hope you don't allow your servants to work on Sundays!' one man called out.

The crowd grew so menacing that some of the ladies in the carriages got frightened. As their horses started to rear up, a titled lady and two of her friends scrambled out of their equipages and continued their journey through the Park on foot.

One of the aristocrats complained to the authorities about 'the disgraceful behaviour of the common people in Hyde Park' and, since the police expected larger crowds on the following Sunday, they drafted an emergency document forbidding any public meetings in the Park on 1 July. A handbill announcing the ban was posted on the Park gates early the next Sunday morning, but it was too late to keep people away.

The poor from every district in London flocked in towards the north side of the Serpentine. They were annoyed by the

* Hypatia Bradlaugh Bonner, *Charles Bradlaugh* (T. Fisher Unwin, 1894).

police placards banning all meetings, and in their new militant mood, it infuriated them to see 'the wealthy ones parading up and down in their carriages'.* It was one law for the rich and one for the poor! The Commissioner of Police, anticipating trouble, had assembled a large contingent of his men, some on foot and some mounted.

Amongst the crowds a gigantic young man with noble features and a powerful voice stood out from the rest. He was Charles Bradlaugh, already well known as a fearless champion of the working classes. Bradlaugh had come to Hyde Park on purpose to see how the day went, being convinced that the Commissioner had exceeded his powers in banning meetings in the Park. He was accompanied by his father-in-law, Abraham Hooper, a genial man of fifty.

Crowds lined both sides of the carriageway and some people broke out into groans and jeers as the superior classes passed by in their carriages. Some ladies in the carriages started screaming—and this was the signal for the mounted police to charge. The police rushed straight at the crowds with the result that a number of men and women were knocked down and trampled over; several others were arrested.

Charles Bradlaugh saw four policemen striking a little man with their truncheons. 'For God's sake don't hit me—take me!' he begged them.

As one policeman continued to hit him, Bradlaugh ran forward and forced the truncheon back with his gloved hand. 'The next man that strikes him I'll knock him down!' he cried.

The police left the young giant alone and took the little man into custody. Later, Bradlaugh was standing on the grass with a crowd when the police made a sortie on them from the roadway. They shouted to the people to hurry along and stop loitering. One man came up to Bradlaugh and started pushing him with his truncheon.

'Don't do that, my friend,' Bradlaugh warned him. 'You've no right to do it and I'm stronger than you are!'

The constable beckoned to two others, who joined him. Charles Bradlaugh seized hold of two truncheons, one in each hand, and said to them, 'If you attempt to touch me, I'll take one of these truncheons and knock you down with it!'

The three policemen, realizing that he meant it, took no

* Report of the Royal Commission on Hyde Park disturbances, July 1855.

further action. The people around Bradlaugh were delighted at his courage in standing up to authority: they picked him up and carried him off on their shoulders, cheering him. They put him down again near the Marble Arch where a big crowd gathered round him and shouted for him to speak. But Bradlaugh said nothing in case it gave the police an excuse to make more arrests. They all regarded him as their leader in the campaign against the New Sunday Bill and it took an effort for him to get away from the crowd. He then walked quietly out of the Park with his father-in-law, Abraham Hooper, who greatly admired him and called him 'the young enthusiast'.

The seventy people who had been arrested in Hyde Park were discharged by the magistrate the following day, and before the week was out Lord Robert Grosvenor had the good sense to drop his Bill. A Royal Commission was set up on the Hyde Park disturbances. Charles Bradlaugh was summoned to give evidence at the public hearing at Westminster; at the end the Commissioners thanked him for his admirable behaviour in the Park.

Charles Bradlaugh and Abraham Hooper both belonged to the freethinkers, a group who did not believe in the organized religions of the world. Bradlaugh lectured all over the country for the Secularist movement: a natural orator with great personal magnetism, he was extremely popular with the working classes. He had revolted against the conventions of his time after being turned out of home at fifteen for daring to question the authenticity of certain passages in the Bible and the Thirty-Nine Articles.

The Secularist movement had been founded as recently as 1851 by George Jacob Holyoake, who had come from Birmingham where his family had been so poor that he was sent to work at the Eagle iron foundry when he was only eleven. He also had rebelled in his youth, objecting to the Victorian concept that everybody should be content to remain in the same station to which it had pleased God to call him. Holyoake moved to London after going to prison for his beliefs in 1843. He had a large following amongst the working classes in the Midlands and the North and was a moving spirit in the growth of the Co-operative movement.

When Charles Bradlaugh was turned out of his home George Jacob Holyoake and his brother Austin befriended him and he joined their group. He had given his first lecture for the freethinkers when only seventeen and ever since then Bradlaugh and the Holyoakes had been close friends and fellow workers in the cause. A frail man of medium height, George Jacob Holyoake was in his late thirties in 1855. The Holyoakes had their own printing press at 147 Fleet Street where they published freethinking pamphlets and their own newspaper. They also published Bradlaugh's pamphlets, written under the name of 'Iconoclast', and the *Investigator*, a new paper later edited by Bradlaugh.

At twenty-two Bradlaugh had just married Susannah Hooper, a vivacious, extremely good-natured brunette of twenty-four. (Some accounts state erroneously that her name was Alice, possibly confusing her with her daughter.) Susannah was generous to a fault, and even before her marriage had been extravagant. The Bradlaughs had a struggle to make ends meet because he only earned £2 a week working as a clerk for Mr Rogers, a solicitor, at Fenchurch Street. They lived in West Street, Bethnal Green, not from choice but because it was cheap. Susannah was incapable of providing him with the intellectual stimulus she felt he needed and, in a childish desire to please him, she entertained more lavishly than they could afford.* Within two years she presented him with two daughters, Alice and Hypatia. However, his young family did not prevent Bradlaugh from working all hours for the freethinkers: there were his pamphlets, his paper and his lectures in London and the provinces.

He returned home unexpectedly one night from a lecture in the Midlands and was horrified to find his wife asleep in the living-room in a drunken stupor. She had become a secret drinker during his frequent absences and used their small store of housekeeping money to buy spirits. Soon the local tradesmen were dunning him for their bills. Although the doctor had ordered Susannah never to touch alcohol again, she continued drinking in secret with a boon companion. When Bradlaugh discovered this he sent her away to a 'cure' establishment: but soon after returning she started drinking again.

His friends began to stay away from the house to avoid being embarrassed by Susannah, who had grown very feckless about money matters. Then it got to the pitch where Bradlaugh could no longer trust her alone with his two daughters. He had to swallow his pride and call on his mother, with whom he had

* David Tribe, *President Charles Bradlaugh* (Elek, 1971).

quarrelled, and ask her to take charge of the household. It was a miserable sort of existence, but even in these circumstances he would not abandon his work for the Secularist movement.

Austin Holyoake, regarded by Bradlaugh as his best friend, still visited the house and knew all about his trouble with his wife. Austin and his beautiful young sister, Elizabeth, were very close and he had persuaded her to join the freethinkers. She soon fell under the spell of Charles Bradlaugh and always went to his meetings at the Hall of Science at 58, City Road. She continued to go there after her marriage to an insignificant tailor's cutter named William Bottomley.

Nobody has ever produced a satisfactory explanation of why the lovely Elizabeth Holyoake threw herself away on William Bottomley. The only certain fact is that her family could not afford to keep her in idleness and that marriage was the only career open to her in 1855. Therefore, when William Bottomley proposed to her she accepted him without necessarily being in love with him. They went to live in St Peter Street, Bethnal Green—the same district as Charles Bradlaugh—and in 1857 she gave birth to a daughter, who was called Florence.

Soon afterwards William Bottomley was seized with a fit of madness and had to be taken away to the Bethlehem Hospital. While he was confined there the Holyoakes supported Elizabeth and her baby.

In 1858 William Bottomley was discharged from the Bethlehem Hospital and returned home. But things could never be the same between him and Elizabeth, although she kept up appearances. William got back his old job with a tailor and she stayed with him. He was the breadwinner and there was Florence to support as well; she was too proud to throw herself on the charity of her family.

The vital question is, did Elizabeth go to Bradlaugh for consolation? If one only had access to the original Bradlaugh papers it could probably be settled one way or another. But Hypatia Bradlaugh, his daughter, wrote his official biography in a spirit of reverence and was so greatly concerned about his posthumous reputation that she censored all his papers, although most of the contents would probably have redounded to his credit. Therefore, one can only attempt to make an imaginative reconstruction of certain events in 1859.

In the first place it seems reasonable to assume that Elizabeth refused to let William Bottomley make love to her after his return because she would not risk conceiving a child by a man subject to fits of madness. Secondly, there is the fact that Bradlaugh's wife had become a dipsomaniac, which cannot have made her attractive to him.* Then it is known that the Divorce Laws of the time did not allow a marriage to be dissolved on the grounds of insanity or chronic alcoholism. Finally, one should bear in mind that Elizabeth hero-worshipped Bradlaugh and they both lived in Bethnal Green.

All this is a prelude to the birth of Horatio Bottomley in March 1860. It is a fact that Horatio never looked remotely like his official father, William Bottomley, but he bore a striking resemblance to Charles Bradlaugh when he grew up. When Frank Harris first met Horatio Bottomley as a young man his 'enormous upper lip' reminded him at once of Charles Bradlaugh.

I think it is quite possible that the unhappy Elizabeth Bottomley fell in love with Bradlaugh, her great hero, and the fact that he was her brother Austin's best friend may have helped their romance. Elizabeth was a beautiful woman and on his side Bradlaugh may well have been attracted by her. Taking all these factors into account, it seems possible that Elizabeth fell in love with Charles Bradlaugh and that he reciprocated her feelings. Perhaps Austin Holyoake knew about their affair, sympathized with their difficulties and helped them to find a secret rendezvous in the district.

The true story will probably never be known, but at least it is possible that Elizabeth Bottomley and Charles Bradlaugh were lovers and that it was as a result of their illicit union that Horatio Bottomley came into the world.

According to the records, Elizabeth gave birth to a baby boy at 16 St Peter Street on 23 March 1860 and he was called Horatio William Bottomley: Horatio after her eldest brother and William after her husband. An examination of his birth certificate shows that Elizabeth registered Horatio's birth—not William Bottomley, as one would have expected. And this was done a month after the event had taken place.

Elizabeth adored the boy and made it perfectly obvious that he was her favourite. Fortunately, his sister Florence had a sweet disposition and was not at all jealous: the two children got on so well together that they were almost like twins.

* 'He found love and respect for her draining away.' (Tribe.)

Elizabeth Bottomley still went to Bradlaugh's meetings at the New Hall of Science and, as a member of the Holyoake family, always sat on the platform with him. Sometimes she took little Florence along with her: later on she carried Horatio there in his long clothes. He was only three when William Bottomley had another fit and was taken back to the Bethlehem Hospital. After he had made a recovery the hospital sent him home, but he had a relapse and died on 14 July 1863 at the age of thirty-six.

William Bottomley left nothing, but the Holyoakes came to the rescue again and supported Elizabeth and the children. However, as none of the family were well off they could only afford to make her a small allowance, and she denied herself necessities in order to make sure that Florence and Horatio had enough to eat. At the beginning of 1865 she was stricken down with an illness which the doctors could not diagnose: they only discovered it was cancer when it was too late. Elizabeth's constitution had been so undermined by lack of proper food that she had no resistance and succumbed to the disease in a few days.

Thus Florence and Horatio became orphans at seven and four respectively and the Holyoakes assumed responsibility for them. For a year they went to live with their uncle, William Holyoake, a successful painter, at Hayter House in the Marylebone Road. Uncle William and his wife were very kind to the children, who enjoyed their stay immensely.* His house seemed like a palace after their cramped rooms at Bethnal Green. However, the Holyoakes had a large family of their own and though fond of the orphans they felt after a year that it was time somebody else took them over.

The Holyoakes in London therefore held a family conference to decide the future of Florence and Horatio; the three who had the children's destinies in their hands were George Jacob, William and Austin. The last-named was too poor to help them, William felt he had done enough and George Jacob was unable to accommodate them because he had seven children of his own. However, he undertook to pay for their maintenance.

Florence was boarded out in Cheapside with the owner of a City chophouse and his wife, who had a daughter of her age. They treated her as one of the family and she was extremely

* Bottomley, article in the *Sunday Illustrated*, 1921.

happy with them: several years later they adopted her. Horatio was not nearly as lucky as his sister. At first he was boarded out in Battersea with Mrs Wormley, a widow. This rather dreary woman looked after him adequately but gave him little affection.

In 1869 George Jacob Holyoake decided it was impossible to support his big family and the two orphans on his slender income. He could only manage to maintain one of the orphans and chose Florence in preference to Horatio. At another family conference the three brothers agreed that the boy should be sent to an orphanage.

George Jacob applied to the Orphan Working School and Alexandra Orphanage at Hampstead, which was near enough for him to be able to keep an eye on Horatio, but they had no vacancy. Then he remembered his old Birmingham friend, Josiah Mason,* the industrial magnate, who had just built an orphanage at Erdington: it had cost a quarter of a million and was reputed to be the best in England. Since Erdington was only a few miles from Birmingham, where some of the Holyoakes were still living, they would be able to visit Horatio if he was admitted there. George Jacob Holyoake wrote to the Governors of Mason's Orphanage on 30 November 1869:

> The votes and interest of the Governors are respectfully solicited on behalf of Horatio William Bottomley, aged nine. The father, following the occupation of a tailor, died in 1863, after recovery from an attack of mania, during which he was confined in the Bethlehem Hospital. The mother died suddenly in 1865, leaving two children of whom the above is the youngest.

Horatio was described on the application form as 'a healthy, promising child, likely to turn out clever and, no doubt, grateful'.

One may wonder why Charles Bradlaugh, who must have known about Horatio's misfortunes from the Holyoakes, did nothing to help the boy if he was his natural father. But in 1869 Bradlaugh was desperately hard up and in no position to offer financial help to anybody. He had lost money on business ventures—one being a loan to the city of Pisa—and in addition his wife had run up large debts with the tradesmen. He was

* Mason was knighted for his services to charity in 1872.

forced to sell up his home to pay their bills and to avoid going bankrupt.

His marriage finally broke up the following year. It was decided that Susannah and their daughters, Alice and Hypatia, should go to live with Abraham Hooper at Cocking, near Midhurst. His only son, Charles, was boarded out with an Army schoolmaster. But in June he caught scarlet fever: due to medical ignorance, no proper precautions were taken and the boy died from a disease of the kidneys. Charles Bradlaugh never recovered from this blow. He supported his wife and daughters and settled down to a frugal bachelor existence in two small rooms in Turner Street, Commercial Road.

On the strength of George Jacob Holyoake's letter to the Governors, Horatio was admitted to Josiah Mason's Orphanage for girls and boys at Erdington. This remarkable building, which could accommodate three hundred children, stood high up over the surrounding country on the Lichfield road. It had thirteen acres of playgrounds, fields, flower gardens and kitchen gardens. Constructed as an irregular oblong in an Italianate style, it had a central tower over two hundred feet high which could be seen for miles. The four ends of the

'This remarkable building . . .'

orphanage were gabled and each had 'a colossal figure of an angel standing with folded wings, as if watching over the happiness of the children'.*

Josiah Mason, who had no children of his own, was an outstanding philanthropist of the period: his intentions were most worthy and he certainly did his utmost for the orphans. However, he took no part in the day-to-day curriculum of the place and by modern standards a Victorian orphanage was a regimented, soul-destroying institution, which had far more in common with a Borstal establishment than a boarding-school. The children who went there were subjected to a harsh régime which could do a great deal of damage to their characters. It was worse for a child who was very sensitive, particularly for one as clever and imaginative as Horatio Bottomley.

Nevertheless one must admit that contemporary accounts speak very highly of Mason's. An article in the *Birmingham Daily Post* of 2 August 1869 shows that the reporter was a fervent admirer of Mason:

> Tender thoughtfulness and loving care is manifested in all respects for the comfort and happiness of the children. The Founder [Josiah Mason] knows all the children by name and is known and loved by them. . . . It is a home from home for those who are homeless, a Family Circle for those who have lost their natural parents.

Hingeley, a Birmingham journalist, visited the orphanage school in 1870 and praised it to the skies:

> There is scarcely a sound as we enter the schoolroom. Scores of little folk are learning their lessons. Their writing is wonderfully neat, there is hardly a pin out of place in the whole school—and as for blots—why they hardly know what they are!

On the other hand the Headmaster, Mr Wright, and his staff at the orphanage enforced strict discipline on their pupils. There were ninety boys and a hundred and eighty girls and however bright or dim they may have been, they were made to learn quickly. A Birmingham educational officer, visiting local schools in the seventies, noted that 'those who failed with their copper-plate writing had their knuckles rapped

* *Birmingham Daily Post*, 2 August 1869.

'Tender thoughtfulness and loving care . . .'

severely. . . . Canes and leather straps were applied with force to emphasize the need for obedience.'

Who can doubt that they used similar methods at Mason's? The boys and girls were only taught English subjects and had to work very hard because the orphanage aimed to produce self-sufficient adults equipped with the basic commercial skills to enable them to earn their own living after they left.

Horatio made excellent use of the elementary education he received there and in later life, when he emerged as Horatio Bottomley M.P., the tribune of the people, he often visited his alma mater and told his old masters how grateful he was to them for giving him such a fine start in life. He used to gossip for hours to Miss Wright, the matron, who had been there during his time.*

Mr H. Searle, who was a boy at the orphanage in 1909, remembers Bottomley visiting them on several occasions. He often brought extra food for the children and gave them strawberry teas. He enjoyed speaking to them in the big hall and would always say, 'Any success I have achieved in life started at this place. . . . When I left the school I went into the Great University of Life called Business.'†

* Henry Houston, *The Real Horatio Bottomley* (Hurst & Blackett, 1923).
† H. Searle, letter to author.

However, one feels bound to add that Horatio Bottomley would have been much better off in a decent home with foster parents to look after him and cherish him. The worst feature of Mason's and the other orphanages of the period was the total lack of human contact and affection. No matter how much time and money Josiah Mason lavished on his orphanage, it still remained an impersonal institution.

The Rules of Visitation at Mason's illustrate this point. The children were only allowed to have visitors twice a year, in January and July, except by written permission, and it goes without saying that few of them ever obtained it. Horatio's only visitors were his Birmingham relations: his aunt, Mrs Caroline Praill, and his uncle, Walter Holyoake. Yet he would have given his right arm to see his sister, Florence, because he missed her dreadfully; but she was living miles away in London with her foster parents and it was six years before he was to see her again.

At the age of twelve Horatio wrote a rather pathetic letter on Christmas Day to his uncle, George Jacob Holyoake, in which he said:

> You are allowed to send a present at any time; but they must be books, toys or fruits, but nothing in the shape of pudding of any kind is allowed to come. . . . I shall be very pleased with anything you can send.
>
> Your respectful nephew,
>
> HORATIO

In *Bottomley's Book** he states that he was happy at the orphanage and well treated. But by then Bottomley had become an incorrigible optimist and looked even at his past through rose-coloured glasses so that he would never admit he had ever been lonely or homesick. One of his favourite phrases was 'I have learned to take my medicine' and one feels that he acquired this philosophy at Mason's. For the five years he stayed there Horatio was simply Number 64 and had to manage to make the best of an orphan's lot.

He did not have a very illustrious record, only distinguishing himself at arithmetic out of all the subjects in the curriculum. He took far more interest in sport than in his lessons; he excelled at running and won several prizes for the hundred yards. His proficiency at arithmetic proved of great assistance to him in

* Odhams, 1909.

'the University of Life called Business', whilst his ability to run fast came in handy at certain stages of his extraordinary career. He was a sturdy, well-set-up boy with little indication that he would grow up into a fat man.

In his book he relates how two unfortunate incidents at Mason's stuck in his memory and, although one must take many of Bottomley's stories with a large pinch of salt, I am inclined to believe both of them. Assuming that these events really happened, they must have had a vital effect on his complex character.

He had been present at the burial of both his parents at an East End cemetery. It was, therefore, a great shock for him to be told, on the day he arrived at Mason's, that he would have to help at the burial of a boy named Taylor who had just died. It was the worst kind of introduction to the 'home for the homeless' and must have disturbed him for a long time.

Bottomley's other unfortunate experience concerned the girls at the orphanage. When he was thirteen he tried to get to know some of them, but could make little headway in the rigid institutional atmosphere. They slept in six large dormitories, being segregated from the boys' dormitories by divisions with sleeping accommodation for the teachers and attendants in charge of the children. Being very high-spirited Horatio and a friend raided the girls' dormitories at night, just for a lark.

His friend took one look at the sleeping damsels and fled, but Horatio stayed on. In the darkness he stumbled on a chair and a girl woke up and immediately raised the alarm. Horatio jumped out of a window and landed unhurt in the garden below.* He had to sleep all night in the shrubbery; but next morning the Superintendent, who administered discipline with a heavy hand, went out and found Horatio in the bushes. The boy had committed one of the most serious crimes in the calendar. The Superintendent called him up before the whole school and gave him a severe beating.

He was then locked up in the Clock Tower for a week and given only bread and water. What had begun as a schoolboy lark had ended in disgrace and humiliation. It must have been a traumatic experience for Horatio, locked up in a high tower for a week without a soul to speak to him.

* This sounds far fetched because Mason's was a high building. Bottomley was probably caught in the girls' dormitory the same night, but felt that his leap from a high window would make a better story.

At last in 1874 he became fourteen, the age at which the boys usually left the orphanage. But Horatio had had enough of Mason's even before the spring was over: he slipped out of the building one morning and ran away. He walked as fast as his legs would carry him and, luckily, he only had to go a few miles to Edgbaston. It was a marvellous moment when he knocked at the door of the pleasant little house of his Aunt Caroline—Mrs Caroline Praill—and found her at home.*

Years afterwards Bottomley told Henry Houston, his original biographer, that his first day of liberty was the most glorious day of his life. And, although he was not exactly the most honest man in London, I believe he was telling the truth.

* One newspaper account states that Bottomley ran away from the orphanage at thirteen to his uncle in Birmingham (presumably Walter Holyoake) who brought him back and that he was soundly thrashed. But I can find no corroboration for this story in any book or other written source.

2 The University of Life

I have not had your advantages, gentlemen. What poor education I have received has been gained in the University of Life.

BOTTOMLEY, to the Oxford Union, 1921

Mrs Caroline Praill and her husband welcomed Horatio into their home at Edgbaston, but their fourteen-year-old nephew was expected to work for his living. He went as an office-boy to Smith's, a firm of builders in Ryland Street, Birmingham. He resented being dogsbody at the builder's and disliked having to work long hours for a pittance. Apart from that, he found it hard to settle down in Birmingham: he missed his sister Florence very badly and though London was only a hundred miles away he felt it might just as well have been on another planet.

Knowing that he was yearning to go back to London, Caroline wrote to her brother, George Jacob Holyoake, and asked if he could arrange it. In the autumn George Jacob sent for Horatio, but as none of his relations could put him up just then he returned to his old lodgings with Mrs Wormley at Battersea. Like any cockney, Horatio was delighted to be back in town and on his first day he went off to Cheapside to see his beloved sister Florence.

A week later he was summoned to Hayter House to see his Uncle William, the painter, who had seen some of the boy's drawings and thought they showed promise. How would Horatio like to be a wood engraver? He was quite willing to try it, so William Holyoake paid for him to be articled to a leading firm of engravers who supplied engravings to the *Illustrated London News* and other journals.

Horatio soon realized he had little talent for this kind of work. During his apprenticeship he had to engrave some special drawings for the *Illustrated London News*, but his hand slipped and one drawing was irretrievably ruined. The wood engraver was very angry with him and gave the work to someone else. Horatio, who was now staying with Uncle William, dreaded going home and admitting his failure. But when his kind uncle heard about it he was not at all angry. It was agreed that Horatio should be released from his articles; then the only problem was to find him a suitable job.

Horatio took the first job offered to him and thus became an errand boy to a haberdasher in Wood Street in the City, who specialized in fringes for ladies' dresses which were imported from France. It was not an inspiring occupation, and Horatio was convinced he was destined for better things, but he resolved to try and stick it out. He began to escape at lunch time to a City bun-shop which was a favourite rendezvous for youths working in offices connected with the law. It became a sort of club for Horatio and he made friends there with a handsome older boy named Dick, 'a mysterious and impressive young gentleman with an excellent position in a solicitor's office'.*

All the youths in the 'club' looked upon Dick as their natural leader. Sometimes he used to invite Horatio to come and see him in his office, which was considered a tremendous privilege. 'Proudly surveying me from the giddy height of the office stool, he would tell me of the mysteries of the legal profession and its golden opportunities.' It was inevitable that Horatio should fall under the sway of this older and far more sophisticated youth, and as a result he grew very discontented with his menial job at the haberdasher's. He even plucked up the courage to have a few rows with his employer.

One morning Horatio was informed that they were moving to new premises in the City, and he was to take the entire stock of French fringes from Wood Street in a handtruck.

The boy set off to trundle his hand-cart through the City streets; it was only a short distance and his employer was supposed to follow him an hour later. At the corner of King Street near Guildhall a policeman held up his hand and brought

* Bottomley's descriptions in *Bottomley's Book*.

Horatio and his truck of fringes to a full stop. Fate decreed that Dick should pass by at this moment and their eyes met. It was a crisis for Horatio, who knew that unless he had the courage to assert himself he would be damned for ever in the eyes of his young legal friends. Leaving the hand-truck in King Street, he ran after Dick to seek his advice.

Could he be compelled to wheel the truck any further? Should he hand it to a policeman? Would they arrest him if he left it on the road? The cynical lawyer's clerk simply advised him to 'chuck it'.

Horatio followed his advice and left his fringes on the corner: he never went back to the haberdasher and never heard from him again. Perhaps the haberdasher had some stolen property amongst the fringes, but the mystery has never been solved.

Dick gave Horatio an introduction to a solicitor in Coleman Street, who engaged him as an office-boy. This gave him a wonderful initiation into the ways of the law.* It was a very small firm consisting of the solicitor, who tippled, the managing clerk, who was as crooked as a corkscrew, and Horatio Bottomley. For years the managing clerk had been levying a fictitious 'County Rate' on a number of City firms, and even rented a tiny office from which he sent out plausible 'demand notices' and 'final notices'. A great deal of the office work fell on Horatio's shoulders, since the solicitor was so often in his cups and the managing clerk so frequently away at his more lucrative business. The boy had such a remarkable flair for the law that he was able to cope with much more complicated work than an ordinary office-boy could have tackled. He soon learnt how to serve a writ and swear an affidavit and before long had mastered the procedure of the Lord Mayor's Court. His instinctive grasp of legal matters at the age of fifteen is very understandable if he was the natural son of Charles Bradlaugh, for there was a tradition of the law in the Bradlaugh family: I have mentioned that Charles Bradlaugh worked for a solicitor in Fenchurch Street, while his father had been confidential clerk to a solicitor in Cloak Street.

The managing clerk in Horatio's office had his come-uppance when a City firm who had received one of his 'final notices' for rates decided to find out if it was genuine. One day a policeman called at Coleman Street and asked to see the

* Houston.

managing clerk. Horatio watched him being arrested and being marched off to Guildhall, where he was charged and given a long sentence. The boy decided he had better look for another job.

Uncle George Jacob, believing it would help Horatio's prospects for him to learn shorthand, sent him to Pitman's College, where he showed a great aptitude for this new feature of commerce. While learning shorthand he went to live with his widowed aunt, Mrs Austin Holyoake, at Johnson's Court in Fleet Street. George Jacob invited Horatio to help him in his publishing activities in his spare time. It was Horatio's first contact with printer's ink, and newspapers always held a fascination for him afterwards. He began by reading proofs of the *Secularist* for Uncle George Jacob; later he did odd jobs for Charles Bradlaugh on the *National Reformer*, the new paper Bradlaugh had founded in 1860, after the failure of the *Investigator*.

This was the first time he had ever met Bradlaugh, who recognized him as a youth of promise and drew him out and encouraged him to read the classics and philosophy. He lent him books by Charles Darwin, T. H. Huxley and John Stuart Mill and discussed their ideas with him. Whether Bradlaugh was his father or not, he had a tremendous influence on Horatio.

'I soon became captivated with the magnetic personality of Charles Bradlaugh, who became my political and spiritual mentor,' he wrote later.

In 1876 Charles Bradlaugh was forty-three, a giant of a man with a powerful physique, and a marvellous orator with a commanding voice. In Victorian times many Englishmen thought it was the height of achievement to become a member of Parliament, but Bradlaugh wanted to get to Westminster because his aim in life was to improve the lot of the working classes and he believed this was the only way he could ever achieve it. He had been adopted as Independent Liberal candidate for Northampton, a seat which he eventually won in 1880. His meetings at Northampton already attracted some of the biggest crowds in the country and it was said that every word of his speeches could be heard half a mile away.

When Bradlaugh and Bottomley stood together people were bound to notice the extraordinary resemblance between them. Bottomley was much shorter, and his height never exceeded five foot five, but they both had the same broad brow and the same enormously long upper lip, and both had a massive jaw and thick hair brushed back without a parting. But when Horatio grew to manhood his face coarsened and his expression became very cynical; he was visibly a very different character to the idealistic Bradlaugh.

At seventeen Horatio started work as a shorthand clerk for a reputable firm of solicitors in Essex Street, off the Strand. He was such an exemplary employee that the solicitors kept for many years an engrossment in which the word *Shares* had been written in Bottomley's copperplate hand—a strange irony. While working in Essex Street Horatio met Alfred Locke Cox, a bright little medical student known to his friends as 'Tommy' Cox. They struck up a friendship which lasted a lifetime.

When Bottomley was eighteen the Holyoakes decided it would be better for him to live on his own. As he earned only a tiny salary he went back to live at Battersea, a cheap district and one that he knew quite well from the past. In September 1878 he stayed with a Mrs Hood in Ashbury Road and paid fifteen shillings for board and lodging, but he had to share a bed with her fifteen-year-old son, Harry. It was a comparatively humble abode after the comfortable middle-class homes of the Holyoakes, but Mrs Hood was an extremely kind landlady and soon regarded him as one of the family.

His City friends had introduced him to a gambling 'hell' near the Law Courts; he started going there once a week and developed a passion for gambling. Sometimes he had a win, but if he had a bad night he would return to Battersea in a horse cab without a penny in his pocket and wake up Mrs Hood, who always paid off the cab and gave him a scolding. He had become a first-class billiards player, by dint of much practice, and started frequenting a billiards saloon at the Ludgate Circus end of Fleet Street. For some reason they nicknamed him the 'Green Stranger'; he would walk in there of an evening and challenge all comers, and he generally won his match. If he won he would collect his winnings and go straight home to Battersea; if he lost he would make a plausible excuse to avoid settling up for a few days.

He often saw his sister Florence at Cheapside and sometimes she came to see him at Battersea. She was being courted by Charles Dollman, a furrier's clerk in the City, but Horatio's vivid imagination led him to improve on the facts: he told

Mrs Hood that his sister was about to marry a City magnate and they were going to live in a splendid mansion on Clapham Common. He also used to boast about his millionaire uncle who had left him a fortune which he would inherit on his twenty-first birthday. But in reality he was so broke sometimes that he could not even find the five shillings for the rent which Mrs Hood had to remit to her landlords, the Shaftesbury Estate. This predicament never worried Horatio, who used to call on the Shaftesbury Estate and persuade them to 'carry' him for a week.

Realizing that he had the gift of eloquence, which he called the gift of the gab, Horatio determined to follow in the footsteps of Charles Bradlaugh and become a public speaker. One evening some friends took him to the Battersea 'Parliament', a debating society which was the equivalent of a local Parliament, where he listened with rapt attention to all the speeches.

He started to practise public speaking in his bedroom at Mrs Hood's, standing in front of the mirror to study his own performance and making Harry Hood prompt him until he knew his speeches by heart. In a few months he was addressing Battersea 'Parliament' on various topics of the day. He progressed so well that he rose to be 'Prime Minister' in his early twenties and resolved that he would become a proper M.P. one day.

At the age of nineteen he fell madly in love with Eliza Norton, who worked on the counter at a dressmaker's at the corner of Lavender Hill and Queenstown. She was a pretty blonde of his own age and he was so carried away with passion that he overlooked her failings; it took him years to realize that she was a silly woman who could never rise above her origins. Eliza also lived in Battersea, only a few streets away from Horatio's lodgings in Ashbury Road, which was very convenient when they were courting. He soon proposed to her and met her family and eventually gained the approval of her father, Samuel Norton, who was a rent-collector for Sarson's vinegar brewery. He kept it all a secret from the Holyoakes, knowing they would be bound to oppose the idea of their penniless nephew's getting married at nineteen, and it was a long time before he told Florence—who had become Mrs Charles Dollman—of his intentions.

The wedding was planned for Christmas Day 1879, and he

went to great trouble to buy the best ingredients for the wedding cake and persuaded the long-suffering Mrs Hood to help him to prepare it. He insisted on stoning the raisins and washing the currants himself. Mrs Hood regarded all her work as a kind of wedding present to him. He had a talk with the local baker, who promised to bake the cake and ice it for sixteen shillings.

But on Christmas Eve he had a night out with his friends in the City and they wound up with a visit to the gambling 'hell'. He had a disastrous session and returned to Battersea in a horse cab absolutely cleaned out. He couldn't ask Mrs Hood to help him pay for the wedding as he was already in her debt—so how the devil was he going to get married next day?

He was too worried to get any sleep that night. On Christmas morning he went to the baker, told him his tale of woe and threw himself on his mercy. Couldn't he possibly pay for the wedding cake next week? But the hard-hearted baker gave him an ultimatum: 'Sixteen bob or no wedding cake!' and even suggested selling his cake in penny slices across the counter.

Horatio decided the only thing to do was to have a diplomatic illness and postpone the wedding till he was solvent again. He confided his plan to Harry Hood, who was three years younger and more or less under his thumb. He asked Harry to go to Eliza's home and tell her that he was so ill they would have to call off the wedding. Afterwards, Harry Hood was to call on the verger of the New Wesleyan Chapel, Wandsworth, with a written message saying that the wedding was cancelled because the bridegroom had suddenly been taken ill.

There was no difficulty with Eliza Norton. Harry convinced her that Horatio was really ill and confined to bed with a high temperature. She was quite willing to wait and marry him when he had fully recovered. However, it was another story when he saw the verger of the New Wesleyan Chapel, Wandsworth. The latter was cross and unsympathetic and was furious at being asked to cancel the arrangements at the last minute, and even threatened to keep the money which Bottomley had paid him in advance for the licence. Harry Hood waited patiently in the vestry until the verger simmered down and agreed to refund it.

Harry returned to Ashbury Road elated with his triumph and gave Horatio back his licence money; he received a shilling for his services and one feels that he had richly earned it. When Harry described his interview with the verger in detail Bottomley laughed till the tears ran down his face.*

* Houston.

3 The Hansard Bubble

I consider that Horatio Bottomley is one of the wiliest men in the City of London.

LEOPOLD GRAHAM, quoted by Frank Harris (1887).

Horatio eventually married Eliza five months later when both of them were twenty. It is reported that they were able to use the original wedding cake for the occasion and all the guests had a merry time.* However, his minute bank balance did not run to giving Eliza a honeymoon, and they started married life in two rooms at Eland Road, Battersea, with a landlady named Mrs Foster who charged them ten and sixpence a week and two and six a day extra for their board. Twenty-eight shillings a week was very reasonable, but even that was a strain on Horatio's finances. He took Mrs Foster aside and told her about the fortune he was coming into on his twenty-first birthday and asked for credit. But the landlady, who had her own way of sizing up a lodger, was not impressed by his fancy talk. Having noticed that his only suit was very shiny and his only pair of boots needed cobbling, she stood firm and demanded a week's rent in advance.

Bottomley had left his firm of solicitors to join Walpole's, a well established concern who supplied the shorthand writers to take down and transcribe the proceedings at the law courts. This was a big step forward for him: he was admitted into the exclusive Institute of Shorthand Writers and sent out to

* Houston.

report the cases held in the Supreme Court of Judicature at Westminster. (It was not until 1897 that the London law courts were all amalgamated and transferred to the Law Courts in the Strand.)

Horatio and Eliza soon left Mrs Foster and moved to rooms in Chancery Lane so as to be near his work. Money was so tight at first that he could only afford to give her a pound a week for housekeeping, but one memorable night he came home with fifty gold sovereigns and she could hardly wait to get her hands on them. Horatio put them on the table and started to divide them up into piles—'five for so-and-so and six for that City bookie'—she didn't realize he had so many debts! Before long nearly all the sovereigns had found their way into one of the piles. Eliza could bear it no longer and cried, 'Oh, 'Orace, do give me some!'

He handed her two sovereigns with great reluctance and commented, 'I can't think what the devil you do with your money!'*

He worked for Walpole's for three years and thus 'got the law at his fingertips'. As a shorthand writer in the courts he was privileged to hear the leading barristers of the day arguing cases and the eminent judges summing up, which was to prove a great asset to his career. The two men he particularly admired were Sir George Jessel and Sir Henry James. Sir George Jessel, who had been appointed Master of the Rolls in 1873, had the distinction of being the first Jew to occupy a seat on the judicial Bench in England. Sir Henry James, a barrister, had risen to the head of his profession as Attorney-General, and later became Lord Justice James.

In a short time Bottomley became a first-class law reporter and Walpole's thought so highly of him that in 1883 they took him into partnership, changing the name of the firm to Walpole and Bottomley. Feeling confident about the future, Horatio moved to a little house in Clapham where his sister, Florence Dollman, was living. He arranged to buy all their furniture on hire purchase and, to please Eliza, they bought a piano. As may be imagined, she was not a serious pianist, but loved to sit down and strum a popular tune.

According to one account, he returned to Clapham one night carrying a little wire-haired terrier in his arms.

'Isn't he a nice little dog?' he said.

* Houston.

Eliza demanded to know how he had managed to pay for it, and he looked sheepish.

'Well, my dear, as a matter of fact, I used the piano money,' he said nonchalantly. 'He was such a nice little dog!'

She suddenly slapped his face.

'What am I going to tell the piano man when he calls for his next instalment?' she asked, almost in tears.

But somehow they paid off the instalment, and in the fullness of time the piano became their own property.

When Bottomley was twenty-four he emulated Charles Bradlaugh and started a newspaper. His first venture was the *Hackney Hansard*, which reported the debates of Hackney's local 'Parliament'. He knew Hackney very well from his early childhood and his public speaking there, and contrived to produce the paper most economically with a staff of two: himself and a shorthand writer. The latter covered the debates in 'Parliament', while Horatio called on the Hackney tradesmen and canvassed them for advertisements. As soon as the *Hackney Hansard* was paying its way he started the *Battersea Hansard*, and for a time his two papers did quite well. Then he ran into a little financial difficulty, as a result of a rash speculation, but extricated himself by merging the two into a single paper called the *Debater*.

During the next two years he acquired a small chain of newspapers, but quickly disposed of any one that was making a loss. The most successful of them was the *Municipal Review*, the national organ of the Town Councils and Local Board, which featured a biography of a local mayor every week and published a colour portrait of him in full regalia. Bottomley persuaded every mayor who appeared in the paper to give him a substantial order for extra copies to be sent to his friends and fellow citizens. And since there were three hundred new mayors appointed every year, and the journal came out only once a week, he was on velvet.

The *Financial News* was read by businessmen all over the country; he founded the *Financial Times* in competition with it, believing that the business world could support two newspapers. However, it took the *Financial Times* a long time to build up a good circulation. Amongst his money-making newspapers was the *Draper's Record*, an excellent weekly with a steady appeal to people in the trade. He also had *Baby, or the Mother's Magazine*, in his group and published it on the

Continent to give English people living abroad something to read in their own language.

In 1885 Bottomley formed the Catherine Street Publishing Association to be the parent company of his chain of newspapers. The following year he was short of capital and called on Osborne O'Hagan, a City financier, to try and obtain fresh finance for the Company. Young Bottomley had cultivated a most engaging manner and O'Hagan was quite taken with him, but turned down the deal because it was too small for him. Bottomley got busy and returned to the financier's office a few weeks later with Douglas MacRae, a forthright Scotsman who owned a printing works, to put up a much bigger proposition: a merger between the Catherine Street Association and MacRae & Co., who printed all their papers, and Curtice & Co., newspaper publishers and advertising agents. The project appealed to Osborne O'Hagan, who needed a printer for his own work; he agreed to float the Catherine Street Printing and Publishing Association with a capital of £100,000 and underwrote half the issue. Horatio Bottomley became chairman and paid a dividend of twelve per cent, which gave everyone the impression that the company had made a good start.

At this period the most discussed journalist in London and perhaps the most brilliant was Frank Harris. An erratic genius with atrocious manners, he inspired one of Oscar Wilde's best mots: 'Frank Harris has been invited to all the best houses in England—once!' Harris met Bottomley at lunch at the Café Royal and was tremendously impressed by him. He described him vividly:

> He was about 5 feet 5, very broad, and threatened to become stout. He had a very large head, well balanced, with good forehead and heavy jaws. The eyes small and grey, the peculiarity of the face a prodigiously long upper lip. He was clean shaven and his enormous upper lip reminded me at once of the great Charles Bradlaugh.*

In the eighties the Hornsey Liberal Association invited Bottomley to stand as their candidate. The odds were stacked

* Frank Harris, *My Life and Loves* (Obelisk Press, 1934). Bradlaugh had been elected as Radical Liberal for Northampton in 1880, but being a well known atheist he was not allowed to take the oath. Although he was re-elected for Northampton he was not allowed to take his seat in the Commons till 1886—he had even been forcibly ejected from the House. He then became the hero of the intellectuals.

against him because Hornsey was a Tory stronghold held by the popular Mr Stephens of the ink family. Bottomley fought very well at the election and managed to get within 3,000 votes of 'Inky' Stephens. He was honoured by a letter from William Ewart Gladstone, the Grand Old Man: 'You have made a good fight, and I am told that but for the outvoters you would have won the seat.'

The local Liberals presented him with a silver tea and coffee service 'in token of their high appreciation of the services you have rendered the Liberal Party in the Division. Coming into the Constituency a stranger, you have made friends who will regard your future career with interest and your success with satisfaction.'

After Bottomley and Douglas MacRae, the printer, had been partners in the Catherine Street Printing and Publishing Association for a year, they had a difference of opinion. Bottomley suggested that one of them should handle the newspapers and the other the printing. According to his account, written much later, 'MacRae was a bit angry, and thought I was desirous of elbowing him out of the journals, so with Quixotic impulse I gave him the choice. He was a printer and I was a journalist—but he took the papers and left me the printing works.'

MacRae became proprietor of the *Draper's Record* and the *Financial Times*, while Bottomley prepared to launch a much bigger combine than the Catherine Street Association. He announced that his printing company had obtained a new Government contract for the publication of debates in Parliament; as this had been the monopoly of Hansard's for years it was a great feather in his cap. In 1886 he arranged a merger between his company, MacRae, Curtice & Co., and four of the leading firms in the newspaper field: Wyman & Co., the printers; Clement Smith & Co., publishers of pictorial posters; Henry Vickers, newspaper publishers; and Vacone & Co., producers of newspaper illustrations. He claimed that his organization of the printing and publishing trades would effect a great saving of overheads and, to commemorate their contract to publish the Parliamentary debates, he called the new company the Hansard Publishing and Printing Union. The next vital step was to try and persuade leading men in the business world to join his board.

He met Frank Harris (a former editor of the *Evening News*) at the Café Royal and asked him, 'Could you get me Lord Folkestone and Coleridge Kennard to be directors? Give me these two names and I'll give you a cheque for ten thousand pounds.'

Coleridge Kennard, the banker, was a major shareholder in the *Evening News* and Lord Folkestone was its proprietor. Coleridge Kennard agreed to join his board, but Lord Folkestone declined. Bottomley managed to secure the services of Sir Henry Isaacs, the Lord Mayor, as Chairman of the Hansard Union. This gave the City more confidence in the venture, although suspicions might have been aroused if they had known that Horatio had paid Sir Henry's brother, Joseph Isaacs, £2,000 to persuade him to take it on. Other well known directors of Hansard were C. Kegan Paul, the publisher, and Sir Roper Lethbridge, Press Commissioner to the Government of India. The managing director of this 'respectable' concern was Horatio Bottomley.

The Hansard Union was given a Stock Exchange quotation in April 1889 and came to market with a capital of £500,000. On the 13th the five companies listed above were sold to the Hansard Union for £325,000 by a certain John Phillips; unknown to the other directors he was a clerk in Bottomley's office, and I shall return to this transaction in the next chapter. With the object of bringing printing firms into the Hansard fold, Bottomley appointed Henry Burt, a leading figure in the trade, as general manager. Burt and Bottomley worked very well together for the first year; Burt's association with Hansard created the impression that the business was being run efficiently.

In May the Hansard board had a letter from a Mr Charles Dollman stating that he was prepared to sell them paper-mills at Cullompton, Devon, and printing-works at Redhill for the sum of £105,000. The reader will no doubt remember that Charles Dollman was Horatio's brother-in-law, but his co-directors seemed unaware of this fact. Bottomley accepted the Dollman offer on behalf of the Hansard board on 26 August, and the money was paid over to Dollman's solicitors—another transaction about which we shall hear more in the next chapter.

After the Hansard Union had paid out £325,000 for the five printing and publishing companies and £105,000 for paper-mills and printing-works on top of their office expenses, there was not much change left out of £500,000. However, the resourceful Bottomley summoned a board meeting in September and persuaded it to pass a resolution to double Hansard's capital to a million. Thus the company was able to declare a dividend of eight per cent in October, and its shareholders were informed that 'suitable mills have been obtained and the business is in a most flourishing condition'.

Bottomley planned that the Hansard Union should merge the printing and publishing trades in Continental centres as well, and formed the Anglo-Austrian Printing and Publishing Union for this purpose. The Hansard Board authorized him to go to Vienna in the autumn to finalize contracts for the company with thirteen Austrian printers, and voted him the handsome sum of £2,000 for his expenses.

Bottomley's visit to Vienna had a touch of comic opera about it. He spoke no German at all and only knew one person in the whole city: a retired Austrian Army officer who eked out his pension by working as a patent and general agent. But the agent rose to the occasion magnificently. Bottomley was met at the station by a Colonel of Hussars and driven off in a gorgeous carriage to the Grand Hotel. The entire staff from the manager to the kitchen scullions greeted 'Milord' Bottomley in the courtyard and they all bowed low as if he were royalty. He was then conducted to the Prince of Wales's Apartments, reserved for Edward, Prince of Wales, on his pleasure-trips to the city. The agent had told everybody in Vienna that he was one of the world's richest financiers and had come there to represent the Lord Mayor of London—Sir Henry Isaacs—who was very nearly as important as Queen Victoria.

The leading Austrian printers called on Horatio next morning and Dr Ludwig Kunwald, a lawyer who spoke perfect English, conducted the negotiations. The following day Dr Kunwald took him to see the leading printers and publishers, and on the third day he signed a working agreement with them. On his last day Dr Kunwald and his colleagues turned up at the hotel and impressed on him that it was vital to the success of their deal for him to meet Count Taafe, the Prime Minister. An audience had been arranged for eleven o'clock and in Vienna it was *de rigueur* to wear evening dress, which they called *Frack*. Horatio had no dress clothes and was afraid that nobody in the city could possibly have a *Frack* that would fit him. However, Dr Kunwald insisted on his meeting the Prime Minister, so it was arranged that he should borrow a *Frack* from a man who was alleged to have the same ample proportions as himself.

When the *Frack* arrived, it was a disaster—the Viennese gentleman was much fatter than Horatio! Since it was unpardonable to be late for the Prime Minister, Horatio did his utmost with the borrowed *Frack* and tucked it round him in every possible place. But it was a sheer waste of time—he left the Grand Hotel for his audience looking like a circus clown.

Having signed 'binding contracts' with the printing firms, he departed for England in a jubilant mood. But at the end of the year the Austrians wrote to the Hansard Union asking for an advance of £75,000 on the sum agreed for the take-over of their businesses. Bottomley called an Extraordinary Meeting of the board in March 1890 and read them the letter from Vienna. After he had convinced them that the Anglo-Austrian Union would be wrecked unless they could find this money, Coleridge Kennard arranged for £75,000 to be advanced to Hansard through various banks and Horatio undertook to forward the money to Vienna immediately.

The Hansard Union held a General Meeting in July, at which the board announced a profit for the year of £40,877 and declared a second dividend of eight per cent. The shareholders never had the faintest idea that the company was almost insolvent and the board had been obliged to issue £250,000 debentures in order to pay the dividend and replenish their coffers. After inspecting the extension to Hansard's premises in Great Queen Street, Henry Burt, the general manager, addressed the shareholders in glowing terms. 'In a short time the Hansard Union will more than double its enterprise,' he promised. 'That organization will make the business the finest of its kind in Britain. . . . There are no more practical men in the country than those who are in charge of this section of the business.' The shareholders would have been horrified if they had known that by the autumn there was only £1,120 left in Hansard's banking account. Once again Bottomley reassured the board about their position and managed to persuade them to borrow £50,000 from the Debenture Corporation. This welcome injection of capital enabled the directors to pay themselves a fee of £200 each, while Horatio drew £2,300 for his salary and an agreed percentage of the two dividends paid by the Hansard Union.

However, this 'snowball' finance could not go on indefinitely. On 15 December the interest was due on the £50,000 which Hansard had borrowed from the Debenture Corporation, but

D

there were no funds to meet it. The debenture holders clamoured for their money, and Henry Burt resigned as general manager and went over to their camp. Ugly rumours were circulating in the City about the Hansard Union, and the Stock Exchange wags called it 'Bottomley's Swindle'. The following February the debenture holders took possession of the company's premises in Great Queen Street; Bottomley's options lapsed on the deal to take over the Austrian business and the £75,000 supposedly paid by the Anglo-Austrian Union to the Austrian printers was liable to be forfeited.

On 2 March 1891 the Anglo-Austrian shareholders appointed a committee of investigation and later published a report marked: PRIVATE, *for use of Shareholders only*. A few items from it show the hopeless state of the company and indicate how Bottomley had manipulated the board:

> The result of our investigations as to 'the conditions and prospects of the company' is to show that its condition is insolvent and its prospect is liquidation. On 13 August 1890 a Board Meeting was held at which Sir Henry Isaacs, Mr Kegan Paul and Sir Roper Lethbridge were present. Mr Bottomley attended and, according to the minutes, received a cheque for £10,000 stated to be for 'working capital'. At that time the company was not in possession of any business, either here or in Vienna.
>
> The payment of the last quarter's Debenture interest almost exhausted the company's funds at the bank; and at the present time the company is in possession of no other assets other than a trifling balance (if any) at the bank. . . .
>
> The company has acquired no business in Vienna or elsewhere, has no property whatever, and its whole capital appears to be lost.
>
> Your committee is of opinion that the present board should not be entrusted with the future management of the company's affairs.

Although Bottomley had taken a total of over a hundred thousand pounds from the two companies, nobody knew where all the money had gone. In the summer he was forced to file a petition in bankruptcy at Portugal Street, Kingsway. He was publicly examined before Registrar Linklater, who was most anxious to see the books of the Hansard Union. Bottomley had several skirmishes with him on this matter.

'I wish to give you a direct answer,' said Horatio at one juncture. 'If you think that I personally kept the books, I personally never kept a book in my life.'

Later, Bottomley was examined at great length by the Official Receiver, Charles John Stewart. As a result of his findings, it was decided to prosecute Bottomley, Sir Henry Isaacs, Joseph Isaacs, and Charles Dollman in connection with the Hansard crash. They were summoned to appear before Mr Justice Hawkins and a special jury to answer charges of conspiring to obtain money from the shareholders of the Hansard Union and the Anglo-Austrian Printing and Publishing Union. The City thought it was all Lombard Street to a china orange that Horatio Bottomley would be found guilty and have to spend a long period as the guest of Her Majesty.

4 Spellbinder in Court

> *The voice is one of singular charm and power. Low, melodious, strong, it is an admirable instrument for an advocate. . . . I could not help feeling what a loss to the Bar had been sustained by Mr Bottomley's devotion to the City.*
>
> 'BARRISTER-AT-LAW', article on the Hess libel trial, 1904

The Hansard trial opened on 30 January 1893 before Mr Justice Hawkins in the High Court of Justice. Sir Charles Russell, the formidable Attorney-General, led for the Crown, assisted by Mr C. F. Matthews and Mr W. Gill. It was said of Russell that 'the power that made him the greatest advocate of his time was best displayed when fraud or perfidy or malice had to be exposed'. In 1894 he was appointed Lord Chief Justice and given the title of Lord Russell of Killowen.

Although Sir Charles Russell was prosecuting, Bottomley conducted his own defence and appeared in person. He had acquired great legal skill and knowledge through working in solicitors' offices and reporting in the law courts, in addition to which he was a natural orator. The jury admired him and even favoured him for having the courage to oppose some of the leading barristers in court, while Mr Justice Hawkins was extremely impressed by the way he conducted his case.

Mr Justice Hawkins (later Lord Brampton) was considered one of the ablest men in the King's Bench Division, although his severity in criminal cases had led to his being nicknamed 'the hanging judge'. He was accused of taking a malicious pleasure in the discomfiture of inexperienced witnesses who appeared in his court. One might have expected Bottomley to have had a rough passage with this judge, but Hawkins was an eccentric of seventy-five who allowed himself to be swayed by the whims and prejudices of the moment.

The other defendants at the trial were Sir Henry Isaacs, the former Lord Mayor, represented by Sir Ernest Clark, Q.C.; Joseph Isaacs, represented by Mr Cock, Q.C.; and Charles Dollman, represented by Mr Lawson Walton, Q.C. The court was packed with a fashionable crowd of spectators who felt that the Hansard case was going to be as good as a play. Frank Harris, who came to listen to it every day, said, 'I was never more amused in my life, or more interested.'

Sir Charles Russell had marshalled an almost cast-iron case against Bottomley and his associates. The various businesses and properties bought by the Hansard Union at an inflated price had resulted in enormous profits to the vendors, which had all been passed on to Bottomley. 'The facts reek of fraud and are incapable of an honest interpretation,' declared Russell. 'Mr Bottomley, with the assent of some of the directors, was manipulating the board in order to put dishonest gains in his pocket.'

Russell began with the purchase of the Bridge paper-mills at Cullompton, mentioned in the last chapter. First Joseph Isaacs bought them, then he passed on the contract to Charles Dollman. Dollman promptly offered to sell the paper-mills to the Hansard Union at a large profit to himself.

'I am most anxious to see the original of this [*Dollman's*] letter,' said Russell. 'If this document was submitted to the directors, why is there no trace in the minutes that it was ever before them? Was it prepared by Mr Bottomley himself? The shareholders' report of that date [*1889*] makes no mention of it.'

Bottomley had visited the Cullompton mills with Sir Henry Isaacs and been introduced to Mr Hall, the owner of the mills, as 'Mr Williams'. Bottómley said in his evidence: 'We had a very pleasant evening. Sir Henry Isaacs sang and Mr Hall prayed.'

'Should not that be "played"?' asked Mr Justice Hawkins.

'No, *prayed* is correct,' replied Bottomley.

There was laughter in court, since Bottomley obviously meant that Mr Hall was praying for them to buy his paper-mills, which had been losing money for years. The mills had to be extended to suit Hansard's requirements at an estimated cost of £50,000. Dollman offered them to the Hansard Union inclusive of the extensions, together with the Atheneum printing-works at Redhill, for £105,000 on 26 May 1889. Bottomley accepted the offer on behalf of Hansard on 26 August, and the money was paid over to Dollman's solicitor, Mr Webb.

'Bottomley was the dominus of the whole matter,' declared Sir Charles Russell.

On 2 September Bottomley wrote to Webb, asking him to return the £50,000 earmarked for the extensions to the paper-mills on the pretext that Hansard were unable to proceed with the work for the present. Dollman paid this money into Bottomley accounts in two instalments. Russell stated that Bottomley had also made a profit of £55,000 on the sale of the paper-mills and printing-works to the Hansard Union.

He dealt next with Hansard's purchase of five printing companies for £325,000 from John Phillips, one of Bottomley's clerks, in April 1889. Since Hansard had spent most of their capital in buying the printing companies and the properties, Bottomley persuaded the board to increase their capital to £1,000,000 and, to hoodwink the shareholders, they paid a dividend of eight per cent in October.

Charles John Stewart, the Official Receiver, testified that the five printing companies in the Hansard merger were sold to John Phillips for £237,000; this meant that there was a profit of £87,000 on the sale to Hansard which was passed on by Phillips in three payments to a Bottomley banking account. Various payments made by Bottomley to Joseph Isaacs had also been traced by the Official Receiver. On 4 July 1890 the Hansard Union held a General Meeting, announced a profit of £40,877 and declared a second dividend of eight per cent.

'This was a complete fiction,' thundered Sir Charles Russell. At that time Hansard only had £1,120 in the bank, but a £50,000 loan had been raised by Coleridge Kennard. Bottomley then cross-examined Mr Stewart, who was largely responsible for instituting the prosecution.

'I have no personal feeling against Sir Henry Isaacs or yourself in this matter,' said Stewart. 'I have never expressed a desire to bring about a prosecution of Sir Henry Isaacs or Mr Bottomley. Most certainly I have never said that if it succeeded it would be a great feather in my cap.' Perhaps he did protest too much.

Sir Henry Isaacs, giving evidence, was questioned about his visit to the paper-mills and said he had not heard Bottomley addressed as 'Mr Williams' there. However, he admitted he had not informed the Hansard board that his brother, Joseph Isaacs, had bought the mills, nor did he tell them later that Charles Dollman, the new purchaser, was Bottomley's brother-in-law and an undischarged bankrupt.

Bottomley opened his defence on 14 February and immediately transformed the atmosphere of the trial; it had seemed a foregone conclusion that the prosecution would succeed, but gradually their case began to weaken. There was no doubt that thousands of pounds had gone into Bottomley's pocket, but 'as soon as he stood up to address the court, all this faded into irrelevance', noted Frank Harris.

'After the dreary legal arguments to which they have listened, it will be the duty of the jury, and I almost said their pleasure, to hear what the defendants have to say in their defence,' Bottomley began. 'The Crown has had unqualified access to all documents of mine and to every scrap of paper, however private. . . . I will satisfy the jury that the Hansard Union was no fraud and I am no criminal.'

He complained bitterly about the way in which the Official Receiver had sworn evidence against him.

BOTTOMLEY Fraud and fraud only was the essence of every question put to the directors of Hansard . . . The report of the Liquidator [Stewart] was sent to the Public Prosecutor, who after twelve months made up his mind to bring this prosecution. . . .

No Hansard director has been called except the defendants [Bottomley and Sir Henry Isaacs]. . . . The whole case rests on the evidence of the liquidator. No auditor or accountant or other director has ever called it a fraud.

'I have gone bankrupt in forwarding the interests of Hansard, in which I glory,' he said, '. . . and though not of an advanced age, I see that I have committed twenty-one pages of crimes.'

'That is nothing,' commented Mr Justice Hawkins, very

amused. 'I remember an indictment with ninety-nine counts.'

An extraordinary event had taken place in court. Hawkins, the 'hanging judge' and the terror of criminals, had established a *rapport* with Bottomley, and as the trial progressed it was obvious that he sided with him against the prosecution.

'For twelve months the stigma of this prosecution has been hanging over me, preventing me from getting my discharge over my bankruptcy or embarking on any fresh undertakings,' said Bottomley later. 'I ask the jury to say by their verdict that I have remained true to my post and done my duty to the company, which has been wrecked by others, and whose assets have been recklessly dissipated.'

Bottomley's manner in making an emotional appeal to the jury was most effective. He distorted the facts to make it appear that he was the innocent victim of a vile conspiracy masterminded by a ruthless man at the top—the Official Receiver.

Harold Farman, a solicitor, whose firm had acted for the Hansard Union and the Anglo-Austrian Union, was called for the defence and testified that he had a conversation with Stewart in 1891.

'Stewart said, "If I could find a criminal case against Bottomley and the directors of the Hansard Union it would be a feather in my cap."'

A juryman caught 'flu and the Hansard trial was adjourned on 19 February. It was resumed on 17 April with the vital difference that Sir Charles Russell no longer led for the prosecution as he was required for another case. He was replaced by Sir John Rigby, the Solicitor-General, which was a tremendous stroke of luck for Bottomley; Sir John Rigby was a Chancery Leader with little experience of jury trials and not in the same class as Sir Charles as an advocate. Mr Justice Hawkins treated him rather patronizingly and allowed Bottomley to interrupt him on several occasions, in contempt of court. When Bottomley asked, 'Is the Solicitor-General addressing your Lordship or the jury?' Hawkins replied, 'I haven't the remotest idea.'

Mr Charles Kegan Paul, a director of Hansard, gave evidence. Questioned about the purchase of the paper-mills at Cullompton, he said, 'We thoroughly and entirely agreed with every word said by Mr Bottomley. . . . I had implicit confidence in the ability and integrity of Mr Bottomley. I cannot say how many shares I held. I bought some a few days before the collapse, so great was my confidence in the company.'

On 19 April Sir John Rigby, the Solicitor-General, summarized the case against the Isaacs brothers. He contended that they were guilty of conspiring to obtain money by false pretences and also of conspiracy, omitting the false pretences. Mr Bottomley had obtained moneys of the company to a very large amount for the Bridge and Atheneum works and he was aided by Sir Henry Isaacs and Mr Joseph Isaacs . . .

SOLICITOR-GENERAL May 22nd is a day of the greatest importance. They go to the mills. An agreement is signed and Mr Joseph Isaacs takes it away. On the same day the report of the managing director [of Hansard] recommending that paper-mills and printing-works should be acquired by the Hansard Union is laid before the board, and the principle is accepted. (Sir Henry Isaacs in the chair.) Therefore on that day Bottomley, Joseph Isaacs and Sir Henry Isaacs were doing things showing that they were in concert.

Mr Isaacs said that he was buying the mills for his son, not Hansard. Sir Henry Isaacs should have said he knew there were negotiations going on that would perhaps put an end to Hansard buying the mills. Joseph Isaacs must have consulted his brother.

On the 24th he sent a telegram that the matter was settled. This was done without any valuation, inspection of the books or other precaution taken such as you would normally do to protect your own money. . . . An agreement was made that Isaacs would hand over the mills to Bottomley for a profit of £5,000.

Mr Joseph Isaacs had never expended sixpence. An account was kept and every farthing was repaid by Bottomley.

. . . Sir Henry Isaacs might not have known what was going on, but the question for the jury is whether he was cognizant of what was going on or was a mere tool.

On 29 July Hansard needed additional capital to acquire the paper-mills. Bottomley therefore put a resolution to his accommodating board. There was no more talk of Dollman's purchasing the mills because Bottomley was successful in passing a resolution and getting consent to the scheme. Then Mr Dalton Easum, an accountant, made a valuation for Hansard of the Cullompton paper-mills.

SOLICITOR-GENERAL The only contribution as to the value of his report was based on what he had been informed, and it did not say by whom he had been informed.

HAWKINS, J. No evidence has been called on either side to show what the value of the mills and works really was. It is a very remarkable omission.

SOLICITOR-GENERAL The insufficiency of the report shows that Easum was in the plan. I do not charge Sir Henry Isaacs with neglect, I charge him with complicity.

HAWKINS, J. The price the mills fetched [when Hansard subsequently sold them] was about the weakest evidence of their value I can imagine.

COCK, Q.C. [*for Joseph Isaacs*] The Solicitor-General has only sketched, not made clear any charge. Joseph Isaacs stood in no fiduciary position to the company. . . . The whole facts show that Joseph Isaacs took up the Cullompton mills as a speculation. He had a perfect right to do this.

HAWKINS, J. Joseph Isaacs had a perfect right to buy the property even if he did so with the intention of getting an exorbitant profit. Bottomley is in a fiduciary position, but I do not understand that this prevents him buying property with a view to making a profit providing he makes a full disclosure. . . .

On 20 April, the twenty-second day of this marathon trial, Mr Justice Hawkins announced that he thought the case against Sir Henry Isaacs had failed.

HAWKINS, J. I do not at present express my reasons. But I have a strong opinion it ought not to go to the jury.

SIR ERNEST CLARK [*for Sir Henry Isaacs*] I ask for a verdict for Sir Henry Isaacs of Not Guilty.

HAWKINS, J. Yes, I think that ought to be done. I have thought this matter well over.

The judge then directed the jury to find Sir Henry Isaacs Not Guilty.

After lunch, Bottomley rose and made his address to the jury.

BOTTOMLEY I hope to induce you to hesitate and even to refuse to brand me as a criminal. . . . I am sure I can convince you that there was no criminal intention on the part of any of the defendants. . . .

Mr Stewart, the Official Liquidator, does not occupy the position of an impartial and fair-minded official. If there is a conflict of evidence between Mr Stewart and any other man in this case, I ask you to prefer that of the other person. Mr Stewart has departed from the truth in several instances. The information he swore was a most specious document. Mr Stewart omitted all sorts of important facts. Was there ever a more degraded exhibition than Mr Stewart in the box? He was the real prosecution. He made the appalling admission that it was by his suggestion that certain witnesses were kept out of this box. I ask you to disbelieve Mr Stewart.

Bottomley had cast Stewart, the Official Receiver, as the villain of the piece. By attacking him at every opportunity he planned to focus the judge and jury's attention on Stewart, so that his own guilt would be played down.

He pointed out that Article 8 of the Hansard Union expressly stated that a director might be interested in the promotion. He then attacked the prosecution for not calling his clerk John Phillips, vendor of the printing companies to Hansard.

'The system of a nominal vendor is universal,' Bottomley contended. 'I had no criminal intention. I did not desert the company, as many promoters do. The jury might consider making an example in this case. I have no desire to be made the Jonah. I ask you, gentlemen of the jury, to say there is no evidence of fraud,' said Bottomley.

He proceeded to give a most lucid account of the origin of the Hansard Union, explaining why it had been considered necessary for the prosperity of the company to buy the various businesses and properties. He convinced the court that it was a serious and enlightened conception.

'I've never heard such a complete statement,' said the Q.C. sitting next to Frank Harris, full of admiration for Bottomley.

Bottomley stated that he had paid £9,000 to advertise the Hansard prospectus and paid a ten-per-cent deposit to the five printing firms before they merged into the Hansard Union. The underwriters had to be paid a high rate of interest for the risk they ran in floating the £500,000 company. In addition he had to spend money on legal expenses making a total of £40,000 to £50,000.

HAWKINS, J. We can see that it is reasonable to surcharge the price of a reasonable amount of expenses. But instead of allowing £100,000 it might be reasonable to allow £50,000. The directors must not sit idly in the chair and allow that.

BOTTOMLEY My argument is that the public subscribe on the faith of the prospectus. They are told the price is £325,000 and they form an opinion as to whether this is a fair price by the valuations.

HAWKINS, J. There are two charges of fraud: one, the fraudulent prospectus; two, that there was deception practised on those who had the provisional contract before them.

SOLICITOR-GENERAL I withdraw Counts 8 and 9.

'The indictment is growing beautifully less,' observed Bottomley, sensing victory in the air. 'It would have been of great assistance to me if there had been a thoroughly trustworthy report made as to the value of the property. If Mr Stewart could have proved that the mills were worth very much less than was given for them he would have produced the evidence.'

Later, he submitted that Mr Webb, Dollman's solicitor, ought to have been called for the prosecution.

'Mr William Webb was smuggled into the court and hustled out of it,' he declared. 'The inference was that though Webb would not have produced the original Dollman offer [for the paper-mills], still he would have identified the copy.'

Bottomley admitted that at the Hansard shareholders' meeting on 29 July 1889 he made a strong effort to persuade them to approve the purchase of the paper-mills and the printing-works.

'But nothing in the contract between Isaacs and Dollman compelled the company to buy the mills. Hansard was free to buy them or not,' he contended. 'The mills were the only suitable ones of which particulars reached the company. It was a matter of complete indifference to me as to whether the Hansard Union purchased or not.'

This was sheer bluff on Bottomley's part, because it was vital for him to get the shareholders to approve of this purchase.

'Why were not the books of the company produced [by the Official Receiver's department],' he demanded. 'They dare not have produced them! There is no evidence that the Hansard Union ever bought a worthless or losing concern.

'If the Dollman offer was a genuine one, it puts an end to the case. It cannot be impeached. No single question has been put to comment on it.'

Bottomley admitted he had made a profit of £55,000 for himself when the paper-mills and the printing-works had been sold to the Hansard Union. But was this a startling sum in regard to the expenditure made? He had to repay a sum of money to Joseph Isaacs (for the paper-mills) and £26,000 of the amount paid by Hansard was settled by giving the vendor their shares.

Bottomley continued to address the jury the following day. Mr Justice Hawkins returned to the matter of Dollman's offer to sell the paper-mills and printing-works to the Hansard Union.

'Every possible twisting of a charge was put in the indictment,' complained Bottomley. 'The Hansard business never failed—it was wrecked! Its business is still flourishing. I refused to be a party to the wrecking and have therefore been singled out for the prosecution.'

This was a clever rhetorical point for the jury, but it was a downright lie to describe Hansard as a flourishing company. They had used up all their capital and could not even pay the interest on their debenture loan of £50,000.

'I would be the last to attack absent men, but circumstances force me to speak,' protested Bottomley. 'I am the first to admit there has been gigantic fraud, although you have not got the right man before you. One at least of the men who took an active part in the wrecking is now fleeing from justice.'

He probably referred to Henry Burt, the general manager, who had resigned from Hansard and supported the debenture holders. Nobody mentioned Burt's name during the trial and he may have gone abroad for some reason; Bottomley, an expert at throwing red herrings across the trail, seized on this as evidence of his guilt.

'I am not going to plead for sympathy or make any artificial appeal,' he told the jury. 'I am simply going to ask you to do your duty and to remind you that your first duty is to me. No home and no reputation has been more wrecked than mine. I assure you no criminal intention ever passed my mind, and I ask with confidence for your verdict.'

At the end of his speech there was applause in the court, which was instantly suppressed. Frank Harris remarked that Bottomley's long speech showed an ignorance of grammar and a cockney incapacity to pronounce the letter *h*.

Mr Lawson Walton, Q.C., spoke on behalf of Charles Dollman, and submitted that Dollman had no idea of joining in a criminal conspiracy. Sir Henry Isaacs was Lord Mayor of London at the time of the deal and Dollman was asked to take part in it with men of the highest position in the City.

Mr Cock, Q.C., spoke next on behalf of Joseph Isaacs. He declared there had never been the shadow of a case against Joseph Isaacs in connection with the sale of the paper-mills to the Hansard Union. The prosecution had failed in their duty in not producing all the evidence which would throw light on the matter, whether it was favourable to themselves or to the prisoner. No witness had been called to show that Bottomley and Isaacs had asked a single penny more than the mills were worth. Mr Cock maintained that the Official Receiver should have placed the evidence of Mr Hall, the owner of the paper-mills, before the law officers for them to exercise their discretion on it.

On the following day Mr Justice Hawkins opened the proceedings. Addressing Sir John Rigby, he said, 'I may as well tell you, Mr Solicitor—I will not explain my reasons, which I may give hereafter—that I think the case ought not to go to the jury in regard to Mr Joseph Isaacs.'

'Your Lordship has not heard me,' protested the Solicitor-General.

'I heard you the whole day!' Hawkins replied. 'I ought to take the responsibility of not letting it go to the jury. I have thought it over seriously. It is quite sufficient to say I have made up my mind.'

Mr Justice Hawkins instructed the jury to find Joseph Isaacs not guilty. Sir John Rigby, the Solicitor-General, then addressed the jury on behalf of the prosecution of the remaining defendants—Horatio Bottomley and Charles Dollman.

SOLICITOR-GENERAL The direction by his Lordship of a verdict of not guilty in the cases of Sir Henry Isaacs and Joseph Isaacs has considerably shortened my task. . . .

He proceeded to do his utmost to press home the charges against Bottomley and Dollman. He contended that the 'Dollman offer' to the Hansard Union of paper-mills and printing-works for £105,000 was the key to the whole case.

SOLICITOR-GENERAL The nominal vendor ought not to be put forward when Mr Bottomley was managing director. If the effect was to keep from the subscribers and directors Mr Bottomley's true position, practically there was no sale at all. . . .

The charges against Bottomley and Dollman are justified under Section 81 of the Larceny Act.

After 29 July, Mr Bottomley was alone interested in the matter, yet he and Mr Dollman went on as if Bottomley was not interested in the property. . . . If the jury come to the conclusion that Bottomley and Dollman were working to a plan . . . the conclusion is that they were guilty of conspiracy. I submit that Dollman knew that Bottomley was going to put over £55,000 into his pocket, subject to what he had to pay out of it. . . .

Why were the contracts signed by Dollman—not Bottomley? It is my duty to suggest that it was not accident, but design—to conceal the true position of Bottomley from the other directors.

If the jury are satisfied that Dollman was a party to the scheme, the prosecution have made out the case against him. I ask the jury to return a verdict according to the evidence.

Sir John Rigby, the Solicitor-General, had been very dull and long-winded. While he was speaking, Mr Justice Hawkins sent round a note to one of the counsel:

PATIENCE COMPETITION

First Prize	Henry Hawkins
Honourable Mention	Job

Mr Justice Hawkins summed up on 26 April, the twenty-fourth day of the trial. He told the jury 'You have to decide:

(1) Was there a conspiracy between Bottomley and Phillips?

(2) Was there a conspiracy between Bottomley and Dollman for the purpose of obtaining a contract from the directors by fraud?'

HAWKINS, J. I think the evidence of a conspiracy between Bottomley and Phillips is as unsatisfactory as it can be. . . . If the prosecution thought Phillips was a conspirator he ought to have been included in the indictment. If they thought he ought to be Queen's Evidence he ought to have been called; but he was not, although he was available for this trial. . . .

The fourth and fifth counts allege that Sir Henry Isaacs, Joseph Isaacs, Bottomley and Dollman conspired to obtain by false pretences the money of the Hansard Union. Those counts are left for your consideration.

The scheme seems to have been rational—to amalgamate into one large company several businesses. Early in 1889 Bottomley took steps to carry out the scheme. At the time there was no company incorporated . . . and I can see myself no objection to a man coming forward and being what is called a nominee for the purpose of carrying out the provisional arrangements if he is willing to take up that position. . . . The vendors had a right to ask as much as they liked, just the same right as a private person had. The properties were thriving and genuine businesses. . . .

The prospectus of the five printing companies set out what is literally true and the price had been fixed at £325,000. On 15 April [Hansard directors' meeting] no doubt the directors ought to have inquired into the provisional contract and to have seen if it ought to be adopted. . . .

I fail to see the evidence of fraud and conspiracy suggested by the prosecution. . . .

If the case for the Crown was that the directors had been deceived, surely one of them could have been called to say so. Not one was called. There must be a conspiracy to defraud to make it criminal. The evidence is flimsy upon this part of the case.

. . . The mere fact of a director [of Hansard] making a secret profit does not make him criminally liable. . . . If he obtained the money by false pretences or conspired to obtain it by fraud, it would be criminal.

Mr Justice Hawkins then referred to the Hansard Union's purchase of the Cullompton paper-mills.

HAWKINS, J. In a complicated matter one is apt to say, 'Well, there is an air of mystery about the whole thing,' but it is necessary for one to say, 'There is the illegality.'

> Suppose Bottomley went to see the mill with the object of buying it and reselling it to the company, there was no illegality. But if he made a secret profit by the sale he would be liable to hand over all his profit to the directors for the benefit of the company, but it is not a criminal offence. On 25 May Bottomley was free to buy or sell or deal with the property as any other person.
>
> ... As to the purchase of the properties ... if the report of Mr Easum, a Chartered Accountant, is attacked, where is the evidence of the value of the mills?
>
> The conspiracy between Bottomley and Dollman to defraud the company is connected with what has been called 'the Dollman Offer'.... The jury must be satisfied that there was an intention to defraud.... Fraud must be established against them both.
>
> I desire to express my view that there is no credit to be attached to the conduct of the directors in this particular case. . . . There is no criminal law which will punish a director who scandalously neglects his duty though he takes the money. . . . Directors ought not to neglect, by what I call criminal negligence, the interests of those who repose confidence in them. . . .

Mr Justice Hawkins then passed on to the evidence of the Official Receiver. 'I am not sure that Bottomley was altogether unjustified in his comments on Mr Stewart's evidence. I would be telling an untruth if I said I saw no traces of hostility in Mr Stewart. I do not like to see something like animus.

'I heartily congratulate the Solicitor-General on his first appearance in a criminal case,' said Hawkins.* 'He said what everyone will agree with—that there ought to be no animus. Fairness is essential to the proper conduct of a prosecution from the beginning to the end. . . . Nothing can be more

* The judge was paying a barbed compliment to Sir John Rigby, whom he had treated patronizingly ever since his replacement of Sir Charles Russell.

horrible than a man being convicted by insinuations which evidence could not sustain. . . . A man facing a criminal charge faces absolute ruin. . . .'

HAWKINS, J. [*turning to the jury*] You must be sure a man is guilty. You are not to find him guilty on evidence you have not got. You are at liberty to say, 'Are we satisfied upon the evidence that is before us, knowing that there is evidence which might have been given?'

The defendants have a right to be acquitted unless the prosecution has satisfied you by the evidence that guilt has been brought home to them. I will not say that they are entitled to the benefit of the doubt—in such cases they have a right to acquittal.

The jury retired at 2.30. They returned at 2.55 and declared a verdict of Not Guilty.

'That makes thirteen of us,' whispered Mr Justice Hawkins.

The foreman of the jury added, 'The jury endorses every word of his Lordship as to the law being amended regarding the duties and responsibilities of directors.'

Friends of Horatio Bottomley swarmed round to congratulate him on his acquittal. The barrister who had listened to the trial every day with Frank Harris pointed across to Bottomley.

'A damned clever *outsider*!' he said.

II

PAPER MILLIONAIRE

5 Champagne and Kippers

> *He had two brains, that man. One linked up with his tongue and the other thought while he talked. . . . You could see the second one reflected in his eye as he wove his spell of words and watched your reaction to the sounds he made.*
>
> SIR HARRY PRESTON (on Bottomley), *Leaves from my Unwritten Diary*

The Hansard trial had been featured in every newspaper in the country, and Bottomley's triumph against all the odds had established him in the public's mind as a financial genius. Ordinary people ignored the fact that he sent the Hansard Union bankrupt in the short space of two years and that out of a capital of £1,000,000 a matter of £600,000 could not be accounted for. Mr Justice Hawkins had called Horatio to his private room after the trial and advised him to take steps to become a barrister; he believed that his gift of oratory and wonderful flair for the law would ensure him an illustrious career at the Bar. A few days later Hawkins sent his clerk round to Bottomley's office with a brown paper parcel. Inside Bottomley found the judge's wig and his notes of the Hansard case, which Hawkins asked him to keep as a memento. This was a unique occurrence. He had been convinced by Bottomley's defence and hoped he would become a leading barrister one day.

'Alas! I went to the City,' said Bottomley, reminiscing later. 'Three years seemed such a long time to wait.'

He was thirty-three and determined to follow up his success

immediately. He believed the quickest way to fortune was to become a company promoter, but first he had to remove the stigma attached to his name in connection with the Hansard crash, which meant trying to persuade the authorities to rescind the winding-up order against the company. He applied to the Official Receiver with the proposal that he should go to Vienna to collect the Austrian assets of the Anglo-Austrian Printing and Publishing Union, which he undertook to hand over on his return. Mr Justice Vaughan Williams agreed to his proposition and he departed to Vienna, but this time he stayed at a very small hotel.

Nobody ever knew what transpired there, but he returned to England empty-handed. Nevertheless, the winding-up order against the Hansard Union was rescinded in August 1893, so his journey had not been in vain.

In the nineties gold was discovered in vast quantities around Kalgoorlie and in other areas of Western Australia. Westralian shares boomed as investors snapped up every share that came on the market, and since communications were then extremely slow and primitive it was a bonanza for unscrupulous City promoters. A hole in the ground in Western Australia could be boosted into a very promising gold-mine, and investors only found out they had backed a loser after the mine had been floated as a public company and they had paid hard cash for their shares. Bottomley called on Osborne O'Hagan, the financier who had backed his Catherine Street Association, and managed to borrow £2,000, which was quite sufficient to set him up as a promoter of Westralian mining shares. At that time men with an option on a gold-mine regarded London as their Mecca; they came to the City with their precious bits of paper and visited Bottomley or one of his competitors and did their utmost to persuade them to float another mining company.

England was basking in peace and prosperity in 1893 and the climate was ideal for the entrepreneurs; investors bought gold shares indiscriminately in the hope of doubling or even trebling their capital. Some of them bought share certificates from Bottomley whose only use was to decorate their walls two years later. Horatio's companies had a way of booming at first and then sinking like a stone. He usually contrived to pay one dividend to inspire confidence and then, after he had milked the company to pay for his personal expenses, of which we shall soon be hearing, he would reconstruct it under a new name.

In one year he floated twenty-three companies with a total capital of ten million pounds. Out of fifty Bottomley companies which were traced, twenty-four had been reconstructed and twenty had gone into voluntary liquidation.

In this way he became a rich man in three years and soon repaid his loan to Osborne O'Hagan. It was true that he occasionally floated a genuine Westralian gold-mine: his Gold Mines of Australia, for instance, was extremely successful and after the re-capitalization he sold his original shares for a million pounds. The greatest money-spinner of them all was Great Boulder Mines: Bottomley brought them out at two shillings a share and at one time in the nineties they rose to £13. Although he had sold out at half this price, he still made an enormous profit on them.

But he had to face a few little local difficulties on the way up. In the first year he was entertaining some City backers to lunch at his flat in Carlisle Mansions, Victoria, when the maid, who had been hired for the occasion, came in and whispered to his wife, 'Two bailiffs outside!' Eliza hurried out and asked the bailiffs if they would wait for a while as they had friends to lunch. 'Sorry, Ma'am,' said one of them, 'but we want to have a look round and see what you've got.' She gave the men half a sovereign and some beer and they agreed to wait in the kitchen. Then she returned to Horatio and whispered the bad news in his ear. 'Keep them outside for another half-hour and then I'll be finished,' he said coolly.

Bottomley announced in the Press that 26 April 1897 was going to be known as 'Hansard Day' because he was holding a meeting of the unlucky shareholders at the Cannon Street Hotel on that day. At the Hansard Relief Meeting he produced a certificate signed by Dalton Easum to the effect that he had examined the Hansard books and that £32,470 had already been distributed to shareholders. There was prolonged applause from hundreds of hopeful shareholders as Bottomley continued:

'I have been perhaps successful beyond the average run of success, having regard to the short time. . . . I have resolved upon the step which I now announce to you, and that is, that out of the proceeds of my success, and inclusive of the £32,000 I have just referred to, I am in the happy position, and it is my intention, to present £250,000 to the Hansard shareholders.' [*Loud and prolonged cheers*]

He ended: 'I hope I shall now be in a position to bring about such changes in the law of our country as will render absolutely impossible a repetition of the great crime which wrecked the Hansard Union.' [*Cheers*]

Later, James Judd, one of his company directors, called Horatio a Napoleon of Finance; but the truth about his splendid gesture was that he only paid out a small fraction of a quarter of a million in cash. Most Hansard shareholders were persuaded to take shares in the West Australian Loan and General Finance Corporation, a Bottomley company that had the doubtful distinction of being reconstructed four times.

The *Financial Times* ran a pictorial supplement entitled 'Men of Millions', and Bottomley was included among the new magnates with Barney Barnato, the South African diamond king, and Whitaker Wright, the financier. But Horatio was only a paper millionaire; he spent money like water.

A few years before he had bought a small country cottage at Upper Dicker, near Eastbourne, and as soon as he made money he started building on to it, until he ended up with an enormous red-brick mansion which dominated the whole village; he furnished it in grandiose taste and called it The Dicker. He bought vast areas of adjacent land to give himself an estate in keeping with the palatial mansion. Six gardeners had to be employed to attend to the lawns and flower gardens and the big kitchen garden. Later, he had a ploughed field converted into an ornamental lake in the grounds; a well had to be sunk in order to fill the lake and they also had to build a pumping-station. He kept cattle on the estate and had his own dairy farm. When The Dicker was completed there was accommodation for thirty guests; he entertained lavishly at week-ends and employed a large indoor staff. Bottomley had the only telephone in the village for a long time and allowed anybody to use it. The train used to stop specially at Dicker Halt in order to pick up 'the Squire'.

One of the joys of being a rich man is that you can afford to indulge your tastes, and Horatio did not stint himself for anything once he had, almost literally, struck gold. At Mason's Orphanage he had been deprived of material comforts and for nearly twenty years it had been a hard struggle before he hit the jackpot. Perhaps his stay at the Orphanage provides the key to his complete recklessness about money after 1896. In his struggling days Horatio had acquired a fondness for wine—particularly for champagne. Now he was able to afford to have vast supplies on tap of Pommery, his favourite champagne. He drank at least a bottle a day and declared he absolutely depended on it to keep him fit. He loved it so passionately that he abstained from smoking in order to preserve the keenness of his palate. He had champagne and kippers for breakfast and kept up this diet as long as he could possibly afford it.

But champagne was only one of his extravagant tastes; the most expensive day of his life was probably when he bought his first racehorse. His horses were trained a few miles across the Sussex downs from him at Alfriston, and he invariably had a bet on them; but being Horatio he did nothing by halves and had at least £250 each way on his own horses. Quite often he backed them for thousands, and whenever he went to a race meeting he used to bet in hundreds or thousands. Another expensive item was his harem of pretty girls whom he kept in flats in various districts in the West End of London.

It is hardly surprising that Eliza Bottomley was unhappy in the ambiance of The Dicker. The workmen were in and out of the place so much that she complained she never had any privacy, and she disliked 'Orace always being up in London on business during the week. He had taken a magnificent apartment at 56a Pall Mall and she nattered because she saw so little of him till the week-end, and at week-ends the house was always so full of noisy guests that they never had time for a cosy chat. Eliza, a simple cockney, was never cut out for the role of Squire's lady in a small Sussex village. She was a fish out of water and often felt miserable and told 'Orace she was much happier in the good old days when they were striving to pay the instalments on the piano. The people in Bottomley's circle—businessmen, racing men, barristers, bookies, theatre people and hangers-on—found her dull and rather stupid. Moreover, her health had begun to deteriorate after the birth of their daughter Florence in the eighties.

Bottomley began his career on the Turf in 1898, informing the Press in his flamboyant way that his horses were being trained with the object of winning both the Derby and the Grand National. He thought he had a great chance of winning the Derby with Hawfinch, whom he had bought as a two-year-old after he had won the Dewhurst Plate in brilliant style. But he was over-enthusiastic and would not let his trainer, Harry Batho, bring Hawfinch up to peak condition by gradual stages. 'I wanted to see a Derby trial every time I went to the stables,' he admitted. Batho humoured him and ran the young horse in so many training gallops at Alfriston that by the time the Derby came round in June Hawfinch was a spent force. But Horatio refused to scratch him. He led the field for the first hundred yards of the Derby, then dropped out and finished last. Horatio had no better luck in the Grand National, where his horse, Gentle Ida, fell at the first fence.

It took him years to realize that he was a complete ignoramus about racehorses. As he preferred racing 'over the sticks' he would often decide to put one of his flat runners to hurdling and expect Batho to have it ready to win a race two months later. If he ever bought a horse on his own judgement it invariably turned out to be a dud. His well advertised interest in racing helped to make him a popular figure with the British public, but what he really liked best about it was that it gave him an excuse to gamble. 'I have always been fond of a gamble and I love taking the odds,' he said.

Incidentally, his racing colours were red, white and black, the colours of the German Emperor. He was told that he should change them during the First World War.

'There is no need for that,' he would say, 'for the German Emperor, like my horses, will never win.'

However, he won the Cesarewitch twice in his racing career and also carried off the Stewards Cup, the London Cup and many minor races. Sometimes he managed to bring off a spectacular betting coup but he never became a good judge of form and was a godsend to the bookies. Although very unbusinesslike about settling ordinary accounts, he always kept faith with the bookies and paid them in the end; in fact he was such a good customer that they gave him unlimited credit in the 'ring'.

Racing had a great influence on his slang. If he had just coped with a difficult situation he would say, 'I got over that fence all right.' If his secretary, W. F. Holland, had to check up on somebody's reference, he would say, 'Find out his form.' If he was beating his opponent in a law case, the man was 'tailed off', and if he thought someone was a failure he called them an 'also-ran'. Most people regard racing as a sport and never expect to win if they have a flutter. But Horatio, being an incurable optimist, always expected to pull off a big coup at the races and never realized that punting was costing him thousands of pounds a year.

Running a harem in the Bottomley manner was another extremely expensive pastime. He kept a number of mistresses in West End flats, mostly in different districts because he liked to carry on two or three affairs at a time and hated any girl to know she had a rival and get jealous. He liked little women with auburn hair of a low social class and his choice generally fell on chorus-girls, barmaids, waitresses and women journalists. His lady-friends called him 'Botty' or 'Skipper' and were given generous presents regularly and special gifts on their birthdays. Whenever he went abroad or left town he sent them affectionate telegrams signed BOTTY or SKIPPER, whichever was appropriate. Sometimes he liked to visit his mistresses in their family circle. He would arrange for flowers and a case of Pommery to be sent on in advance of his arrival, and when he arrived and saw the champagne he would say coyly, 'Now I wonder who on earth could have sent that bubbly?'

Considering the number of lady-friends he acquired over a long period it is extraordinary that their names have remained a dark secret. Henry Houston, who was to become his political secretary, knew him as well as anybody in his entourage and wrote a book about him, but he was most discreet and never revealed the name of a single one of these charmers. Horatio was very fickle and often changed his mistresses; he was never seriously in love with anyone in the harem until he met Peggy Primrose, of whom we shall hear in later chapters.

West End flats were rented for the harem, very discreetly, by 'Tommy' Cox. When Bottomley had first met Cox in the eighties he was a medical student and Horatio was working for a solicitor. Tommy Cox never qualified as a doctor, and instead joined Horatio in his first venture into the financial world, the Catherine Street Association. Tommy had been one of its directors and was also connected with the ill-fated Anglo-Austrian Union. When Horatio went into the City Tommy Cox became his right-hand man and was made a director or officer of every one of the Westralian mining companies, which got him the nickname of 'Bottomley's Rubber Stamp'. A sharp little man of only five feet, he was a hard drinker and just as susceptible to a pretty girl as his chief. Tommy Cox called Bottomley 'H.B.' and was absolutely devoted to him.

Another of Cox's functions was to organize Bottomley claques at his law cases and his shareholders' meetings; members of the claque got three shillings an hour in the nineties, but in the new century the rate went up to ten shillings. The claque also sprang into action when Bottomley was backing a show; its members occupied most of the gallery on a first night and applauded at the top of their voices.

Horatio began his career as a theatrical angel by backing a light comedy called *The Bungalow* which failed to draw the public. He tried again with *The Judge*, starring W. S. Penley, one of the leading comedians of the day. Penley, an extremely selfish actor, complained to Horatio over lunch at Romano's that the other people in the company were getting too many laughs.* Horatio therefore told them all to underplay—with the result that *The Judge* was condemned after a very short run.

Romano's in the Strand was his favourite restaurant. W. S. Penley came in there one day at lunchtime specially to ask Horatio to back him in a new farce.

'Is there a good part for you in it, Penley?' asked Bottomley.

'It's the part of my life!' the comedian assured him.

'Sorry, old chap, but I won't put up a penny.'

'But why not?' demanded Penley, very disappointed.

'Because if any of the others were to get a laugh you'd wreck the show!' retorted Bottomley.

Though he had scored over Penley, he had missed a golden opportunity: the farce was *Charley's Aunt*, which was first produced on 21 December 1892 and is still revived eighty years later.

Nobody could accuse Bottomley of being a highbrow, yet the only time he ever made a real profit as an angel was when he backed Forbes Robertson in *Hamlet* in 1897. He arranged to lease the Lyceum Theatre from Sir Henry Irving, who very generously gave him the sets for the play at a nominal cost. Forbes Robertson was acclaimed as the finest Hamlet of his generation, the public flocked to see him and Horatio made a profit of £5,000. Fired with enthusiasm for Shakespeare and Forbes Robertson, he agreed to back *Macbeth* at the Lyceum the following year. Mrs Patrick Campbell played Lady Macbeth opposite Forbes Robertson, and, despite the tradition that *Macbeth* spells disaster in the theatre, Horatio just managed to break even on the production.

By the time Bottomley was described as 'a new millionaire' he had acquired an entourage of men who would do anything

* Guy Deghy, *Paradise in the Strand* (Richards Press, 1958).

for him without asking questions. He called them his 'bodyguard' or, more often, his 'stable'. An original member of the stable was his brother-in-law, Charles Dollman, one of the defendants in the Hansard trial. Another was Saul Cooper, an Austrian furrier. Dalton Easum, the tame accountant who appeared at the Hansard Relief Meeting, was also in the stable, which included several accountants and solicitors, as Bottomley never knew when he might require their services. He also had a squad of ex-boxers and ex-policemen, who could be very useful in an emergency. And there were a few boon companions who did nothing in particular, but were tolerated because they flattered Horatio and amused him. All these men more or less depended for their livelihood on him; Tommy Cox, Dollman and Saul Cooper called him 'H.B.', the others called him 'The Chief' or 'The Guv'nor'.

When Bottomley had to cope with an awkward shareholders' meeting his claque, under the management of Tommy Cox, was invaluable. At the end of 1898 he came under fire in connection with the Westralian Market Trust, a mining finance company which had recently been reconstructed. On 24 January 1899, he addressed a crowded shareholders' meeting at the Cannon Street Hotel and made this plausible speech:

BOTTOMLEY It is sufficient to remind those of you who may not be acquainted with all the facts that after a brief and, one might say, brilliant career, our progress was somewhat rudely interrupted and we found ourselves confronted by a crisis which threatened our very existence. But we came to you, the shareholders in the company: we put all the facts before you and thanks to the response which you have made to our appeal, I am content today to give you the assurance, in the presence of every one of my colleagues on the board, *that our difficulties have been completely overcome*. [*Loud applause*]

And I should like to say a little more than that. . . . I think, with the concurrence of my colleagues, I can say this—that not only have our difficulties been overcome, but that we are once more on the road to prosperity. [*Applause*]

But I would like to go a step further than that, if you will not misunderstand me, and if my colleagues will not misunderstand me, I will say that, but for my colleagues on the board, I would promise you a very early dividend on your shares. [*Shouts of 'Hear, hear'*]

You must understand that the troubles to which I have referred have given some members of the board a little shock, and they are determined to be extremely cautious in any official utterance which may receive their sanction in the future. Therefore, for the moment, voicing the directors of this company, I will say no more than this—that we have got over all our troubles, that we are well on the road to success, and that we anticipate at a very early date being able to say something even more satisfying than that to the shareholders in these companies. [*Applause*]

. . . I say, without hesitation, that the new business we have in hand, the large amount of new business which we are entering upon, will *much more than earn us sufficient money to pay you a handsome dividend indeed upon the shares you hold in this undertaking*. [*Applause*]

And I think that if that turns out to be true you will feel that you have acted wisely when you responded to the appeal we made to you at a time of trouble and decided that the Market Trust should not be wrecked. [*Hear, hear*]

. . . I am going to try very hard to get you those dividends before inflicting another speech upon you. . . . I am going to conclude by telling you in the simplest language that we have got over our troubles, we are doing well, and we shall soon be paying dividends again. [A voice: '*When?*'] You must ask my colleagues that, sir. [*Laughter*]

We shall soon be paying dividends again, and if you are wise people, you will buy all the Market Shares you can get under par, and having got them, I hope you will keep them

> until you have the accounts of the companies. [*Loud applause*]

It was a speech well calculated to keep the shareholders happy: the Market Trust had turned the corner and could even pay a dividend if only Bottomley could persuade his ultra-cautious directors to loosen the purse-strings. The truth was that Bottomley packed his boards with easy-going directors, and if the company could really have paid a dividend it would have done so like a shot. One also notices that he went out of his way to tip the shares as a good lock-up investment . . . yet only five months later the Market Trust shares (£1) had fallen to 1*s.* 6*d.*, and Bottomley was being asked some searching questions by a Dr Alexander of Putney on behalf of the dissatisfied shareholders.

> *Holly Lodge,*
> *Putney*
> *27 June 1899*
>
> DEAR MR BOTTOMLEY
>
> I am in daily receipt of letters from shareholders of the 'Westralian Market Trust' and the 'Joint Stock Trust', asking for information and advice, or expressing doubt and apprehension: and it becomes increasingly difficult to reply—not only because of their number, but also because of my own want of special knowledge and of the feeling which I share with my correspondents that the continual fall in the price of the shares must have some definite cause—other than mere depression of mining shares. . . .
>
> If these doubts and fears, therefore, are unfounded, it would put many anxious minds at rest to prove them so. If, however, the case is otherwise than it should be, the correct course should be to get the real facts of the situation. I desire, on behalf of the numerous shareholders who are in communication with me, to have an opportunity, if you will kindly afford it to me, of looking into the position of these companies, for I will not disguise from you that considerable uneasiness prevails on the subject. I again disclaim any inimical feeling . . . and I hope you will see fit to give me an appointment in the course of next week.

Bottomley replied promptly from his City offices.

Broad StreetAvenue, E.C.
29 June 1899

MY DEAR SIR

. . . In regard to the Market Trust, the directors are now considering the question of either calling a meeting of the shareholders or issuing an interim report, and pending their decision I do not feel at liberty to say more.

With reference to your request for an opportunity of looking into the position of the two companies [Market Trust and Joint Stock Trust] whilst I do not doubt your statement as to the representative capacity in which you make it, you will not, I hope, misunderstand me when I say that before such a request can be considered I am sure the boards of both companies would require more definite information as to the character and extent of the representative authority which you claim.

Of course the very last thing Horatio wanted was for Dr Alexander to be allowed to look at his mining companies' books. But he had not yet heard the end of the self-appointed watchdog of the shareholders.

DR ALEXANDER TO BOTTOMLEY *4 July 1899*

MY DEAR SIR

I would have wished that you might be able to give some definite assurance that the wretched prices and prevalent uneasiness in no way reflect the true position of these companies. I do not, of course, read your letter in the contrary sense, but I am sorry it was not more precise. . . .

I am in daily receipt of letters from numerous shareholders . . . and though I do not pretend to have any formal mandate, I cannot be insensible to the requests, and even appeals, which reach me in such number. . . . I feel, therefore, that a duty is laid upon me, and I cannot but respond to it. . . .

I propose—unless you decidedly object—to send a copy of this correspondence to the shareholders, and if you will kindly state the amount, I shall send you a cheque for the list of shareholders in these companies, which I now beg to order, and request be at once sent to me.

BOTTOMLEY TO DR ALEXANDER *11 July 1899*

MY DEAR SIR

I must apologize for not having answered your letter of the 4th inst. earlier—but I have been very much occupied during the past week. In the meantime . . . there has been a considerable appreciation in the quotation for the shares—and I trust that at this juncture my efforts to restore the fortunes of the two companies are not to be interrupted by anything in the nature of internal agitation. Under these circumstances I do not think any great purpose would be served by your communicating with the shareholders in the manner you suggest, although, of course, I cannot prevent you doing so should you be so advised.

If you are in touch with a considerable number of shareholders, and you will furnish me with their names, I will look up their holdings and consider how far I may be justified in meeting them with you for the purpose of an informal, and I trust friendly, conference upon the present position of affairs.

In brief, whilst I strongly deprecate anything in the nature of a 'movement', I would rather welcome the assistance of any bona fide group of shareholders in the difficult and somewhat wearing tasks upon which I am engaged.

This was a clever attempt to play for time with Dr Alexander by asking him not to rock the boat just as the shares were starting to rise again. However, Dr Alexander was not to be fobbed off quite so easily:

DR ALEXANDER TO BOTTOMLEY *14 July 1899*

MY DEAR SIR

On the 12th inst. I received your letter. I at once accepted your implied challenge, and went to your office to satisfy you that I was expressing the views, and fears, of many hundreds of shareholders, but you were too busy with your boards and I could not see you.

Yesterday, I at length procured speech with you and I must say that . . . I do not think it right that any one man should be subjected to such continual strain and tension; and I do not think it safe from the shareholders' point of view that their interests should so greatly depend on one man's brain or health or life. . . . I am deeply disappointed at the futility of my efforts to prevail on you to take the shareholders into your complete confidence. . . .

Let me again appeal to you, so that I may not have to appeal to the shareholders who, after all, are the real masters of their concerns. There is a weak spot—perhaps several—somewhere. . . .

At the risk of offence I speak out boldly and plainly. I only hope that you will be able to demonstrate that I am mistaken along the whole line. If you do I shall be rejoiced, and will properly and frankly apologize: if you do not I shall . . . ask the shareholders to take up the common cause by common action.

This letter must have sounded rather dangerous to Horatio: he mulled it over for a few days before sending a reply.

BOTTOMLEY TO DR ALEXANDER *20 July 1899*

MY DEAR SIR

I have duly received your letter of the 14th inst. I do not in any way question the sincerity of the attitude you have taken up, nor do I altogether dispute that there may be force in some of the contention which you have tabulated in your letter.

In the best interests of the shareholders, however, I would strongly appeal to you at this juncture, as I hope that in a few weeks from now the boards of the two companies will have arrived at a decision in reference to certain proposals of a very important character, the outcome of which would be to remove most of the weak spots to which you refer, and the official announcement of which will afford you and your friends, together with the shareholders generally, ample opportunity for ventilating any questions affecting the interests of the shareholders.

DR ALEXANDER TO BOTTOMLEY *20 July 1899*

MY DEAR SIR

We are getting on something like common ground and I, therefore, cheerfully comply with your wish to do nothing in the meanwhile. I truly hope that the outcome of what you contemplate will be speedy and satisfactory.

Thus Horatio, without really doing anything positive on the lines requested by Dr Alexander, managed to play for time. Their correspondence shows us that Bottomley's Westralian mining companies were running into trouble, but apart from that the Boer War broke out and was casting its shadow on the Stock Exchange.

It was at this period that Horatio wrote to his stock jobber partner:

> MY DEAR HARRY
>
> What on earth have you done with our nugget—the one we used to show to shareholders in the old days? I've got hold of a promising client, all he wants is a sight of the stuff.

There is a revealing anecdote about Bottomley at this period. When he walked into his office one day he found the office-boy in tears, being rebuked by the Company Secretary for stealing stamps.

'We've been losing stamps for months, and I've got to make an example of the brat,' he told Bottomley.

'Give me a chance, sir,' said the office-boy to Bottomley. 'I won't do it again, I promise you.'

Horatio sent the boy out of the room, then said to his colleague, 'You'd better give him another chance.'

'No, I can't do that—we must make an example of him!'

'Oh, don't take any notice of it,' said Horatio. 'After all, *we've all got to start in a small way*.'

Horatio had a domestic problem on his hands. Eliza's health had continued to deteriorate and the doctors advised her to leave England and go to a warm climate. Horatio therefore bought a large, attractive villa named Bell'Aria at Roquebrune in the Alpes-Maritimes near Monte Carlo and transported her there. Eliza was much happier in the south and it proved most beneficial to her health. She remained on excellent terms with Bottomley, after closing her eyes to his peccadilloes in town. He went abroad every year and often used to stay with her at the villa. Their daughter Florence, who had grown up into a charming, good-natured girl, preferred to stay on at The Dicker rather than join her mother; she used to act as hostess for Horatio at weekends. Prosperity had made him a super-optimist and he felt that everything had happened for the best.

He enjoyed seeing Eliza now and then, but it was a treat to be able to entertain his lady friends for week-ends at The Dicker without having a guilty conscience.

Being very keen on tennis, Bottomley had a grass court specially designed for him, and held tennis-parties at week-ends. He played a good game, moving about the court with surprising agility for a man of seventeen stone. He was determined to win, and often called a good return 'out'.

He had an impressive billiard-room, and delighted in showing off his skill on his fine table. Thanks to some coaching he had become almost professional standard and was rarely beaten. His butler generally marked the score—left to himself, Horatio was apt to cheat. The family doctor once discovered that the score had been reversed to give Bottomley a lead of 68–56. 'Oy, just a minute! You haven't scored for a quarter of an hour,' said the doctor indignantly.

Visitors to The Dicker were shown into a neo-gothic hall with imitation stained-glass windows. On one side there was a gigantic organ, probably never played; opposite there hung a life-size portrait of Bottomley. At the back of the house was a 'museum' with several portraits of Bottomley himself and Charles Bradlaugh; the place of honour was occupied by Mr Justice Hawkins's wig and his notes of the Hansard case. Bottomley was to appear before dozens of judges during his unique career, but he never again found one as sympathetic as Hawkins.

6 The People's M.P.

> *In many ways I consider Mr Horatio Bottomley to be one of the most attractive speakers to whom I have ever listened. . . . His House of Commons style was almost ideal.*
>
> F. E. SMITH, *Cambridge Review*, 1912

Whatever the faults of Horatio Bottomley, one cannot help admiring his amazing energy. Just consider some of his activities in the new century: he was managing director of over twenty Westralian mining companies; he became the proprietor of an evening newspaper, the *Sun*; he frequently went to see his racehorses in training and always watched them run; he backed theatrical shows and took a personal interest in them; and he supervised the alterations and improvements being carried out at enormous expense at The Dicker. Nevertheless, he still found time to try and achieve his great ambition: to become a Member of Parliament.

I have mentioned that he stood for the Liberals at Hornsey in 1887 and only lost the seat by a small majority. Impressed by his promising debut, the North Islington Liberals invited him to represent them at the next election. North Islington was rather a forlorn hope at that time; the Tories held the seat with a clear majority, and the sitting member was very popular. But Bottomley accepted the challenge and for two years he worked hard to gain the goodwill of the constituency. He developed a man-to-man style which went down remarkably well at meetings and never refused an invitation to appear at a local function, however boring it might be. There were certain traits of the actor about Horatio Bottomley. Whenever he spoke to the working classes he dressed for the part and wore a simple dark grey suit, with a black tie and black boots to create the impression that he was an 'ordinary bloke' like the people in the audience. He changed out of all recognition if he had to meet financiers in the City, greeting them in a huge, opulent fur coat under which he wore a frock coat and morning trousers. His political meetings in the country called for a different rigout: he usually appeared in an old tweed suit, brown boots and a soft hat.

He made such a striking impression on the electors of North Islington that the Liberal agent began to think he might manage to win the seat. But when the Hansard Union crash forced him to go bankrupt in 1891 he had to resign as a parliamentary candidate. Tommy Cox had given him splendid support at North Islington and had found a useful recruit for the 'stable' in John Harrison, a street-corner orator generally known as 'the People's Perkins' and reputed to have lungs of leather.

After Bottomley had made his mark in the City in the nineties the Liberals invited him to represent South Hackney, a much more promising seat, and he soon made himself very popular in the constituency. He answered every begging letter and sent money to anything that looked like a deserving cause, and it was rumoured that by the turn of the century he was paying out seventy pounds a week. He gave a big Christmas Party every year at which he appeared as Father Christmas and gave costly presents to the children. Tommy Cox made sure that his generosity to the poor was well publicized and organized a claque at all his meetings, while the People's Perkins spoke frequently and was ready to burst his lungs for the Guv'nor. Bottomley's cockney wit and down-to-earth oratory made him an ideal candidate for the working-class population of South Hackney.

He fought his first campaign there in the 'Khaki' Election during the Boer War in 1900, which resulted in a landslide for the Tories. He lost the seat by only 280 votes after being violently attacked in a newspaper article in the *Critic* by Henry Hess. The latter described Bottomley as a fraudulent company promoter, a share-pusher and a bucket-shop keeper. 'This barefaced swindler has engineered one imposition after another on the credulous public,' said Hess. 'Many of his victims are now in the workhouse . . . and now he is bribing with their money the unwashed of South Hackney. His place is at the Old Bailey, not at Westminster.'

Bottomley sued Hess for libel, conducting his own case. A barrister who heard him in King's Bench Court IV throughout the trial, which opened on 4 March 1902, was so carried away by his eloquence that he wrote a newspaper piece. This was his impression of Horatio's address to the jury:

> The voice is one of singular charm and power. Low, melodious, strong, it is an admirable instrument for an advocate. . . . For the most part he was conversational: now and again the low voice would rise to indignant heights . . . as the litigant appealed to the noblest instincts of the jury, or declaimed in accents of scathing reproach and scorn against the flimsiness of the case he had to meet, his voice would be hushed almost to a whisper (which only the startled silence of the court made audible).

There was also a telling passage about Horatio outwitting Mr McCall, K.C., Hess's counsel.

> Mr McCall's cross-examination was one long, unbroken triumph for Mr Bottomley. . . . Presently Mr Bottomley got on Mr McCall's nerves. Papers were mislaid, references got lost, important dates could not be fixed. Long pauses ensued while counsel consulted his colleagues, or listened to the eager advice of Mr Hess or his solicitor. . . .
>
> Mr Bottomley stood calm and impeturbable in the box, rarely glancing at a note, relying almost entirely on a marvellously exact memory, never at a loss for a date, a fact, a figure, an explanation.

Hess, an Austrian with a poor command of English, never got in touch with the jury from start to finish. Mr Justice Grantham cautioned him: 'Your voice is too weak and your dialect is too strong.'

Bottomley boldly challenged him to prove a single allegation in his article and Hess failed abysmally. Bottomley cross-examined him ruthlessly and demonstrated that Hess's charges were founded on hearsay and unsound evidence based on incomplete information. When Henry Hess made a statement to the jury Judge Grantham kept interrupting to ask him to draw the line between what he 'alleged', what he 'charged', what he 'submitted' and what were the 'facts'. After Bottomley's address to the jury it was a foregone conclusion that he would win the case.

Mr Justice Grantham, summing up, remarked that Mr Bottomley always appeared to win while the shareholders lost. But there might not be any dishonesty in it at all and Bottomley might have had perfectly bona fide transactions. On 9 March the jury returned a verdict for Bottomley with damages of £1,000. This verdict was a great asset to him; after his acquittal in the Hansard trial and his victory over Hess, it was a long time before anyone tried to institute proceedings against him.

By 1906 the British public had grown tired of the long Conservative administration, and the Liberals under Sir Henry Campbell Bannerman were poised to take power. At the General Election Bottomley again stood as a Liberal for South Hackney, his principal opponent being Herbert Robertson, the Tory member. At the last moment a breakaway faction of the Liberals brought in the Rev. William Riley, who was supported by the *Daily News* and the *Daily Chronicle*, although the other papers called him 'the Cuckoo Candidate'.

Tommy Cox and the People's Perkins and other members of the stable worked day and night for Bottomley, who was in fine form during the campaign. Half the population turned out and cheered when his racehorses marched in procession down the High Street, each with a notice round his saddlecloth: VOTE FOR MY OWNER. He also scored with the racing humour in his pamphlet:

LATEST SPORTING INTELLIGENCE

South Hackney Stakes

RUNNERS

Mr John Bull's HORATIO (dark horse by Vox Populi out of Fairplay)

Mrs Robertson's HERBERT (grey horse by Clap-trap out of South Hackney)

Mrs Grundy's RILEY (H.b. by Crank, out of his mind)

> Horatio, the favourite, continues to go strong. He is daily doing some excellent gallops, and yesterday went the full course of the constituency, pulling up sound and well. His party are very confident.
>
> Herbert, on the other hand, travels badly. All sorts of sinister rumours are afloat. It is said that his fiscal ligament is very dicky, and yesterday he was confined to gentle exercise round the Chinese compound. Certainly his recent outings in public are not calculated to inspire confidence.
>
> Apart from a strong disinclination to face the crowd, he has more than once shown a strong desire to bolt. He is probably stale and requires rest. Every effort will, however, be made to get him to the post.
>
> CLOSING PRICES
>
> 20 to 1 on Horatio
>
> 20 to 1 against Herbert (offered freely)
>
> 1000 to 1 Riley (offered)

The indispensable Tommy Cox made some amusing alterations to two of Herbert Robertson's election posters. One of them read:

VOTE FOR
ROBERTSON
YOUR OLD AND TRIED MEMBER

Cox changed a letter so that it became:

VOTE FOR
ROBERTSON
YOUR OLD AND TIRED MEMBER

Another poster read:

VOTE FOR
ROBERTSON
AND REPUTATION

an allusion to Bottomley's City reputation which was rather dubious at that time. This was changed to:

VOTE FOR
ROBERTSON
AND REPETITION

The angry Tories did not discover this hoax for several hours. Horatio drew big crowds to his meetings who delighted in his quick repartee. At one meeting he was asked:

'Is the candidate in favour of mixed bathing for the unemployed?'

'I am quite unable to consider the possibility of their being unemployed under such conditions,' he replied.

South Hackney elected Bottomley by a big majority, the figures being:

Horatio Bottomley	6,736
Herbert Robertson	3,257
Rev. William Riley	804
Majority	3,479

The Liberals were returned to power and Horatio was congratulated on his large majority. He was forty-six when he rose to make his maiden speech in the House of Commons.

> I have been sent here by the largest majority secured by a metropolitan member sitting on this side, to give the Government an independent and, I hope, an intelligent support, so long as it proceeds on the lines of robust and healthy democracy, but I am here also to oppose all fads and 'isms and namby-pamby interference with the liberty and freedom of our common citizenship.

Members heard the outsider from South Hackney in chilling silence and did not take him seriously at first; they thought him too trivial and were prejudiced by his shady reputation, which had preceded him. During his first Parliamentary session he lay low, waiting until he had got the 'feel' of the House. He first gained attention by calmly asking for a public holiday on Derby Day. He then explained that that particular day was the anniversary of our peace treaty with the Boers and also the birthday of Alfred Austin, the sub-standard Poet Laureate. The House roared with laughter at this form of wit and afterwards they listened to him.

He spoke much more often during the second session in 1907, particularly in criticism of Mr Asquith's Budget Speech. On 13 May he complained about the Government's miserable record on Old Age Pensions.

> The Liberals have had nearly two years of office in a period of unparalleled prosperity. Mr Asquith has said, 'as regards Old Age Pensions, to which I am pledged to the hilt, the utmost I can do is to provide the nucleus of a fund and to lay the foundations of this reform'—language about as vague as any Minister could possibly use.
> . . . We have been told, Sir, time and again, on behalf of the Government, that a system of Old Age Pensions of *five shillings a week* to every person of sixty-five and upwards will require a sum of at least *twenty-eight millions*. I do not agree with that figure. . . .
> . . . Last year the President of the Board of Trade . . . read to the House an elaborate set of figures . . . and I gather that at least *ten millions* is at present spent in the maintenance of old paupers, criminals and lunatics, and as that is already provided for, it follows that the twenty-eight millions will be considerably reduced.
> . . . Taking all considerations together, I have come to the conclusion that *twelve millions* is the outside sum which would be required for a scheme of five shillings a week at the age of sixty-five.

After damning the Government for their attitude towards Old Age Pensions, Bottomley suggested a number of ways in which they could obtain the required funds: an Employer's Tax of a penny in the pound on all wages; super-tax on Investments; Stamp Duty on Share Certificates; a tax on Racing and Betting stakes; State appropriation of all dormant Bank Balances and Securities.

It is a tribute to the acumen of Horatio Bottomley that nearly every one of his suggestions has subsequently passed on to the statute book in some form or another. Next day, the *Daily Chronicle* sang his praises.

> A very striking speech from Mr Horatio Bottomley. The freshness of outlook and originality of idea greatly pleased the House. The Member for South Hackney had a large audience, which he held to the last. Mr Asquith and Mr Balfour, and Mr Lloyd George, and other Front Benchers did him the compliment of listening to him very intently.

During the session of 1907 a newspaper poster proclaimed:

> MR BOTTOMLEY'S ADVICE TO THE CHANCELLOR OF THE EXCHEQUER. HOW TO RAISE £50,000 STERLING.

This prompted Edward Roll, a solicitor's clerk of Tunbridge Wells, to write to him:

> DEAR SIR,
>
> I see you are about to raise £50,000 sterling for the Exchequer: in the magnitude of your financial operations it may have escaped your memory that you still owe my client £50, for which I shall be glad to receive a cheque forthwith.

Bottomley replied immediately:

> DEAR SIR,
>
> Your argument is irresistible: please acknowledge cheque for £50.

Bottomley made some effective speeches in the Commons on licensing reform. He was strongly opposed to any prohibiting and restricting legislation, and objected to the compulsory closing of public houses on a Sunday.

'It does not lessen the consumption of drink,' he contended. 'If Sunday closing, why not Saturday closing? That is the big drinking day.'

He also introduced the first reading of a Bill to authorize the wives of men sentenced to long terms of imprisonment to be able to marry again. The Bill got no further, being years ahead of its time. In fact this only became law in 1970, so Horatio could have claimed to have been sixty years ahead of public opinion. By 1908 he was receiving more notice in the Press than any other back-bencher in Parliament. He once confided to that arch-cynic Frank Harris that his ambition was to become Chancellor of the Exchequer.

'You haven't an earthly chance,' said Harris crushingly. 'All the leaders of the parties will turn the cold shoulder to you, and to get to the top from your standpoint seems to me utterly impossible.'

However, Frank Harris could not prevent Bottomley from having his dreams. He had begun to feel that he was a man of destiny, an idea which was encouraged by his sycophantic associates, who flattered him and overrated his achievements.

At South Hackney he organized annual excursions for the poor people to Epping Forest and the Crystal Palace and ran special trains for them. Five hundred women and their children turned up regularly: Horatio always appeared at these outings and used to pour out the beer himself. His Christmas parties continued and begging letters still received sympathetic treatment. He had become so popular in the constituency that he seemed to have taken an option on it for life.

7 The Birth of *John Bull*

In the end we hit upon John Bull. *We liked the ring of it; it suggested common sense and warm blood and no humbug.*

BOTTOMLEY, *John Bull*, 1906

Although Bottomley had made his fortune as a company promoter he was still fascinated by journalism. In 1902 he bought the *Sun*, an evening paper in competition with the *Evening News* and the *Star* but not nearly as popular; it was then losing £300 a week. Bottomley had the *Sun* printed in green to distinguish it from its competitors and appointed Theodore Dahle, a lively journalist from Leeds, to edit it. He believed he could make the *Sun* a success by specializing in newspaper stunts and sensational stories.

'We stoked the fires to white heat,' he said. 'Be our sensation for the day what it might be, we taught our readers to expect another one tomorrow.'

One of his first stunts was very simple, but it succeeded in putting up the circulation. The office cat walked out of the building one day, so the *Sun* ran a feature—*Has Anyone Seen Our Cat?* They gave ingenious clues as to its whereabouts and aroused tremendous interest which kept the public cat-hunting. The stunt went on for four days, by which time the cat had been found. Sometimes readers wrote in casting doubts on the veracity of items in the *Sun*, and this led Bottomley to coin a slogan: 'If you see it in the *Sun*, it *is* so.'

Many of the stunts in the *Sun* were inspired by the crimes of the period, particularly the murders. When Samuel Dougal was tried in 1903 for the brutal murder of an old lady at the Moat Farm he pleaded Not Guilty, but the jury found him guilty and he was hanged. On the same day the *Sun* published a facsimile of his confession to the murder. Some of Bottomley's murder stunts were worth while: for instance, the case of William Gardiner, a Sunday-school superintendent accused of murdering a girl pupil in a Suffolk village. Although two juries had failed to find him guilty, Gardiner was still kept in prison. The *Sun* appealed for funds to help his defence for the third trial and raised a substantial sum. Gardiner wrote to Bottomley from Ipswich Prison:

27 January 1903

SIR,

No one knows how much I feel the awful agony of this cruel suspense as to my fate. Please let the public know, through the Editor of the *Sun*, what I am suffering.

For the third time I am to be put on trial, though they say that the last time ten were for me and only two against me. Do ask the Editor of the *Sun* if he will let me appeal to the public to assist my wife in getting some funds for my defence. We are all penniless and of ourselves we can do nothing.

Yours obediently,

WILLIAM GARDINER

New evidence in the case was discovered by an eminent lawyer and was submitted to the Attorney-General. The latter decided to abandon the prosecution and William Gardiner was freed.

TO THE EDITOR

Ipswich Prison,
Thursday night

The Governor has sent me out tonight and once more I am free. I can never be grateful enough for what you have done, and your readers.

Yours faithfully,

WILLIAM GARDINER

Another case in which the *Sun* intervened was that of the Grimme brothers, who had been convicted of stealing chests of tea in the East End of London. Henry Grimme had a previous conviction, which first led the police to suspect the brothers, and Henry was then identified by a Stepney warehouse-keeper. A team of *Sun* reporters who investigated the case found that both brothers had very strong alibis, so they prepared a full statement maintaining their innocence and sent it to the Home Secretary. The latter decided to free the Grimme brothers, who wrote to the *Sun*:

12 Sheridan Street,
TO THE EDITOR OF THE *SUN* *Shadwell, E.*
February, 1902

We are glad to tell you that we are out of prison, having been released through your kind efforts for us, for which we cannot be too grateful.

If any employer can give us work and help us we shall be pleased to serve him well.

Yours truly,
HENRY GRIMME
CHARLES GRIMME

One of the most celebrated crimes of the era was the Yarmouth murder. A man named Bennett had strangled his wife with a mohair bootlace on Yarmouth Beach, in order to be free to marry his mistress. Having been found guilty, Bennett lamented in the condemned cell that his little daughter Ruby was doomed to be a penniless orphan when he died. This human story touched the heart of Bottomley, who knew what a wretched fate it was to be an orphan, and he started a fund for Ruby Bennett in the *Sun*. Subscriptions for Ruby poured in and they received enough money to enable them to make her a Ward of Court.

The *Sun*'s racing correspondent, under the nom de plume of 'The Scorcher', had a big following on the strength of his successful tips. He failed to turn up at the office one day and threw the staff into a panic. But the imperturbable Bottomley stepped into the breach; he produced his hat, drew six horses out of it for the meeting of the day and got four winners. As a result of all these stunts the *Sun* increased its circulation, but it never made a profit. The Westralian mining boom had petered out by 1904, and as Horatio was very hard up he sold the paper to the proprietors of the *Globe*. In a few months the *Sun* had set, never to rise again.*

* The *Sun* was an evening paper and had no connection whatsoever with the *Sun* which rose from the ashes of the old *Daily Herald*.

I related in the last chapter how Bottomley became M.P. for South Hackney. Although he was in the red in 1906 he felt he was on the crest of a wave and planned to start a new weekly paper which would be the poor man's *Truth* and expose the evils and injustices of the day. It would sell for a penny and be called *John Bull*, to identify it with the typical Englishman or the man in the street. The John Bull character on its cover, who had a dog at his side, looked remarkably like Horatio himself in a masterful pose. The motto was a quotation from Byron:

The world is a bundle of hay,
Mankind are the asses who pull;
Each tugs it a different way,
but the greatest of all is John Bull.

The slogans on the masthead were:

Politics without Party—Criticism without Cant;
Without Fear or Favour—Rancour or Rant.

Bottomley had the dummy of *John Bull* ready only two months after his election for South Hackney. The next thing to do was to find a printer and a backer, and he was advised to go to Odhams Press, then only in a modest way of business, at Long Acre, Covent Garden. Odhams asked him to call and discuss the proposition with their managing director, Julius Elias (later Lord Southwood). However, Bottomley insisted that Julius Elias should come and see him at his Pall Mall flat. Elias, a small, dapper, hard-working Jew, had never met anyone like Bottomley in his life and dreaded having to deal with such a formidable character. He walked up and down Pall Mall for a long time on the morning of their appointment before deciding to stop at the flat.

Horatio received him at 11.30 in a vivid dressing-gown, just finishing his breakfast of champagne and kippers. He offered Elias a glass of champagne, which was refused because Elias was determined to keep a clear head and concentrate on business. Bottomley wanted Odhams to print *John Bull* and to back it for £50,000. He showed Elias the dummy and outlined the type of paper he intended to produce. He estimated a first print order of 50,000, but was sure it would soon be much larger. Then he mentioned that he had registered a *John Bull* company in Guernsey with a capital of £100,000 and that the principal shareholder was Ernest Terah Hooley.

This immediately put Elias on his guard. Ernest Hooley was an undischarged bankrupt with a shocking reputation; we shall hear a good deal about him in later chapters. Elias also knew that Bottomley was a bad risk: a man who was sitting on a keg of gunpowder which might go up at any time. On the other hand, he liked the format of the paper, admired its lively and provocative point of view and thought it had great possibilities. He appreciated Bottomley's flair for popular journalism and it was an asset that he had become a household name since getting into Parliament. After weighing up the pros and cons, Elias decided to take a gamble and promised that Odhams would back *John Bull*. Having clinched the deal, Elias accepted a glass of champagne from Horatio and they toasted the success of the new paper.

The two men who had just become partners could scarcely have been more different. Elias was a slight, red-haired little man of five feet four and Horatio overshadowed him; he had developed an enormous corporation and weighed eighteen stone. Elias was extremely respectable and quiet, never gambled, hardly drank, and never looked at another woman because he adored his wife. Whereas Horatio was a great womanizer and a great guzzler of champagne; he had a pathological dislike of being alone and was generally surrounded by a lot of people, and he would bet on anything.*

Bottomley started editing *John Bull* from his flat at 56a Pall Mall with Ernest Wray from the *Sun* as his only assistant, using contributions from his journalistic friends. Frank Harris proved a tower of strength in the early days; he advised Bottomley on the make-up and other details, wrote the leaders and also reviewed the books and plays. Another regular contributor was Theodore Dahle, the ex-editor of the *Sun*. Herbert Vivian, one of the principal staff writers, devised an entertaining feature called 'Prisoner at the Bar' which put a famous person on trial every week and then passed sentence on him. The principal feature was 'The World, the Flesh and the Devil':

> The Editor reviews the events of the week and the passing topics of the hour. In these notes we shall be no respecters

* R. J. Minney, *Viscount Southwood* (Odhams, 1954).

> of persons, of place, or of power. If we think a man a thief, we shall not say he is lacking in the power of differentiation between 'meum' and 'tuum'. But we shall never be spiteful, or petty, or bad tempered.

Written by Bottomley, 'The World, the Flesh and the Devil' lambasted politicians, company directors, judges and magistrates. The paper covered many interests; there was John Bull in Parliament, John Bull in the courts and John Bull in the City. 'Racing Notes and Ideas' were contributed by William Lotinga, a well known racing correspondent who also wrote as 'Larry Lynx' for the *People*.

Another feature was the Open Letter to a celebrity. The first one was addressed diplomatically to King Edward VII:

> With Your Majesty on the throne, Parliament is almost a redundancy. You are more of a democrat than most of its members.
>
> GOD SAVE THE KING
>
> Your faithful liege,
> *John Bull*

John Bull was fearless, dogmatic and rather sensational for its time. It had a lively style and, although sometimes guilty of bad taste, was always entertaining. It promised to expose any form of humbug and always took the side of the under dog. *John Bull* first appeared on Saturday 12 May 1906 and was sold out in a few hours; it had caught the public's fancy and the circulation rose steadily. In the first issue Bottomley related how he had arrived at a name for his paper:

> In the end we hit upon *John Bull*. We liked the ring of it; it suggested common sense and warm blood and no humbug. There, in a sentence, is our policy.

In the second issue he wrote an Open Letter to the Prime Minister, Sir Henry Campbell Bannerman. 'In view of the fact that the Liberal Party has been returned by an overwhelming majority, the country expects you to institute new and vigorous policies.' Since Campbell Bannerman was rather a half-hearted politician, the letter ended: 'Enough of this fooling! As you are strong, be Brave. Wake up!'

Ben Tillett, the Labour Trade Union M.P., contributed a piece on A. J. Balfour, the Leader of the Opposition, in which he said: 'Mr Balfour says nothing so beautifully, I could listen to him for hours.'

Herbert Vivian wrote an amusing series entitled *John Bull's Auction*. One week his subject was Joseph Chamberlain, who had changed his politics from Radical Liberal to High Tory.

Sale of Joseph Chamberlain's Coat and Oddments.

> Sixpence did I hear? Why, his coloured coat alone is worth that sum. . . . Well, you will always find him ready to change it at a moment's notice. When new, it was a brilliant and revolutionary red, it is now true blue (more or less) and no man knows what it will be next.

The third issue of *John Bull* contained a specimen of Bottomley's chauvinistic leanings—an article by 'Jim Crow' which was a crude libel on the French people.

The Foul French

> Cordial understanding may be all very well for political purposes, and I join in admiration of Edward VII's diplomacy, if only because it means an economy in armaments.* But it will be well to remember that the French are corrupt, tyrannical, bloodthirsty, sycophantic, unmannerly, treacherous and lecherous.

After the first month Editor Bottomley felt it was time to beat the big drum about his paper. '*John Bull* is a month old and he has come to stay. The success of the journal has been quite phenomenal. No other newspaper in modern times has come near it.' In the same issue he printed a prospectus of the John Bull Investment Trust. (*Managing Director*—Horatio Bottomley, M.P. *Minimum Subscription*—£10). Subscribers were promised the benefit of 'that special and exclusive information which is obtainable only as the result of an intensive City experience'. Since the boom in Westralian mining shares was

* A reference to the Anglo-French Entente Cordiale which had been signed in 1903.

over, *John Bull* gave Bottomley an opportunity to utilize his talents on the small investor who was often too frightened to visit a legitimate stockbroker, but trusted Horatio Bottomley. In the early days of the paper 'Jim Crow' wrote a companion piece to his article on the French.

The Gentle German

> . . . They are not deterred from aspiring to dominate the destinies of Europe. . . . The only future which I can anticipate for them is to go on providing the world with cheap clerks, nasty waiters and other philosophers. . . .
>
> All character has long been battered out of them. They are all machine-made, with lives and habits fashioned in the same ugly mould.... They are enslaved, body and soul, by hordes of offensive officials, who in their turn are the vassals of other bureaucrats. . . . Their language is the harshest and clumsiest in the world.

In July *John Bull* chose a rising young Liberal politician named Winston Churchill as its Prisoner at the Bar. He was accused of 'travelling too rapidly', a reference to the fact that he had made such a success as Under-Secretary for the Colonies at the age of thirty that he was tipped for Cabinet rank. 'Counsel of the Prosecution' stated that 'in this country it is in the interests of every imbecile that progress should be *slow*'. The 'Judge' decided that Winston Churchill should 'be sentenced to public servitude for the rest of his natural life'. Bottomley had the greatest admiration for Churchill, and if he had lived to see World War II he would certainly have been proud at the way in which he 'served his sentence'.

When Bottomley first met Elias he had mentioned a *John Bull* company in Guernsey of which Ernest Hooley was the main shareholder. The latter had persuaded an old man named David Powell to put £10,000 into the shares. But when the old man read the paper for the first time he was shocked by its 'blasphemy'. It praised Charles Bradlaugh and freethinkers and agnostics and seemed to have the utmost contempt for Christianity. Powell asked Hooley to come and see him at his home in Watford.

'Mr Hooley, I'm afraid I can't keep these John Bull shares,' said the old man.

'What's the matter?' asked Hooley, alarmed.

'Why, this man Bottomley is an infidel. I bought a copy of the paper last week and I was simply horrified. He doesn't seem to believe in anything!'

Ernest Hooley went to see Horatio immediately and gave him a lecture.

'You must have more respect for people's feelings, my dear fellow. You are losing readers.'

'My dear Ernest, d'you really think I care tuppence about Bradlaugh or anyone else? If you want us to preach orthodox religion then by all means let's have it.'

The following week *John Bull* published a moving article about the red blood of Christ. Old Powell read every word of it and decided to keep his shares after all.

John Bull became so popular that Julius Elias decided to transfer the editorial offices from Bottomley's flat to Odhams' premises at 67 Long Acre. Before the summer was over he had to buy new printing-presses to cope with the increasing public demand for the paper.

8 A British Institution

It thinks by infection, catching an opinion like a cold, and there is nothing so little that it will not roar itself wild about it when the fit is on: nothing so great but it will forget it in an hour, when the fit is past.
JOHN RUSKIN, Essay on 'The Mass Mind'

'We have a positive genius for taking risks,' wrote Editor Bottomley on the first anniversary of *John Bull*. 'When, after many successes and many disappointments, we had at last said good-bye to the City and its sordid life, and had fought our way into Parliament, we determined to return to our first love and to start a paper. . . . *John Bull* is the greatest success of modern journalism.' He announced that the circulation had reached over half a million. *John Bull* had become an institution.

The British public showed their confidence in it by subscribing £100,000 for shares in the John Bull Investment Trust, which was extremely gratifying to Horatio even if it did not make up for the lean times he had encountered since his fall from grace as a company promoter. His remarks about the 'sordid life' of the City might have led his readers to imagine that Bottomley had been the innocent victim of City sharks, but Horatio Bottomley hardly ever admitted his own misdeeds; from the time of the Hansard Union he had practised a dangerous form of self-hypnosis.

John Bull continued to debunk people in authority and to expose any matter which Horatio considered a public scandal. There was an open letter to Rudyard Kipling, whose great literary reputation had slumped after the Boer War, stating that he 'murdered the King's English' in his poetry. Kipling was maliciously described as 'a Fourth-form singer, simply the Poet Laureate of boys from 12 to 16'. He was castigated for writing doggerel and warned that if he was not careful he would suffer the fate of Macaulay: '. . . in a single generation after his death he is forgotten and only remembered to be sneered at . . . and his fate will be yours.' Of course this was a foolish judgement, but it was typical of Bottomley to run with the tide and proclaim that Kipling had had his day. When the First World War broke out Bottomley became a great patriot overnight and lamented that we lacked a young poet with Kipling's genius for expressing pride in Britain and the Empire.

In the summer season *John Bull* wrote open postcards instead of open letters to the famous. Two examples would have upset our Diplomatic Service if they ever read the paper:

> TO THE KAISER OF GERMANY—I hope in your mercy you will not invade London in 1910 as forecast by William Le Queux in his book.
>
> TO H.M. KING OF THE BELGIANS—The King of a people very often has nothing to do with the land except cover himself with the mud. . . . We hear of your vices, of Congo horrors, of the persecution of your family.

The Post Office, the Income Tax and even the Salvation Army were examined by *John Bull* and found wanting. The first article on Income Tax was entitled 'The Grand Inquisitors of Income Tax and How To Deal With Them'. After publishing critical articles about the Salvation Army, *John Bull* wrote an open letter to General Booth on the eve of his departure on a grand tour of the United States: 'If you do not first visit the State of New York you will run the risk of killing your movement in America. . . . Tell us straight, what do you do with the money?' General Booth was warned of the dangers threatening him if he refused to face the music in the State of New York. 'Do, like a good man, go to New York and face Satan,' *John Bull* advised him.

The paper had started a new feature, the John Bull Exposure Bureau, whose object was to investigate any organization or individual suspected of acting nefariously. It was ironical that a man with Bottomley's shady reputation should set up an unofficial detective agency. The Bureau employed a team of retired policemen and private detectives; its chief investigator, Captain Edmondson, had served in the Boer War and still carried a revolver in his belt, and there was an unkind rumour that he had been cashiered for deserting his post in South Africa. As a result of the Exposure Bureau *John Bull* received an enormous readers' postbag, and hordes of undesirables began turning up at the office, most of them cranks or crooks or petty blackmailers. Soon Elias had to find extra accommodation for the staff. The Exposure Bureau resulted in many writs for libel being served on *John Bull*. When they began coming in at an average of four a week the Odhams brothers grew very worried and so did Elias, but Horatio remained as cool as a cucumber and told Elias, 'I don't mind how many libels we get. I'll go to court and defend them myself!'

He seemed to revel in fighting libel actions. As he was reputed to be the best lay lawyer in England by then, he probably felt he needed plenty of practice to keep up to concert pitch. In defending these libel cases he used a brilliant technique of turning logic upside down and cross-examined witnesses with consummate skill.* This combination generally enabled him to win the verdict, and even when he lost the plaintiff often got awarded a farthing damages and it was all good publicity for *John Bull*. However, after Bottomley had been fighting the paper's libels for a few years the Odhams brothers thought it would be better to keep his name out of them and F. E. Smith (later Lord Birkenhead) was briefed to defend them. This magnificent advocate nearly always won his cases; gradually fewer writs for libel came into the office and the Odhams brothers heaved a great sigh of relief.

To give Bottomley his due, the Exposure Bureau did some admirable work in showing up various types of frauds and swindles and in calling the public's attention to cases of outrageous conduct by institutions or individuals.

The most famous scandal was in connection with the *Akbar* reformatory training ship which lay in the Mersey. In 1910 the headmaster gave *John Bull* a dreadful account of conditions in *Akbar*; boys were gagged and birched for minor offences until the blood came, and another punishment was immersion

* It is significant that Charles Bradlaugh 'had a talent approaching genius for the cross-examination of lying witnesses'.

in ice-cold water for a long period. After *John Bull* had exposed the scandal it was brought up in the House of Commons. Winston Churchill, the Home Secretary, agreed to hold an inquiry into conditions there and C. F. G. Masterman, the Under-Secretary of State for the Home Department, was put in charge of it.

Masterman did not issue his report for four months; in the meantime the two men accused of brutality were left in charge of the *Akbar* and a boy who had been sentenced to be birched tried to cut his throat. Masterman's report recommended that the two men in charge should be removed. But, on account of his personal prejudice against Bottomley, he said that the charges made in *John Bull* regarding the *Akbar* were 'random and reckless'. Bottomley accused Masterman of 'doing his best in the way of whitewashing' and from that day on pursued a vendetta against him and attacked him in open letters in *John Bull* as 'the Whitewasher'. Eventually, Bottomley succeeded in ruining Masterman's political career. He never forgave Masterman for trying to dismiss his charges against the *Akbar*, because he knew from his early life at the orphanage how badly children could be treated in institutions.

Before the *Akbar* affair Horatio had written an open letter to Mr Tennyson d'Eyncourt, Metropolitan Police Magistrate at Clerkenwell, for sentencing a man of good character to two months' hard labour for stealing two loaves of bread worth ninepence halfpenny.

'Are you not ashamed of yourself? If not, we are certainly ashamed of you!'

Despite the phenomenal success of *John Bull* Bottomley still had money troubles. Although he had been served with forty bankruptcy petitions in 1906, he refused to change his ways and cut down his living expenses. Elaborate improvements were still being carried out at The Dicker; his harem still flourished; and he still backed horses as if he was John D. Rockefeller and sometimes lost thousands in a week. When the bookies sent in their bills on a Monday morning it was agony; he called it 'going through my garden of Gethsemane'. But he had a special code of honour about racing bets and always settled them promptly because he was determined to keep his own commandment, 'Thou shalt not knock a bookmaker'. He was often so hard pressed on settling day that he either sent the bookies a postdated cheque on his *John Bull* bank account or resorted to the money-lenders and had to pay over the odds in interest.

He often called in for lunch at the Royal Albion Hotel, Brighton, on his way to The Dicker or when he was going to a Sussex race meeting, and thus became a great friend of its sporting owner, Harry Preston.* Sometimes he motored over to The Dicker with Preston, who would marvel to see so many men working at the place. Once they saw Bottomley's artificial lake being completed; another time a private racecourse was being made.

'My dear fellow, this must be very expensive,' remarked Harry Preston.

Horatio waved his huge hand airily and assured him, 'The public will provide.'

Horatio had a magnificent board-room at *John Bull* in Long Acre, which was panelled throughout in oak and furnished in green leather; a large bust of Charles Bradlaugh dominated the mantelpiece and all round the room there were photos and cartoons of Bottomley. His private secretary, W. H. Holland, had a small room next door. Bottomley and Holland always wore correct frock coats in the office, and Holland had the manners of a diplomat of the old school. George Wedlake, the new assistant editor, had his office two doors away.

The construction of Bottomley's suite of offices was a tribute to his resourcefulness. On one side of his room he had a 'dummy' door which enabled him to make his getaway in an emergency by the rear exit into Anne Street. It was a marvellous way of dodging process-servers, cranks, crooks, and discarded mistresses, and considering he was over eighteen stone Horatio could move surprisingly fast if he had to leave by the back way.

When Bottomley owed Odhams Press £50,000 for printing Elias felt it was time they had a straight talk. Being thirteen years younger, Elias felt diffident about broaching such a delicate subject; but as soon as he walked into the room Horatio guessed the reason for his call.

'I know what you've come for, Elias—it's the money'†

'Yes, Mr Bottomley, I have.' Elias was delighted that the ice had been broken.

'My dear fellow, I am providing the brains. It is up to you to provide the money,' said Horatio brazenly.

* Knighted for his services to sport and charities in 1933.

† Minney.

'But Mr Bottomley, you ought to have told us this before.'

Horatio wagged his huge finger at Elias. 'Ah, if I had told you that, you wouldn't have agreed to print us at all!'

'Well, if you could give me a cheque on account—say for £5,000 . . .?'

'My dear Elias, I haven't got five thousand pence!'

Elias suggested a solution for their predicament: Odhams would take over the management of *John Bull* and run all the advertising, and then give Bottomley the net proceeds. Horatio was delighted with the proposal and called Elias a genius.

'Agreed!' said Elias with less than his usual modesty.

Everybody at Odhams called Elias 'the little man' and all the staff had an affection and respect for him. The partnership of Elias and Bottomley was one of the strangest in the annals of the newspaper business; and the contrast between them even extended to their social habits. Elias generally lunched alone and had a plain meal with a glass of stout, while Bottomley favoured a rich repast with plenty of champagne at Romano's or the Café Royal in the company of convivial friends and pretty girls. And while Elias and his wife Alice invariably went to the Grand Hotel, Eastbourne, for their holiday, Horatio usually went abroad, often accompanied by one of his lady friends. One would have thought the two men had nothing in common, yet a friendship developed between them in the course of fifteen years. Julius Elias occasionally had a night out with Horatio, leaving his wife Alice at home because she could not abide his associate. Bottomley once took him to Epsom for the Derby, which was the only time Elias ever visited a racecourse.

Although Elias liked Bottomley, he was a businessman first and foremost and had to draw the line somewhere. He therefore left private instructions about the procedure if Bottomley called at *John Bull*'s offices on a Friday night. On those occasions Horatio would summon the cashier and tell him, 'I must have money. I need it for a special investigation.'

This was a euphemism: what he really meant was that he was going racing. He would open the cash box and take out heaps of sovereigns. The cashier, acting on instructions, would say feebly, 'Let me count them, sir,' and take hold of Bottomley's great wrist to try and restrain him, but it was a waste of time. Bottomley just ignored him and cried, 'More—I want more! Now come on, let me have it.' It was always impossible to get rid of this massive man until he had pocketed all the gold sovereigns he required for his week-end.

The Odhams brothers thoroughly disapproved of Bottomley's behaviour and kept writing memos urging Elias to control him. It was beyond the powers of Julius Elias to do so and, to make things more difficult, Bottomley started to leave the routine editorial work to his assistant, George Wedlake, and rarely came into the office. Elias turned a blind eye to Horatio's faults and counted his blessings: *John Bull* was far and away the most successful publication in the whole building. He decided that since Odhams was now on a businesslike footing with Bottomley it was worth spending more money on advertising *John Bull*, and ordered special posters, which were displayed in London and all over the country, of the paper's famous slogans:

WRITE TO *JOHN BULL* ABOUT IT
IF *JOHN BULL* SAYS SO, IT *IS* SO

This advertising helped to push sales even higher. Julius Elias was confident that in the near future their circulation would be up to a million.

9 Bottomley's Law

Words are like leaves; and where they most abound,
Much fruit of sense beneath is rarely found,
False Eloquence, like the prismatic glass,
Its gaudy colours spreads on ev'ry place;
The face of Nature we no more survey,
All glares alike, without distinction gay. . . .

ALEXANDER POPE, *Essay on Criticism*

The Joint Stock Trust and Finance Corporation was one of the best-known Bottomley mining companies. It called itself a finance company and never pretended that it produced any Western Australian gold, but it would be more accurate to describe it as a bucket shop. Every few months glowing circulars would go out to faithful subscribers about the Trust's new 'stock operations', and many subscribers believed them and sent Bottomley their money, expecting to make a fortune. This money was either gambled in Westralian gold-mines or used for any purpose Bottomley might have, such as settling his pressing racing debts. When the bottom fell out of this market in 1903 he kept reconstructing the Joint Stock Trust and his other Westralian mining companies.

It should be explained that Horatio had an unique method of reconstruction which amounted to 'intentional fraud'. The first company would exhaust its funds and run into debt because Bottomley had taken large sums out of it under the heading 'for services rendered' to settle his private debts. Then he would incorporate the second company with the same capital as the first one, and the original shareholders would be asked to take shares in the new company for fifteen shillings paid, thus only having to pay five shillings for a one pound share. But if the first company had a capital of a million pounds, it meant that £250,000 came into Bottomley's possession every time it was reconstructed and he could then pay off another series of private debts.

However, by 1906 the Joint Stock Trust and the Selected Gold Mines of Australia, which it had taken over, were both bankrupt, and Bottomley intended to put them into voluntary liquidation in order to prevent an awkward investigation by the authorities.

This ploy would have worked as successfully as usual if he had not had the bad luck to come up against an incorruptible solicitor, Edward Bell of Carter and Bell, who practised at Idol Lane in the City. A tall, formidable man with a strong face, Bell was an expert in Common Law and at forty had acquired a flair for unravelling fraudulent ventures. He represented a shareholder in Selected Gold Mines, and had become very suspicious of the way Bottomley had been running the company.

When Selected Gold Mines were a day late in paying the interest on their debentures, Bell sent his clerk to the Law Courts first thing in the morning. As soon as the courts opened his clerk went in and applied for a writ against the company. A friendly debenture holder, who had been sent there by Bottomley, arrived a minute after Bell's clerk but he was too late. When he reported this misfortune Horatio hurried along to Idol Lane to see Bell in his office. He said he had come to ask Mr Bell a great favour in connection with Selected Gold Mines of Australia: he would appreciate it if Mr Bell would agree to the appointment of a certain Mr X as the Liquidator. Edward Bell, knowing that this was a solicitor whom Bottomley could twist round his little finger, did not warm to the suggestion.

'Appoint this man and I am your appreciative friend,' said Bottomley.

His huge hand went delving into his wallet for a ten-pound note. Bell, who had never taken a bribe in his life, was disgusted and told his clerk to show Mr Bottomley out of the office. Convinced that Bottomley was a rogue, he pursued him relentlessly from this time until his downfall.

Seymour Salaman, an accountant, was appointed independent Receiver of Selected Gold Mines, which was a large creditor of the Joint Stock Trust; Edward Bell met him and promised to give him every assistance. Bottomley, sensing danger in the air, called an Extraordinary (Liquidation) Meeting of the shareholders of the Joint Stock Trust on 20 March 1906. There was a phenomenal vote in favour of the resolution: the count was 1,812,255 shares voted by proxy or in person, although only two million shares had been issued. Salaman and Bell, convinced that something nefarious was going on, persuaded the Winding-up Court to authorize them to inspect the transfer and share registers of the Joint Stock Trust and Finance Corporation.

They found tremendous confusion at Bottomley's offices at Blomfield House in the City. After spending a whole day putting the transfers in numerical order, they returned next day to find all the papers had been disarranged; it looked as if Horatio and his clerks were playing a practical joke on them.

> The earthquake amongst the transfers was not sufficient, however, to dissipate the effect of observing upon the transfers the names of five persons who appeared to have been transferring away the whole of the company's share issue.*

Salaman and Bell addressed a petition to the court alleging irregularities in the share issue of the company; Bottomley protested that he was being victimized and filed a number of affidavits. Nevertheless, Mr Justice Buckley decided on 8 May to direct that the Joint Stock Trust should be wound up compulsorily. The judge directed the Official Receiver to collect the books and papers of the company, 'but by a remarkable coincidence the five ledgers containing the five names of transferors were missing'.

The Official Receiver made an order for the investigation of the Joint Stock Trust books. Mr Fox, his chief examiner, an extremely conscientious official, regularly worked overtime over a period of eighteen months and overcame the difficulty of the missing ledgers by checking through the counterfoils of the issued share certificates. He found that nearly ten million shares had been issued in excess of the capital of the company; all these duplicates or forged certificates were held by thousands

* 'Tenax', *The Gentle Art of Exploiting Gullibility* (David Weir, 1923).

of shareholders all over Britain who had paid cash for their shares. This money was traced after passing through many hands to—Bottomley.

Bottomley was publicly examined by the Official Receiver in October and November 1907 and was asked a total of 3,267 questions about his companies. He and three of his associates were then summoned for trial at Guildhall Justice Room on 1 December 1908 on a charge of conspiracy to defraud the shareholders of the Joint Stock Trust and Finance Corporation. Bottomley again defended himself and appeared in person. George Fewings, secretary of the company, and William Stevenson, a clerk, were defended by F. E. Smith, K.C., and Leslie Scott, K.C.; Dalton Easum, auditor of the company, was defended by E. G. Hemmerde, K.C.

Frederick Edwin Smith, a distinguished lawyer and a brilliant advocate, was noted for his biting wit and withering scorn. He had a marvellous gift of oratory and his speeches were perfectly delivered in a melodious voice which always made a great impact on judges and juries. His mind worked at high speed in court; this mental agility was a great asset to him and often led to arguments with the Bench and altercations with judges.

The prosecution was conducted by Horace Avory, K.C., and Richard Muir. Horace Avory, who was nicknamed 'the Acid Drop', never made a joke throughout his long career as a barrister and later as a judge. Although a sound lawyer and an astute and courageous advocate, he lacked eloquence and his voice was generally in the corner of his mouth. His arguments commanded the attention of judges because he never indulged in irrelevancy. However, he was not at his best on this occasion; he had been sent on a sea voyage to recuperate from a nervous breakdown, but had to cut it short for Bottomley's case. Consequently the 'imperturbable' Horace Avory was nervous and irritable and allowed himself to be drawn by Bottomley.

The Joint Stock trial, which lasted twenty-eight days, opened under Alderman Sir George Smallman. The general opinion in legal circles was that if the prosecution had concentrated on a single charge—the duplication of the share issue of the Joint Stock Trust and Finance Corporation—and had simply called the original shareholders (to produce their certificates), the stockbrokers and others who had bought shares in the market bearing the same serial numbers, and the old men and young heirs whom Bottomley had gulled into buying big holdings of the shares, a magistrate would certainly have found there was a strong enough case to commit him for trial to the Old Bailey, and it would have been merely a question of how long a sentence he received. However, Horace Avory for the prosecution decided to charge Bottomley on a number of counts and entirely miscalculated the effect of Bottomley's eloquent speech on the Aldermen at Guildhall.

The main charges were that Bottomley had obtained debentures of the Selected Gold Mines* from the shareholders by false pretences and fraudulently converted them to his own use; that he and his three associates had obtained money by false pretences from the subscribers to stock operations of the Joint Stock Trust; and that Bottomley had duplicated nearly ten million shares of the company.

Fifty-four debenture holders in Selected Gold Mines had sent their certificates to Bottomley on the understanding that they would be converted into Ordinary shares; but they received neither shares or cash, while Bottomley raised £14,000 from the sale of their debentures. Horace Avory stated that Bottomley and his associates had circularized shareholders of the Joint Stock Trust and told them that any subscribers to the 'stock operations' were guaranteed against loss and they were bound to make a profit of at least twenty-five per cent. The three stock operations in 1904 netted nearly £14,000. 'Then,' said Avory, 'it became necessary to complain of the state of the market, and to explain why operations entered into had not been carried out.'

Finally, Avory outlined the charge that Bottomley had duplicated the five-shilling shares in the Joint Stock Trust; there should only have been two million shares in operation as the capital was £500,000. Fewings, the company secretary, told a clerk in the office in 1906 that the shares had probably been over-issued six times.

The principal witness for the prosecution was Leonard Levie, a clerk who had been working for the Joint Stock Trust and other Bottomley companies for ten years. When confidential clerk to Fewings, the secretary, in 1905 he had to put special numbers on shares. Fewings once told him he had some dirty work to do, but 'they didn't trouble him so long as they got

* Selected Gold Mines of Australia had been taken over by the Joint Stock Trust.

what they wanted'; Levie assumed 'they' meant Bottomley. In August 1906 Fewings told him that the share capital of two million shares was grossly over-issued.

LEVIE An accountant and a solicitor [Salaman and Bell] came to the office early in 1906 and wanted to see the register. An appointment was made for the inspection of the books and Fewings instructed me to have them ready.

'Don't place them all together, just place them here and there and say, "Here are the books, you can see them," and during the examination you can take some of the books out of the office and say they are wanted and generally to baulk them.'

If Mr Salaman and Mr Bell wanted to see the transfers, Fewings instructed me to mix them up. . . . When the register was asked for, Mr Bell would be told it would be in use for half an hour.

F. E. SMITH [*for Fewings and Stevenson*] I object to the witness saying what 'would be' done. We want to know what exactly occurred.

LEVIE Messrs Salaman and Bell never saw the whole of the transfers. A small bundle was tied up and kept back by Mr Fewings. It was placed in a locker a little while before the winding-up, and Mr Easum said: 'If they see these transfers it is all up!' [*Laughter*]

The day of the winding-up Bottomley came into the office and said, 'Have you been to lunch yet, Levie?' 'I don't usually go till one o'clock, sir.' 'Well, never mind, I've got a meeting of gentlemen coming from the court to inspect the books and you'd better go now, I want the room.'

On my return I saw Mr W. W. Davies, who had just finished tying up a brown paper parcel. A cab was standing at the door and Davies went away carrying some large books which looked like registers.

In March 1907 Levie received a letter from Bottomley dispensing with his services. When Bottomley cross-examined him Levie admitted he gave a statement to the Winding-up Department in February 1906, but denied saying that if he received a certain sum he would give evidence for Bottomley.

BOTTOMLEY Please consider this question. Throughout the whole of that period were you ever asked by me to do any act which you considered wrong or improper?

LEVIE It is a long period. I shall want time to consider it.

BOTTOMLEY May I say that at the moment nothing occurs to you?

LEVIE I might not have considered it wrong at the time?

BOTTOMLEY Have you written many letters expressing lifelong gratitude to me?

LEVIE I may have said I was grateful.

BOTTOMLEY At any time during the whole period you were in my service did you ever report to me any irregularity in the office?

LEVIE Not to my recollection. I looked to Mr Fewings as my master and presumed he had instructions from you.

BOTTOMLEY Did you ever have a little lapse?

LEVIE I might have done. I once had a little too much to drink.

BOTTOMLEY Were you suspended for being intoxicated and fighting in the office?

LEVIE I was knocked about and I did not understand the position at all. I think it was arranged somehow.*

* It is practically certain that Bottomley had arranged to get Levie intoxicated in the office because he wished to get rid of him, but he was an expert at covering up his tracks.

Levie admitted that when the Official Receiver dispensed with his services in 1906 he wrote to Bottomley begging for employment. He was engaged as a shorthand clerk for a year, then fell ill. Bottomley gave him a month's salary and guaranteed to continue paying him till he found another job, but Levie wrote to him and complained it was a low salary considering his 'special services'.

BOTTOMLEY After Levie had said four times that his position was *desperate*, he wrote, 'I trust you will not ignore this letter. That is all I have to say at the moment.' Then, getting no answer, he has gone to the Official Receiver about my terrible crimes.

[*to Levie*] In a letter of 23 January, you say, 'I am now in a desperate position,' the word *desperate* being underlined, and you end up by saying, '*I trust you will not ignore this letter. That is all I will say at the moment.*'

Now I am going to put to you my version of that phrase in your letter of 23 January about your being then in a 'desperate position'. Did you ever express the opinion to anybody—not having received any reply to your last letter—that I contemplated taking proceedings against you for blackmail?

LEVIE No, to no one. Never at any time did I have the thought of blackmailing.

BOTTOMLEY Will you tell me whether, just after seeing the Official Receiver, you called at Mr Fewings's house and saw Mrs Fewings?

LEVIE I did. . . .

BOTTOMLEY Did you ask her to use her influence with her husband to get some more money for you?

LEVIE I think I did.

BOTTOMLEY Did you say you had been several times to see me and I had refused to see you?

LEVIE No.

BOTTOMLEY As a matter of fact, had you called at my flat several times and been refused admittance?

LEVIE Yes.

Further cross-examined, Levie admitted he could not say if Bottomley had anything to do with the destruction of the Joint Stock Trust documents. Bottomley stated he had never sent Levie off early to lunch on the day of the winding-up order because he was attending before Mr Justice Buckley.

LEVIE I do not remember that . . . I distinctly remember Davies tying up a parcel and taking it out of the office.

BOTTOMLEY And if Mr Davies comes here and says he was left in charge of the books, would that be incorrect?

LEVIE Yes.

BOTTOMLEY You are smarting under a sense of my injustice to you?

LEVIE You turned me off at a moment's notice after ten years' service.

BOTTOMLEY If I had gone on giving you money you would never have gone to the Official Receiver and made your statement?

LEVIE If I thought I was going to be included in this I should.

BOTTOMLEY But you never thought that until I stopped giving you money.

This concluded Bottomley's masterly cross-examination. He had succeeded in throwing considerable doubts on the evidence of Levie, the chief witness for the prosecution, by establishing that Levie was probably trying to blackmail him. The dismissed clerk had been hard pressed to parry Bottomley's questions, and then he had to face the formidable F. E. Smith, cross-examining on behalf of Fewings and Stevenson. Levie said he had called on Fewings for help because he believed he was an honest man.

LEVIE I did not ask Mr Fewings to get me money from Mr Bottomley. I asked him to use his influence. I wanted assistance from Mr Bottomley . . . a few days after I had failed to get it I went to the Official Receiver.

F. E. SMITH If you had got money from Mr Fewings at that time, do you suggest to the court that you would still have gone to the Official Receiver?

LEVIE I should not put it that way.

F. E. SMITH This is what you said in your last letter to Mr Bottomley: 'I trust you will not ignore this letter. That is all I will say for the moment.' Do you say that was not intended as a threat?

LEVIE On my oath, no.

F. E. SMITH We will soon see how much value can be attached to your oath. When you found the money was not forthcoming, you formed the plan of going to the Official Receiver?

LEVIE It was all along in my mind to go if anything happened.

This ended the third day's proceedings. Levie must have been overjoyed to get a respite, but Bottomley and F. E. Smith between them had already discredited him as a witness. Avory, realizing this, re-examined him next day; but it was too late to make any difference.

LEVIE . . . I told shareholders things were in such a muddle [at Bottomley's office] it would take some time to put them right. I sent my notebooks, containing notes of letters to shareholders, to Mr Bottomley and have not seen them since.

AVORY I call for the production of those notebooks because I have been informed that they have never been handed over to the Official Receiver.

BOTTOMLEY The Official Receiver can have them at any time he cares to send for them.

SIR G. SMALLMAN [*to Bottomley*] You will have them here next Monday.

BOTTOMLEY If you express that wish, sir, they shall be here.

This concluded the evidence of Levie. Edwin Bennett, who had bought £2,793 debentures in the Joint Stock Trust but never received his certificates, gave evidence later. He was petitioning creditor in the compulsory winding-up of the company and was in court on 8 May 1906 when the application was made. After leaving the court he saw Bottomley, Fewings and another man in a corridor.

AVORY What happened?

BENNETT I turned round and walked towards them when Mr Bottomley was emphasizing these words: 'We must not allow them to get these ledgers under any circumstances.'

AVORY Did you soon afterwards meet a Mr Bush?

BENNETT Yes, a few minutes later. I had jotted down the words I had heard in a rough notebook before I had left the spot.

Bottomley then cross-examined Bennett.

BENNETT I swear I am a shareholder, but have not got my old certificate. Mr Bell, the solicitor, has it. I have a good memory, although I am getting old. . . . When I presented the petition it had to be withdrawn and my wife's name substituted.

BOTTOMLEY Did you know the reason was that the shares were in your wife's name and you were not on the register at all?

Bennett stated that he called and saw the Treasury Solicitor and gave him particulars of the corridor conversation. Mr Bell already knew of it. . . .

BOTTOMLEY . . . This is my last question to you. . . . I suggest that at the moment the winding-up order was made I left the court accompanied by one of the counsel in wig and gown and went straight off to that counsel's chambers. Now, was there a gentleman in wig and gown among the crowd?

BENNETT No.

BOTTOMLEY I am now going to put a question to you which the learned counsel will probably tell you not to answer. If I call the counsel and solicitor I have referred to and they swear to what I have suggested, you would swear it is false?

AVORY [*agitated*] No, no, do not answer that! [*Laughter*]

Later, during the evidence of Frederick Ellis, a wool merchant who had £200 debentures in Selected Gold Mines, E. G. Hemmerde (for Dalton Easum, a defendant) asked, 'Will the Official Receiver be called?'

AVORY Yes.

BOTTOMLEY Then I withdraw my objection.

AVORY His representative will be called. [*Derisive laughter*] I am not going to be snapped up in this ridiculous way. When I said the Official Receiver I meant his representative and any such witness as I think necessary will be called.

BOTTOMLEY Then I understand the Official Receiver will not be called at all?

AVORY Mr Bottomley will be good enough not to understand anything! [*Laughter*]

BOTTOMLEY I was anxious to know if I should see the Official Receiver in the box.

AVORY Mr Bottomley will find that out when the time comes.

Horatio was employing one of his regular tactics: baiting the opposing counsel and making him look foolish so that he would lose his temper and lose his grip of the issue.

During the following days Horace Avory, for the prosecution, called a number of small tradesmen who had subscribed money to the Joint Stock Trust 'operations' and never had a profit from them. Several of them retained their faith in Bottomley despite losing their money.

'Anything I can say in your favour, Mr Bottomley, I will say,' said William Fletcher, a paper-merchant.

Thomas Lean, an architect, had lost money in Bottomley companies and made no profit on the stock operations. In cross-examination he admitted, 'I always thought a great deal of you, Mr Bottomley.'

Leonard Levie, recalled by the prosecution, quoted from his shorthand notebook a letter from Fewings to Bottomley.

LEVIE 'DEAR SIR, I have been keeping things quiet during your absence, but the end of the month is fast approaching and I have before me several letters demanding payment of debenture interest amounting to £500 and threatening the appointment of a Receiver. I am sorry to have to trouble you but if I can keep them at bay I will do so.'

BOTTOMLEY [*to Sir George Smallman*] Is it suggested, sir, that this has the remotest bearing on the charges before you?

AVORY I should not have read it if it had not.

BOTTOMLEY . . . It is utterly irregular evidence, because if these letters had been sent the person who received them should have been called. . . .

AVORY The witness has already sworn that he acted on instructions and I am simply calling attention to the instructions he received.

The trial was becoming a duel of wits between Bottomley and the pedantic, rather pompous Horace Avory. Bottomley was needling his opponent at every opportunity. Later, Mr Platt, a seventy-eight-year-old retired wool-merchant, gave evidence of how Bottomley and Ernest Hooley, his confederate, had tricked him into paying £7,960 for worthless Joint Stock Trust shares. On 27 January the prosecution called Arthur Bowden who, like Levie, had been a former clerk of the Joint Stock Trust. Bowden testified that he had made out share certificates in the name of Stevenson (a defendant), taking the numbers from existing certificates. . . . When a shareholder applied for his certificate after November 1905, there were already some in existence with the same number, so new numbers from 1 onwards were allotted and written in red ink at the request of Fewings.

BOWDEN After 5 November I asked Fewings what to do in case of any shareholder's complaint about the alterations in the numbers and he said, 'Oh well, it is a clerical error. There has been a muddle in the shares.'

MUIR [*prosecuting counsel*] Apart from the use of these numbers for Stevenson's shares, had there been any muddle?

BOWDEN No . . . on one occasion I objected to register a transfer as the shares did not stand in the name given. Fewings said, 'You need have no fear, Bowden, Bottomley will put it right.'

Bowden was cross-examined by Bottomley.

BOWDEN I appreciate that Levie and I are the only two witnesses who have been able to speak as to what went on in the office.

Bowden stated that he bore Bottomley no malice and swore he had never threatened that if Bottomley did not pay him money he would give evidence against him. He had left the office after a little friction with Fewings. Bottomley read a report of Guildhall proceedings against Bowden; he had been fined ten shillings for being drunk and molesting women in the City.

BOWDEN I admit this is substantially true. Fewings . . . suspended me on 15 January 1906. Later I was discharged. . . . When I was dismissed at your instigation, as I understood, I wrote as follows: 'I must say I expected a little better treatment from you *taking everything into consideration.* I again ask you to grant me an interview which, I think, is due to me.'

You did not reply to me and I made several attempts to see you, but they all failed. On one occasion I sent up a message to you: 'Not hearing from you, I again ask for an interview. My dismissal is apparently treated very lightly and as there are my wife and children probably starving, to me it is of total importance. If you don't intend to see me will you please say so, and then I shall know what to do. *Perhaps my late position in the office as transfer clerk is worthy of consideration.*'

BOTTOMLEY What did you mean by saying you should know what to do?

BOWDEN That I should have to go to another quarter for financial help. I should have to go to my father.

BOTTOMLEY Why did you underline in your letter the fact that you had been transfer clerk?

BOWDEN I thought that after all the dirty work—

BOTTOMLEY You thought it would be wise for me to square you?

BOWDEN No, certainly not. I thought that at least you ought to have given me an interview and helped me in some way temporarily. I thought my dismissal was somewhat uncalled for and that is still my opinion.*

Bowden said it was just a coincidence that both he and Levie went to work later for the Prudential Insurance Company and denied saying to somebody, 'I am working with Levie and if Bottomley doesn't see me we shall know where to go. Mr Fox [the chief examiner] will give anything for our evidence.'

* It is quite possible that Bottomley had arranged for one of his 'stable' to frame Bowden in order to justify sacking him.

BOTTOMLEY Did you ever say to anybody that it would be better to wait and see if you could get any money out of me before you made a statement?

BOWDEN Not to anyone.

BOTTOMLEY Did you see Levie in a public house in February 1908 and say to him—speaking of this matter—'Tell him [Fox] I can be a very useful witness?'

BOWDEN No, certainly not.

BOTTOMLEY Did you ever certify a transfer out of Stevenson's name which at the time you knew was out of order?

BOWDEN I did. I can't give an instance, but I know the numbers were taken from an unissued certificate.

BOTTOMLEY Do you know of any case in which numbers were taken from any unissued certificate and that certificate has been claimed?

BOWDEN No I don't.

Bottomley had managed to destroy the force of Bowden's testimony, particularly when he led him on to admit that he thought he deserved a reward for doing the dirty work in the office. The fact that he and Levie, the other clerk, had both gone to the Prudential also told against him. The impression created by the two clerks under cross-examination was that, after failing to blackmail Bottomley, they had put their heads together and made statements to the Official Receiver. On 2 February the prosecution called Seymour Salaman, the chartered accountant who had been appointed Receiver of Selected Gold Mines on behalf of the debenture holders.

Salaman was cross-examined by Bottomley.

BOTTOMLEY Did you have any agreement with Carter and Bell [Bell's firm] as to getting your costs?

SALAMAN [*angry*] You ought to be ashamed of yourself for asking such a question!

Salaman and Bottomley proceeded to have a heated discussion about Bottomley's 'unorthodox' methods of running his companies. Salaman thought the agreement by which the Joint Stock Trust took over the assets of Selected Gold Mines was a scandalous fraud on the public. 'Another scandalous matter was the way in which the Selected Gold Mines was tricked out of £10,000,' said Salaman. He was uncertain how much blame should be attached to Fewings, Stevenson and Easum but he thought Mr Bottomley dominated the whole transaction.

Alderman Sir George Smallman was taken ill and the trial was adjourned till 25 February, having already lasted eighteen days. On the 25th W. Cash, an accountant, gave evidence that he had examined the books of the Joint Stock Trust.

Cash was examined by Richard Muir (prosecuting) about the various stock operations of the Joint Stock Trust and also about other stock operations by Bottomley companies. While they were discussing a maze of figures Sir George Smallman suddenly clutched at his desk and rose to his feet. He was obviously very ill and slowly left the bench.

'You adjourn till Monday, sir?' asked Muir. Sir George replied faintly, 'Yes,' and retired to a private room where Lady Smallman was waiting.

On 1 March the court resumed under Alderman Sir Horatio Davies, who had full notes of the case. Bottomley said he had hoped that Sir George Smallman would be able to return to the case. The defence did not propose to call any evidence.

Sir Horatio Davies said he regretted that Sir George would not be able to undertake the case again: 'His doctors have prohibited him from doing any kind of work for a long time.'

Horace Avory proposed to inform Sir Horatio of the nature of the charges and to recall two or three witnesses to give samples of the frauds alleged. He would then conclude the evidence they were upon at the time of adjournment.

SIR H. DAVIES I shall come to a decision upon the evidence brought before me.

BOTTOMLEY [*to Sir Horatio*] If the learned counsel says he discounts the evidence already given and proposes to rely exclusively on the evidence he calls before you, of course I have no objections

> to make except that one must assume that the other evidence was unnecessary, or redundant, or unsatisfactory. [*Laughter*]

'Of course one must not assume anything of the kind,' said Avory, extremely annoyed. 'Nobody but a lunatic would!'

'This is mere vulgar abuse,' retorted Bottomley.

'I think, Mr Avory, you should withdraw that,' said Sir Horatio Davies.

There were cheers from the public; Bottomley's claque had been very well stage-managed by Tommy Cox. At this critical stage of the trial, with a new magistrate in charge, Bottomley had scored by making Avory lose his temper.

'I said nothing to the effect that I propose to discard any evidence, or that I regarded it as redundant or anything so ridiculous!' Avory declared. 'I protest against such an idea being foisted on me!'

Mr Hemmerde (for Easum) thought that the present inquiry should be treated as an entirely new case. 'Any other proceeding might result in the greatest injustice to the defendants. How can the new magistrate form an opinion on "sample evidence"—not having had the same advantage as his predecessor?'

'The prosecution are satisfied that they can be acting regularly in recalling some of the witnesses, having their evidence read over, and leaving the defendants to cross-examine them if they like,' said Horace Avory.

BOTTOMLEY — Why, if it was thought necessary to call a hundred witnesses before Sir George Smallman, does the prosecution now think it enough to call four or five before the new magistrate?

F. E. SMITH — [*for Fewings and Stevenson*] The accumulative force of the evidence depends mostly upon the testimony of discharged clerks who have deposed to certain alleged conversations. I think my clients would be grievously injured if the magistrate was deprived of the opportunity of judging of the evidence of these witnesses. The judicial discretion of a magistrate must be based on the evidence before him.

An argument ensued between F. E. Smith and Sir Horatio Davies. It was finally agreed that an application should be made to the High Court on behalf of the defence for a ruling on whether a witness should be shown his deposition.

Sir Horatio Davies went down with flu on 3 March and the case was once more adjourned. It was resumed on 8 March under Alderman Sir James Ritchie, who was determined to speed up the trial which had already lasted twenty-five days. The illness of the two Aldermen was a great stroke of luck for Bottomley. If Sir George Smallman had still been on the bench, having heard all the evidence, he would have been far less lenient.

AVORY The High Court has approved of the procedure suggested by the prosecution. I am going to indicate the main charges, then recall certain witnesses and have their depositions read over.

SIR J. RITCHIE My idea was to have the fresh witnesses you are going to call and then, if I am not satisfied with their evidence, you may recall any of the others you choose.

AVORY Perhaps you will reconsider that, because the witnesses from whom money was obtained have in fact all been called, and it will be necessary to recall them as the basis of the foundation of the charge.

SIR J. RITCHIE You are not going, surely, to try this case all over again?

AVORY No, and I hope you are not either. . . . The difficulty about that is that I have summoned here today witnesses from different parts of the country to have their depositions read over. The High Court has expressly approved of that course.

SIR J. RITCHIE I rather gather the discretion is left in my hands.

Later, Sir James Ritchie decided that prosecution witnesses should be re-sworn to their depositions and he would read them over privately. The cabman who was supposed to have transported the Joint Stock Trust's books from Bottomley's office on the day of the compulsory winding-up admitted he had left the job to a man he had picked up in the street. Cross-examined by Bottomley, he admitted he had made no further effort to trace this man. A number of witnesses were recalled and swore to their depositions.

The following day W. Cash, the chartered accountant, was recalled to resume his evidence about the company's books, and reported that although the Joint Stock Trust debentures had a value of £54,636, only £4,420 remained in the account. Bottomley's indebtedness was £40,743 in 1904, but by means of some faked book entries it appeared that he was a creditor of the company for £1,500. There were still some share ledgers missing. Bottomley held only 113,000 shares but he delivered 870,000. Stevenson delivered 1,700,000 shares, of which 765,963 had been acquired by transfer and not allotment.

Bottomley cross-examined Cash, who stated he had traced a very large duplication in these shares.

BOTTOMLEY I ask you to point out to me any piece of paper in the world purporting to be a certificate of this company which is a spurious document.

CASH I say there have been these shares issued more than was required.

BOTTOMLEY Can you, in order to assist the court and in justice to me, put us in the way of ascertaining the name of any person who has held a spurious certificate?

CASH [*after a long time*] I personally cannot do that. I know of no instance of anybody coming forward since the prosecution started and complaining that he had a fictitious certificate. . . .

SIR J. RITCHIE I have read the depositions of Levie and Bowden [Bottomley's clerks] and come to certain conclusions about them. I do not want to see them in the box.

After lunch Bottomley rose to speak for his defence.

BOTTOMLEY . . . This is a Treasury prosecution, and if the Treasury with all its resources, wealth, facilities and legal ability has not after all this time been able to make out a more complete case against me—and I am going to submit that they have grotesquely failed to justify one of the charges against me—what would have been the state of things if the matter was in the hands of a private prosecution?

I contend that there are no grounds upon which I and my co-defendants should be asked to stand our trial. If, after the speeches for the defence, the magistrate does not definitely come to the conclusion, I would ask him to suspend his judgement while I have had an opportunity of going into the box and denying on oath every one of the suggestions made against me, and giving the counsel for the Treasury an opportunity of cross-examining me.

. . . Why was the charge one of conspiracy? The device introduced a monstrous law of evidence under which anything said by or to any of the alleged conspirators was evidence against the whole. But day after day the other defendants have not even been mentioned by the witnesses. . . .

Out of 110 or 112 witnesses for the prosecution only the odd 10 or 12 have had any communication with the Treasury before the case was opened. Witnesses, when they came to be cross-examined, said, 'I have never complained to any one of being defrauded. I was dug up by Mr Pearce of the Treasury, or a police officer, I have come up here reluctantly and I make no charge.'

A great deal of animus and feeling has been shown against me by the prosecuting counsel, and every forensic trick has been resorted to in this case.*

Some methods have been adopted which

* Bottomley regularly complained that the prosecution were showing animus against him in his cases. It gained the sympathy of the jury for him, and in this case, the sympathy of the Alderman.

> might be permissible in Russia, but it was a terrible shock to me to see them adopted here. . . . The Treasury have relied on two discharged clerks, one of whom was admittedly a disappointed blackmailer. Even the Treasury have now disowned Levie and with him has been dropped the most absurd and wicked story of the destruction of books and conversations to which he had deposed. . . . The only other witness [Bowden] who knew of what went on in the office has been twice arrested for drunkenness. . . . Before he went to the Treasury he told me that if his former position was not worthy of consideration 'he would know what to do'.
>
> There is not one iota of evidence to show that any of the Joint Stock debentures ever found their way into my hands. . . . There are many hundreds of subscribers to the stock operations, and the Treasury, after scouring the country, has brought up a few who said they expected a profit in cash.

Bottomley continued his speech for the defence on 13 March, the twenty-eighth day of the trial. He complained bitterly because Mr Brougham, the Official Receiver, who had made serious charges against him, had not been called as a prosecution witness.

'I have had to do the best I can with junior clerks. . . . Where would the prosecution have been if I had not given them permission to investigate my accounts with my brokers?' he asked.

BOTTOMLEY As to the question of the stock operations, I have asked all the subscribers called by the prosecution, 'Do you say you have been defrauded?' . . . These witnesses have not only said that they had not complained to anyone of being defrauded, but in the witness-box they made no allegations of fraud. . . .

Why am I, of all the directors, singled out? I do not disclaim the circulars concerning the stock operations, but I had no more to do with them than the other directors. . . . Now—regarding the disappearance of the books——

SIR J. RITCHIE The removal of the books from the company's office by the Official Receiver's staff seems to have been carried out in a very slovenly way. In my opinion, there is insufficient evidence as to the destruction of the books.

BOTTOMLEY It has been stated that £50,000 came to me as the proceeds of the alleged duplication of the shares. . . . I have asked Mr Cash why he did not add up every certificate issued by the company and deduct from the total every certificate returned by the company. Would not the balance tell the number of shares then out? 'Yes,' said Mr Cash, 'it would, but that is not my way.' [*Laughter*]

According to the prosecution, Stevenson has been selling me duplicated shares and I have foisted them back on Stevenson, so apparently we ought to be prosecuting each other! [*Laughter*]

No duplicated shares have turned up and the Stock Exchange does not regard the re-numbering of shares as a *de facto* indication of anything suspicious.

The Joint Stock Trust is a reconstruction of the Associated Finance Corporation and in order that it should take over the undertaking the latter had to go into liquidation. . . . That was why I became so large a creditor because I paid off the debts of the company and the sums 'traced' to me have been the amounts repaid. . . .

I consider it an insult to the Alderman to commit the defendants for trial on such evidence, for I don't think there is much to choose between a committal and a conviction. I don't know why my co-defendants were dropped into the case. Perhaps it was hoped that they would turn King's Evidence; but, as it happened, they were neither Bowdens nor Levies.

Radical and Democrat as I call myself, I have always revered the traditions, prestige and power of the Corporation of the City and I do not hesitate, hunted and hounded and harassed as I am, to go to one who is not the least respected of a bench of eminent magistrates to give me sanctuary. [*Cheers, which were suppressed*]

Sir James Ritchie retired from the court. He returned fifteen minutes later with three Aldermen and gave his decision.

SIR J. RITCHIE I have very carefully considered this case in all its bearings. Of course I did not hear Mr Avory open it, but I have, as I say, considered every part of it in all its bearings. This is a very complicated case. I fail to see that the Crown have proved their charge of fraudulent misrepresentation in relation to the affairs of the company in question, and if I can't understand the case I don't suppose a jury will. I have come to the conclusion that in this case no jury ought to convict. [*Loud cheers*]

MUIR [*for the prosecution*] I will take the instructions of the Attorney-General as to what course the prosecution ought to pursue. [*Laughter*]

BOTTOMLEY [*to Sir James Ritchie*] You dismiss the summons?

SIR JAMES I do.

There were loud cheers in court and cries of 'Hurrah!' and 'He's a jolly good fellow!' Friends pressed forward to shake hands with Bottomley. He was cheered again in Guildhall Yard as he drove away. He had achieved another spectacular victory against the odds.

Richard Muir, who had assisted Avory in the prosecution, said afterwards, 'It will be a long time before anyone dares to prosecute Bottomley again. But he might, like some of the others, grow careless and then he will fall.'

10 Lambs to the Slaughter

I like this man; I have heard him speak; I won't have you say a word against him; anyone who says a word against Bottomley I will quarrel with. I am not sorry I lent him the money, and I would do it again.

OLD MAN, to his family after losing £40,000, 1907

Bottomley never reduced his standard of living in the new century and as Westralian mining shares went off the boil in 1903 he had to find a new source of revenue. In the first phase of his financial career he had formed the Hansard Union and exploited the leading ranks of the City, such as Lord Mayors, bankers and company directors. Then in the nineties he had become a company promoter and battened on successful merchants and middle-class investors. In his third and most sordid phase, which lasted from 1905 to 1911, he became a high-class confidence trickster and persuaded senile magnates and youthful heirs to part with their money; he usually worked hand in glove with Ernest Terah Hooley, the chief shareholder of John Bull, Guernsey (among other things).

Ernest Hooley was tall, dark and bearded and had an attractive air of Mephistopheles about him. In the late Victorian era he had been a very successful entrepreneur and brought to market firms which became household names, such as Dunlop Tyres, Bovril and Schweppes. He became the Squire of Risley in Nottinghamshire and was accepted in society. An enthusiastic Tory, he was elected to the select Carlton Club after being proposed by a peer of the realm. The British public first heard of Hooley when he bought the Prince of Wales's yacht,

The Honourable Member for South Hackney arriving at the House of Commons for the debate on the Home Rule Bill, 11 April 1912.

Horatio Bottomley (*left*) and Charles Bradlaugh—these photographs, taken when each man was in his fifties, suggest that Bottomley's birth certificate (*below*) may not be an entirely accurate record.

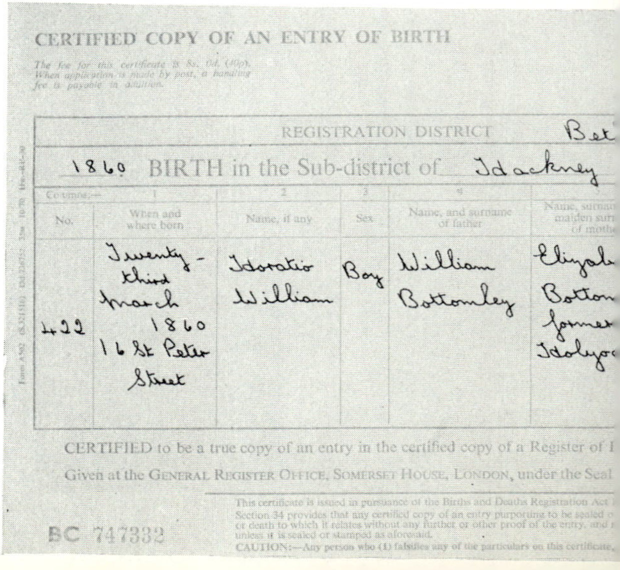

CERTIFIED COPY OF AN ENTRY OF BIRTH

The fee for this certificate is 8s. 0d. (40p). When application is made by post, a handling fee is payable in addition.

REGISTRATION DISTRICT Bet

1860 BIRTH in the Sub-district of Hackney

Columns:—	1	2	3	4	5
No.	When and where born	Name, if any	Sex	Name, and surname of father	Name, surna[me] maiden sur[name] of mothe[r]
422	Twenty-third March 1860 16 St Peter Street	Horatio William	Boy	William Bottomley	Elizab[eth] Botto[mley] forme[rly] Holyo[ake]

CERTIFIED to be a true copy of an entry in the certified copy of a Register of

Given at the General Register Office, Somerset House, London, under the Seal

This certificate is issued in pursuance of the Births and Deaths Registration Act

Section 34 provides that any certified copy of an entry purporting to be sealed o[r] ... or death to which it relates without any further or other proof of the entry, and ... unless it is sealed or stamped as aforesaid.

CAUTION:—Any person who (1) falsifies any of the particulars on this certificate,

BC 747332

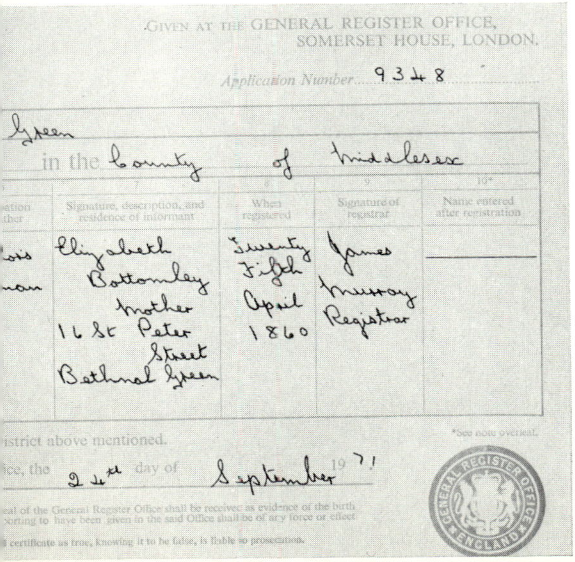

GIVEN AT THE GENERAL REGISTER OFFICE,
SOMERSET HOUSE, LONDON.

Application Number 9348

Green

in the County of Middlesex

6	7	8	9	10*
...ation ...ther	Signature, description, and residence of informant	When registered	Signature of registrar	Name entered after registration
...ois ...man	Elizabeth Bottomley Mother 16 St Peter Street Bethnal Green	Twenty Fifth April 1860	James Murray Registrar	———

...istrict above mentioned.

...ice, the 24th day of September 1971

*See note overleaf.

...eal of the General Register Office shall be received as evidence of the birth ...porting to have been given in the said Office shall be of any force or effect

... certificate as true, knowing it to be false, is liable to prosecution.

GENERAL REGISTER OFFICE • ENGLAND •

William Lotinga, *John Bull*'s racing correspondent, leading in his horse, March 1917. Like Bottomley, he lost a fortune on the Turf.

Peggy Primrose in 1918.

Queuing to join the colours, Southwark Town Hall, 1915.

ENGLAND'S RECRUITING SERGEANT

The ship's company of H.M.S. *Queen Elizabeth* cheering Bottomley on his visit to the Grand Fleet, December 1917.

Bottomley stands with Henry Houston among the graves of British soldiers in Étaples cemetery, September 1917.

Bottomley arriving at Bow Street with (*left to right*) Arthur Newton (tame accountant), George Rawson (manservant), and an unidentified member of the 'stable'.

BIGLAND ON TRIAL

Reuben Bigland and supporters leaving the court.

Horatio Bottomley, a pathetic figure at seventy-two, doing his turn at the Windmill Theatre in September 1932. He collapsed on stage after a few nights.

Britannia, for £10,000; later, he had the honour of dining with His Royal Highness.

But in 1898 his group of companies went into liquidation and Ernest Hooley filed his petition in bankruptcy; when he was examined at Carey Street great irregularities in his companies came to light. He was tried for fraud at the Old Bailey, found guilty and sentenced to twelve months' imprisonment. When he came out he had lost his place in society, but was crafty enough to retain his mansion at Risley and other assets which had all been placed in his wife's name. It was rumoured that Hooley had become very disreputable and rumour did not lie: from 1900 he lived entirely by his wits and flourished like the green bay tree; he was a superb salesman who could sell almost anything to anybody. His speciality was persuading rich old men to part with their gold or their gilt-edged stock in exchange for his promises and dud shares. He conducted his operations from a luxurious first-floor flat over a jeweller's in Bond Street and seemed to put a spell over his victims. An old man whom he had swindled out of thousands confessed to his secretary:

> You may think me foolish, but the reason is that I am eighty-three years of age. I have been a student of human nature and life since my youngest days and the conclusion I have come to is that life is a complex system, and that *anticipation is its greatest joy*: and Mr Hooley can give me plenty of that, so I am prepared to pay for it.*

In May 1905 Bottomley met Hooley through a mutual friend. At that time Hooley was 'nursing' an aged land-dealer named William Carter and told him, 'I have just met the smartest man of business I have ever come across—his name is Horatio Bottomley—you ought to meet him!' Carter fell in with the suggestion and Hooley introduced him to Bottomley in June.

A description of a visit to Horatio's suite of rooms by one of his victims would have applied equally well to William Carter:

> Upon the door being opened, he was ushered into a wigwam sort of a tent of red cloth with a light outside. Inside was a brazier and the victim was asked to warm himself and compose his feelings until the great man was able to appear. In the ruddy glow, Hooley spoke of the difficulties of the introduction and tentatively feared that the great

* 'Tenax'.

> man was too busy to be seen. However, the curtain of the tent was opened by a plumaged servitor and in the red light Bottomley was seen. He approached Hooley and told him how he had torn himself away from urgent business of national importance but he would give him five minutes. . . .
>
> From the wigwam he was ushered into a drawing room with blue and gold furniture. There was a large armchair in the middle of the room.

The victim was always invited to sit down in this armchair and Bottomley used to refer to it humorously as the 'extracting chair'. He switched on his considerable charm for old Carter; it was very hard to resist his twinkling blue eyes when he smiled at one of his 'lambs'. In July Bottomley bought the Basingstoke Canal from Carter, paying for it with a million shares in the Joint Stock Trust. All these shares were duplicates and therefore worth precisely nothing.

The Basingstoke Canal was undoubtedly thirty-five miles long, but unfortunately it had been dry for years. Bottomley renamed it the London & South-Western Canal and floated it as a company with a capital of half a million. He had recently taken under his wing two exceedingly wealthy young brothers, Vincent and Reginald Eyre; Vincent was in the Lifeguards and Reginald was a gentleman of leisure. He strongly advised the Eyre brothers to buy several thousand London & South-Western Canal shares, assuring them he had inside knowledge and they were certain to go up in the next few weeks. The two 'lambs' were invited to his suite of rooms in Pall Mall where he managed to create an impression of unlimited wealth. Two manservants were in attendance and champagne flowed like water, which all helped to inspire confidence. He generally made important telephone-calls in the presence of his victims and engaged in long conversations with 'tycoons' about imaginary big deals.

In this way Vincent and Reginald Eyre were induced to buy 50,000 worthless shares in the London and South Western Canal, and in exchange for his bits of paper Bottomley obtained an impeccable portfolio of gilt-edged stock. . . . The Eyre brothers eventually found out they had been swindled and sued him a few years later, but by then Horatio had found fresh 'lambs' to be sheared.

Another of his victims was James Platt, a retired wool-merchant aged seventy-eight. Bottomley and Hooley had sold him duplicated shares in the Joint Stock Trust; he lost £20,000 when the company went bankrupt, and had been a witness for the prosecution when Bottomley was tried at Guildhall. Bottomley and Hooley had assured him the shares were worth two shillings each and he had bought 300,000 from them in 1906 at prices around one and sixpence. Horatio once asked Hooley to give Platt a contract note for some shares.

'My word is my bond. No contract is needed,' said Hooley solemnly.

When Platt realized he had lost thousands of pounds in the Joint Stock Trust he called at Horatio's flat, vowing to shoot him. Horatio seemed delighted to see him.

'My dear fellow, you're the very man I've been looking for. Where on earth have you been all this time?'

'Don't try and put me off,' said Platt furiously. 'I want my money back and I'll kill you if I don't get it! You've been humbugging me quite long enough.'

'Come, come, what's all the excitement about? Of course you can have your money. Just wait a minute while I get my cheque-book. In the meantime'—Horatio pushed a bell—'we'll have a bottle.'

A manservant appeared with a bottle of champagne almost as if he had been waiting in the wings. Horatio kept replenishing Platt's glass and soon the old man was squiffy. He forgot all about the money he had come for, and at the end of the evening wrote Bottomley a cheque for £4,000 for shares in a new company which were 'guaranteed to go up'.

However, James Platt was luckier than many of the other 'lambs': he lived long enough to obtain justice. After Bottomley had been acquitted of fraud at the Joint Stock Trust trial at Guildhall, Platt brought a test case in July 1909 for the recovery of the sum he had paid for his bogus shares to Bottomley's stockbroker. Platt was most ably represented by the Hon. Frank Russell in the Chancery Division of the High Court of Justice. Mr Justice Swinfen-Eady gave judgment for Platt on 28 October 1909, and the stockbrokers had to repay him for the duplicated and fictitious shares he had received. This was a passage from the judgment:

> Mr Horatio Bottomley, the chairman of the company, stated that he had dealt in some twelve million shares of

the company, that his title to deliver shares frequently depended upon a mass of transfers to himself, which had not been entered up, that on Stock Exchange settling many shares would be delivered mainly for his account, and that to facilitate the transfer of shares out the share department of the company would use the numbers most available. But such a proceeding is wholly irregular and illegal. . . .

The Plaintiff, having . . . paid money for a worthless transfer, is entitled to recover it. The purchase money for the 13,000 shares was received by Chapman & Rowe, who delivered the transfers, and they are liable to refund this money.

Another of Bottomley's 'lambs' was eighty-three-year-old George Parker, a retired insurance broker, whom he fleeced of £20,000. But this swindle came to light only after Parker had died; when his executors discovered it they decided to sue Bottomley in 1910. The case was tried before Mr Justice Darling, and Bottomley was defended by F. E. Smith. Bottomley managed to produce two extremely ingenious letters and the whole case hinged on their interpretation. The first letter, signed by Parker, said:

7 November 1906

DEAR MR HOOLEY

I confirm the arrangements contained in Mr Bottomley's letter of this date as regards the settlement of accounts between him and me.

Yours truly,

G. W. PARKER

Witness:

A. L. Cox.

The letter referred to by Parker read:

56a Pall Mall,
London, S.W.1

DEAR MR HOOLEY

You are aware that a dispute has arisen between Mr G. W. Parker and myself as to the state of the accounts between us. We have today agreed that everything shall be treated as finally settled upon the condition that I am to authorize you—which I hereby do—to deduct from any moneys which may from time to time become payable by you to me out of any business in which we may be mutually interested 25% (twenty-five per cent) until you have in this way paid Mr Parker—which I hereby authorize you to do—the sum of £10,000 (ten thousand pounds) and subsequently to your having done this, you are to pay him a further sum of £10,000 (ten thousand pounds) of any moneys so becoming due to me from you: Mr Parker agreeing in consideration of this authority to take no further steps of any kind against me. His receipt is to be equivalent to mine in respect of any sums you pay him under this authority. I attach his confirmation of the arrangement.

Yours faithfully,
HORATIO BOTTOMLEY

Witness:
A. L. Cox.

It was extremely significant that the late George Parker did not sign Bottomley's letter to Hooley. This was an ingenious move by Bottomley because Parker was dead, and so he and Hooley were the only people left to dispute the authenticity of the documents, both of which had been witnessed by Tommy Cox. Hooley swore that both letters were forgeries and made very rude comments about Bottomley. But Mr Justice Darling told the jury that the case was a peculiar one and that Bottomley and Hooley made peculiar arrangements between themselves. The jury found that the agreement was valid; thus Horatio got away with it and was absolved from paying a penny to Parker's executors.

In 1910 the Liberals called a General Election on the issue of Lloyd George's Budget. Despite his crop of sordid law cases, Bottomley again offered himself as the Liberal candidate for South Hackney. His campaign was supervised by Tommy Cox, and the People's Perkins supported him with lusty speeches at the street corners. Conway Wertheimer, his Tory opponent, was of German origin and the anti-German prejudice brought extra votes to Bottomley. But Wertheimer discovered a leaflet about Horatio's wicked past and had copies of it printed for distribution to the electorate. Just as Bottomley was going to make an election speech he got a copy of the leaflet and cleverly turned it to his advantage.

BOTTOMLEY Ladies and Gentlemen, as I was coming into the Hall tonight I was given a leaflet issued by my opponent. He warns you not to vote for me until you have heard some startling revelations he is going to make about my past life. He tells you he has something up his sleeve.

Now, ladies and gentlemen [*long pause*]—if the revelation he is about to make *concerns his nationality*, about which I have already asked him a number of awkward questions during the election, *the sleeve is the last place I should look for the evidence*.

It was announced that Austen Chamberlain, a leading Conservative and the elder brother of Neville Chamberlain, was coming to South Hackney to speak on behalf of Wertheimer. Bottomley and Tommy Cox made plans to wreck the occasion. They engaged fifty men at three shillings each and sent them to have their heavy boots weighted with iron tips and heels. After being inspected by Bottomley and Cox they were placed in the front seats at Wertheimer's meeting.

Austen Chamberlain spoke without any interruption, but as soon as Wertheimer rose to speak the first man with weighted boots got up and left the hall with a great clatter. Amid shouts of 'Silence!' he returned and told the audience he was going out as quietly as he could. The second man then got up and drowned the opening words of Wertheimer's speech. There were cries of 'Silence' and he returned and apologized to the audience, but as he left the hall the third man got up and drowned Wertheimer with the clatter of his boots. The other men repeated this performance until poor Wertheimer lost his nerve and abandoned his speech. Bottomley arranged as usual for his racehorses to walk in procession down the High Street carrying notices saying *Vote for my owner*, and the people thronged the streets to cheer them. The election resulted in another win for the Liberals and Bottomley got in with a comfortable majority.

During 1910 he started the John Bull League: readers of the paper could join it for a shilling a year, for which they got a membership badge. The object of the League was to introduce 'commonsense business methods into the government of the country'. Tommy Cox wrote a special song for the League's first meeting at the Albert Hall:

If you would to Parliament
Businessmen of grit be sent
Join the John Bull League.
Men and women who despise
Party tactics, party lies,
Foolish fake election cries,
Join the League.

After the election was over Bottomley sent for one of his voluntary helpers, a young man named Henry Houston. He was of medium height, very thin and of a somewhat delicate appearance.

'I've been watching you,' said Bottomley. 'You did about three times as much work as anybody else! How would you like to join my staff? I want you to become one of Bottomley's Bodyguard.'

Henry Houston, who greatly admired Bottomley as a politician, was very pleased to join his 'stable'. Bottomley was so impressed with his abilities as a political organizer that he appointed him his political secretary a few months later. Houston gave him years of loyal and devoted service and they became close friends, although Houston was young enough to be his son. Houston called him 'H.B.', like the other élite in the stable.

Bottomley was lunching with Houston one day at Romano's when he noticed a very pretty girl who came into the restaurant with an older man. She was small with auburn hair and merry, laughing eyes. Her features were delicately modelled, her complexion was perfect and she was well endowed.

'What a pretty girl!' Horatio remarked. 'What a fine figure! I wonder who she can be.'

The girl was just his type and he was so intrigued by her that he forgot to finish his *Sole bonne femme*. Her stage-name was Peggy Primrose: she was twenty, unhappily married to a 'gentleman of leisure', Aubrey Lowe, and in the chorus of *The Dollar Princess*, a musical comedy which was on tour. When she left Romano's Horatio hurried after her. He went to ground for a whole week and neglected all his business activities, including *John Bull*.

Julius Elias and the staff were greatly relieved when he phoned up the office at last because the paper was due to go to press that day. George Wedlake, his assistant, hurried over in a taxi to a flat in Bedford Court Mansions off Tottenham Court Road which Horatio had just taken for Peggy Primrose. Wedlake and Bottomley got right down to work and managed to get *John Bull* to press. Bottomley was so enamoured of Peggy Primrose that he followed her musical comedy to the provinces: he joined her at Stafford and insisted on taking the whole cast out to supper.

His financial needs were so great that he again joined forces with Ernest Hooley to plunder an old man's fortune. They picked on Robert Masters, a retired Indian Civil Servant in his eighties who had lost his memory. Bottomley and Hooley entertained him lavishly and through plausible stories they fleeced him of £90,000 in the course of a few weeks. All he got for his money was dud shares in the John Bull Investment Trust and the John Bull Agency, and shares in two bogus companies named Carter's Deep Leads and Hadon Park Estate.

After this catastrophe Masters left town and never told a soul how he had been conned by the two scoundrels. A year later Horatio wrote him one of his standard letters to 'mugs', a cunningly worded document which read:

> DEAR MASTERS
>
> I have been going over the names of my old supporters and it struck me that I might now be able to do something for those people who lost money in my companies. Would you mind letting me know approximately the amount you consider you are out of pocket and I will see what I can do towards recovering your losses.

Masters, owing to his loss of memory, had forgotten everything that had happened in the past. He swallowed the bait and called at Bottomley's flat next day. He noted in his diary that 'Bottomley was most cordial and offered to repay my losses'. Bottomley then brought Hooley on to the scene and they dined and wined the old man for a week. Another note from his diary says:

> Walked to Bottomley's chambers in Pall Mall. Took me small hotel in Coventry Street where we had much cham-

pagne and gorgeous lunch. After discussing business went home.

During that week Masters gave Bottomley and Hooley a series of bills for £41,772 which were discounted immediately. The old man received thousands of worthless share certificates, but was too proud to complain to anyone, and in 1909 he died a pauper. His daughter, Mrs Curtis, who had always assumed he was a rich man, was horrified when his will was proved and the truth came out. She consulted her solicitor, Mr Dade, and on his advice sued Bottomley and Hooley in June 1911.

Hooley managed to settle the matter out of court, but Bottomley decided to contest the claim. The case was tried before Lord Chief Justice Alverstone and a special jury, and Horatio was much too wily to risk going into the witness-box. On 30 June the jury gave a verdict against him and assessed damages at £50,000. His appeal was dismissed on 31 July; but he told members of his 'stable' that Mrs Curtis would be lucky if she ever got a penny from him because he was on the brink of bankruptcy.

On the night Horatio lost the Masters case he was accosted in the Strand by Aubrey Lowe, the estranged husband of Peggy Primrose. Lowe had brought a cab driver along with him as a witness.

'I've got you at last!' cried Lowe, and knocked him down in the road.

Although the papers reported the attack on Bottomley, he refused to bring a charge against Lowe, saying he had had enough bad publicity for one week. He continued his affair with Peggy Primrose just as if this had never happened: she was established as first favourite of the harem and was to become the love of his life.

The Odhams brothers were always asking Julius Elias to try and keep Bottomley in order for the sake of *John Bull*, so Elias thought he had better have a word with him about Aubrey Lowe's attack.

'I wonder how the public will react to these revelations about you if they go on,' said Elias gravely.

'The public are not affected by one's personal affairs,' said Bottomley, laughing. 'Take it from me, they buy the paper for the articles it contains and the service it offers.'

By 1912 Bottomley's financial position had become hopeless.

The last straw was when he had to pay the penalty for his frauds in the Joint Stock Trust. On 1 February Mr Justice Swinfen-Eady ruled that, despite his acquittal at Guildhall, he was liable to the shareholders of the Joint Stock Trust for damages for fraudulent breach of trust and misfeasance in the sum of £36,373; he also had to pay 5 per cent interest thereon from April 1905, making a total sum of £49,290. He was forced to file his second bankruptcy petition with liabilities of £233,000.

Amongst his creditors were the Prudential Assurance, who had sued him for a libel in *John Bull*; he had subsequently been unable to pay their costs. The Prudential instructed J. M. Astbury, K.C., and H. M. MacCardie to appear at his examination. Before this took place Astbury had seen Osborne O'Hagan, the financier, and asked his advice on how to handle Bottomley.

'He has a way of dealing with you gentlemen of the Bar which not only floors you, but also wins the sympathy of the judge and jury,' said O'Hagan. 'The only way to beat him is to control yourself: smile when he scores off you or insults you, but keep pegging away. . . . You must keep your temper with him.'

When Horatio arrived at Carey Street for his examination he told the meeting, 'This is about the first meeting I have attended where I have not been received with cheers!'

'Unfortunate I may have been, but never dishonest,' he protested later.

J. M. Astbury appreciated Osborne O'Hagan's advice when he examined Bottomley in February and March. Astbury questioned him gently but firmly about his extravagant mode of living; he admitted keeping six gardeners, six indoor servants and two chauffeurs at The Dicker alone. Then Astbury dealt with his complicated banking accounts, and asked why great sums of money had been paid over to his friend Saul Cooper. Astbury mentioned the Masters case and asked if Bottomley would like to have a copy of the judgment.

BOTTOMLEY No: I know the wretched thing by heart.

ASTBURY You can have a second copy of mine.

REGISTRAR Mr Bottomley does not appear to want any assistance.

BOTTOMLEY It is Mr Astbury's assistance that I do not want, sir.

ASTBURY Quite right. Don't you take my advice about anything.

Astbury managed to keep his temper through the many weeks of the examination, although Horatio did his utmost to annoy him, as in this well known passage:

ASTBURY You keep racehorses, Mr Bottomley?

BOTTOMLEY No.

ASTBURY You do not keep racehorses?

BOTTOMLEY Certainly not.

ASTBURY Then you did keep racehorses?

BOTTOMLEY No, never.

ASTBURY You have a place in Sussex called The Dicker?

BOTTOMLEY Yes.

ASTBURY You breed horses there—racehorses?

BOTTOMLEY Yes.

ASTBURY Then why did you tell me that you never kept racehorses?

BOTTOMLEY I gave you a correct answer. I never kept race-horses. *They keep me.*

Astbury made a point of joining in the general laughter.

After being declared bankrupt Bottomley was obliged to apply for the Chiltern Hundreds. It was a sad blow for him to leave the House of Commons; F. E. Smith, K.C., paid tribute to him in the *Oxford and Cambridge Review*:

> In many ways I consider Mr Horatio Bottomley to be one of the most attractive speakers to whom I have ever listened.... His House of Commons style was almost ideal, self-possessed, quiet, irresistibly witty, and distinguished equally by common sense and tolerance. He made for himself a position in the House of Commons of which

nothing but the loss of his seat could deprive him. His absence from the House of Commons has impoverished the public stock of gaiety, of cleverness, of common sense.

But in the House of Commons Ramsay MacDonald, the Labour leader, had made a malicious speech about Bottomley in revenge for past attacks on himself in *John Bull*. Ramsay MacDonald called him 'a man of doubtful parentage who has lived all his life on the threshold of jail'.

Stung by the insinuation that he was a bastard, Bottomley summoned Henry Houston and told him to drop all political work for the present because it was vital for his reputation to establish that he was legitimate.

'You're an expert at digging up facts, Henry,' he said quietly. 'Help me to clear the names of my father and mother.'

Houston was empowered to go out and discover the necessary proof regardless of expense. He applied for Bottomley's birth-certificate, on which Elizabeth Holyoake and William Bottomley appeared as his parents; this was photographed and a copy of it published in *John Bull*. After a long search Houston managed to locate the East End cemetery where William Bottomley was buried. Horatio accompanied him to the cemetery and when they came to William Bottomley's grave he broke down and wept. Houston, who had never known him to be so sensitive, could hardly believe it.

'I can't remember much about him, but what I do remember is good,' Bottomley said in a broken voice. 'I can't help feeling that half the money I spend in a week would have saved his life. He was too poor to have the rest and nourishment he needed.'

They noticed that the grave had been sadly neglected.

'We must put up a proper stone for him,' said Horatio as they left the cemetery.

John Bull reported that William Bottomley had died from consumption, although the truth was he had died in a fit of madness. After publishing these 'facts' in his paper, Horatio Bottomley never went near the grave again.

However, one should mention that when his sister, Florence Dollman, had died in 1909 he had been heart-broken. His love for Florence was one of his redeeming features and he never forgot her. Houston related that on the anniversary of her death Horatio always went to Highgate Cemetery to put flowers on her grave.

11 How to Win at Lotteries

There is an art of sophistry by which men have deluded their own consciences by persuading themselves that what would be criminal in others is virtuous in them.

DR JOHNSON

Bottomley's bankruptcy was not nearly as disastrous for him as the newspaper headlines made out. He had to give up his flat at 56a Pall Mall—sometimes known as his 'den of iniquity' —and to move temporarily into a small hotel in the West End, but this was about the only 'hardship' he had to endure. He still retained The Dicker, which had been previously transferred into the name of his son-in-law Jefferson Cohn, a well known City man and racehorse-owner. However, he sorely missed being M.P. for South Hackney and was determined to regain his old seat as soon as he could raise the money to get his bankruptcy annulled. An ordinary man would have been depressed at the prospect of raising £20,000, let alone £233,000, but Bottomley was confident that it would be only a matter of time before he was back at Westminster.

It is most important for a politician who intends to make a come-back to keep his name before the public, and Bottomley opened his campaign by holding a meeting of his supporters at the Queen's Hall on 11 May, 1912. After being given a marvellous reception, since every member of his claque was present, he explained that he had been forced to retire from the House of Commons owing to his bankruptcy. Although he regretted this, he was convinced that Parliament was almost played out, and he intended to address meetings up and down the country at which he would advocate his solution for all Britain's troubles—a Business Government run by businessmen.

Henry Houston organized Business League meetings for him in the principal towns of Britain and accompanied him on his travels. Bottomley went everywhere by train and made a point of drawing £100 from *John Bull* for each engagement. He justified this self-awarded bonus by introducing the name of the paper into all his speeches, as in this example:

> Ladies and gentlemen, I'm Bottomley! Having said that, the individual who stands before you tonight has neither horns in his forehead, nor, as far as you are able to judge, cloven hoofs!
>
> Certainly those of you who read the law reports have seen my name, because I hold the unique distinction of having gone through every court in the country—except one—and here I touch wood!—because that exception is the Divorce Court.
>
> Some of you may have heard of me in the City. There was a time when I was called the Napoleon of Finance. That was when the few companies with which I was connected were paying attractive dividends. Then came a time when the shares fell so fast—but not as fast as Consols—that I was dubbed an unscrupulous company promoter. That is a way they have in the City.
>
> Some of you may have heard of me as the editor of a more or less obscure journal—I forget the name for the moment [*shouts of* 'JOHN BULL!' *from the audience*]—through the columns of which I advocate each week the cause of the bottom dog and the man-in-the-street.

Later in the speech he said, 'I don't mind letting you into a secret. Although I am nominally a bankrupt, *I never had a better time in my life*—plenty of money and everything else I want as well!'

He had huge audiences everywhere he went and always put himself across as a sportsman—racing and his horses and boxing got into every speech—and a man of the world who knew how to get the best out of life. At the same time he convinced the working classes that he was 'one of us'.

Bottomley was in such demand as a speaker at Business League meetings that he and Houston had to work to a most strenuous itinerary. Houston noted that during one week their schedule was:

TUESDAY	10.30 a.m.	Leave London
	6.00 p.m.	Arrive Glasgow
		Deputation of leading men at hotel
		Rehearse speech
	8.00–10.00 p.m.	Meeting
	11.00 p.m.	Return train to London (sleep)
WEDNESDAY	a.m.	Session with secretaries at station
	10.15 a.m.	Leave London, Cornish Riviera Express
	p.m.	Arrive Plymouth
		Same routine as at Glasgow
		Return to London

Houston handled the petty cash on these trips. 'H.B.' had the most extravagant notions of how much they needed for travelling expenses and before setting out Houston had to cash a large cheque for the 'getting-away' money. Horatio tipped porters and railway attendants a pound, saying it was good propaganda for him, and sent affectionate wires from the station to the girls he was leaving behind, signing them BOTTY or SKIPPER, as appropriate. And whenever they stayed a night at a hotel in the provinces he cashed another cheque for his 'getting-home' money.

He was very sorry to hear that the train attendant on a northern line, who sometimes cashed his cheques, had gone to prison.

'Ah, we shall miss him, Houston. You'd better send his wife some money.'

'But he's in prison for bigamy!'

'What a hero!' Horatio declared. 'Ah well! Send both his wives some money!'

By autumn of 1912 the circulation of *John Bull* had reached a million and a half. Bottomley won the Cesarewitch at Newmarket and made £70,000 on the day, but it only helped to balance his betting losses. It was vital for him to find a new way of making money. After taking his annual cure at Carlsbad he stopped at Lucerne on the way back; hearing that the Swiss lottery promoters were making a fortune, he thought it would be worth studying their methods.

He was staying at the Hotel National when an unknown admirer, Reuben Bigland, called to see him. He was a small printer from Birmingham, tall, broad-shouldered and bulky and about the same age as Bottomley. Bigland had been a jack-of-all-trades; once a crossing-sweeper, he had also been a bookmaker and a professional punter in his time. In the latter capacity he had won a lot of money, sometimes by backing the winner after it had passed the post; this was done by a telephone code with a confederate and earned him the nickname of 'Telephone Jack'.

Bigland waited down in the hotel lobby until the unmistakable figure of Horatio Bottomley descended the stairs.

'Mr Bottomley, I believe?'

'That's me.'

'My name is Bigland—Reuben Bigland of Birmingham.'

'Birmingham! . . . yes, that is a city I know very well. . . . I was reared and educated at Sir Josiah Mason's school. But what can I do for Mr Bigland?'

On learning that Bigland had a proposition to discuss, Horatio took him to his suite of rooms. Reuben Bigland suggested that *John Bull* should run a big sweepstake on the Derby on the same lines as the Calcutta Club sweepstake. The money for the tickets would be sent to Switzerland in order to get round the Lottery Act.

'We could take ten per cent for our expenses—there's a fortune for us both!' declared Bigland enthusiastically.

But Bottomley dismissed the idea with a majestic wave of his hand.

'It's a great scheme, Bigland—but it's no use to me. But perhaps you can do something for me that might lead to other developments. Introduce some of these football bookmakers to me, and you will have done me a service.'

Reuben Bigland put him in touch with some of the Swiss bookmaking fraternity, and Bottomley told them he would arrange for some of his 'special commissioners' from the 'John Bull' Exposure Bureau to come over and study their methods. This was a crafty device to make the Swiss bookies advertise in *John Bull* and thus ensure a favourable reference from the paper.

In return for Bigland's help, Bottomley took him to meet some Swiss racing men. 'My friend Mr Bigland is a large printer in Birmingham, a man I have known for twenty-five years,' he said with his usual disregard for accuracy. 'I want you to give him some of your printing—see what you can do for him.'

Meanwhile, *John Bull* had started a novel kind of competition known as 'Bullets', which were a form of puns; every week the paper gave its readers a phrase and the first and last words of the Bullet each had to include two letters from it. A good example was IN THE SWIM, for which the winning Bullet was MILES WITHOUT SMILES. Another example was MARRIAGE BELLS for which the Bullet was I'LL ALTER HIM. The Bullets became so popular that *John Bull* awarded a weekly prize of £500 for the best one.

The paper also ran football and cricket competitions and gave £2,500 in prizes to readers who forecast the correct results of a number of games. But after rumours that Bottomley's *John Bull* competitions were being rigged, *Truth* magazine investigated the matter. They unearthed some extraordinary facts about the winners of £1,700 on twenty football matches.

> Whatever the odds may be against the persons picking out by chance the winners of twenty football matches, I do not believe in the practical possibility of their being picked out by men who all depart from London at the same time to spend a few days respectively in lodgings or hotels at Torquay, Leicester and Manchester.

Bottomley did his best to scotch these dreadful revelations by publishing an outraged article in *John Bull* the following week. It stated that the John Bull Exposure Bureau had gone into action and brought every one of these football cheats to justice.

When Reuben Bigland returned to Birmingham he had a letter from Bottomley asking if he would call on him in London. Bigland arranged to come down at once and in gratitude for the Swiss printing orders he had received he brought with him two water-colours painted by a well known Birmingham artist as a present for Bottomley. When Horatio saw the first one he asked if it was an oleograph. Bigland, very annoyed, told him to scratch it and he'd find out if it was real.

'Now, Mr Bigland, it's very nice of you to present me with

these lovely pictures by your local artist, but if you can let me have a monkey [£500] it'll do more good than pictures,' said Bottomley brazenly. 'This is an expensive office and I'm an expensive man.'

'A monkey, sir?' asked Bigland, leading him on.

'Yes, and I am your friend for life,' said Bottomley eagerly.

Reuben Bigland turned on him.

'A monkey-on-a-stick is all you'll get from me before you've earned it!'

Bottomley, furious at being made to look a fool, bustled him out of the office.

Bigland felt most disillusioned about Bottomley, whom he had regarded as a superman, and never expected to see him again.

'I felt he was socially head and shoulders above me—a big man in his own circle, boosted to the skies by the Press . . . and then when I came to meet him, I had to say, "Well, where is his cleverness? I could beat him myself!"'*

William Lotinga, *John Bull*'s racing correspondent, was a big gambler on the Turf like Bottomley, and once lost £40,000 in one week, but in other ways they were very different characters. Lotinga had been up at Cambridge and was a champion amateur runner in his youth. A devoted husband and father, he loved to entertain sportsmen at his house at Roehampton. However, Lotinga was very independent and outspoken and sometimes fell out with his associates; on several occasions he went to law when he thought he had a just case. Bottomley had recently bought his racing paper, *Lotinga's Weekly*, and the two men were on good terms.

In October William Lotinga suggested to Horatio that they should go into partnership and run sweepstakes on the big English races, making Switzerland their headquarters in order to get round the Lottery Act. Horatio replied he was not interested in sweepstakes at the moment, although they had distinct possibilities. But either he changed his mind suddenly or else he was lying to Lotinga.

In December he happened to meet Reuben Bigland at the Queen's Hotel, Birmingham, where he had come for a Business League meeting. He greeted Bigland cordially and invited him to call and see him the following morning. Bigland was ushered into his hotel room at the Queen's at seven. Horatio, who was

* Reuben Bigland, *Bottomley* (Farwood, 1922).

working in bed, said he had decided to run *John Bull* racing sweeps after all, and the first one would be on the Derby of 1913. He asked Bigland how much he ought to charge for tickets.

'Half a crown each, or ten tickets for a pound,' replied Bigland.

'And how much should I pay my agents?'

Bigland told him the rate and answered all his other questions about the economics of sweepstakes. Having picked his brains, Bottomley asked him to quote for printing a million books of ten tickets. However, this was an empty gesture: he never gave him an order for a single book. He had just been using Bigland, whom he regarded as a small-time operator in a different class to himself.

John Bull offered a first prize of £15,000 for their sweep on the 1913 Derby, which was being organized from Switzerland by Patrick O'Brien, described as an expert with years of experience in running sweepstakes. Their readers had no notion that Patrick O'Brien was really an ex-convict named Harry Bennett, also known as Bangham, and was in Bottomley's 'stable'.

There was a sensational result to the 1913 Derby: a suffragette ran on to the course during the race and killed herself; and the Stewards later disqualified Craganour, the winner, and awarded the race to the second horse, Aboyeur. Horatio decided that the first prize should be divided between the ticket-holders of Craganour and Aboyeur—a taximan and a brewer's drayman. As the total receipts were £270,000, Horatio had made a most auspicious start to his new venture. Nevertheless, he decided to run the next sweep himself and 'Patrick O'Brien' was paid off with a cheque for £5,000. Patrick O'Brien alias Bennett alias Bangham happened to meet Reuben Bigland at the National Dog Show at Bigley Hall, Birmingham, and complained bitterly about the way he had been treated.

'Horatio wants the middle and both ends, and it's his greed that will bring him down,' said O'Brien.

Henry Houston had agreed to run the English side of the Derby sweep, after being assured that the whole thing was 'perfectly legal' and that Bottomley had taken counsel's opinion on it. Many months later Houston discovered that this opinion had been written by Bottomley himself!

Immediately after the Derby sweep Bottomley announced

a 'remnant' sale of tickets at three for five shillings and sent out 200,000 books; later he asked Houston to come over to Switzerland to help him deal with the tickets. He had booked a luxurious suite of rooms at the leading hotel at Geneva and had two lady-friends and the ubiquitous Saul Cooper in his party. Houston saw the remnant tickets being sorted out in three bedrooms, in one of which Horatio was seated at a desk stacked with piles of money: a mixture of gold sovereigns, pound notes, cheques and postal orders. Sacks of money had been arriving for him every day at the post office at Geneva. Houston made out tickets for all the subscribers and placed them in a tombola. Horatio collected all the sovereigns, pound notes and postal orders and carried them off in relays to his lady friends in the bedroom opposite; only the cheques were left on the desk. Houston went in later and watched Horatio and the girls making up the cash and postal orders into amounts of £7,000 and putting them into separate baskets.

'"H.B." personally took these baskets back to England, and that was the last I saw of them,' said Houston.

Once again Bottomley was making money hand over fist, but in July 1913 a small cloud appeared on the horizon. Some dissatisfied shareholders of John Bull, Ltd, presented a petition to wind up the company on the grounds that there had been grave irregularities by the management. Certain allegations in their petition are most illuminating.

> The following is a further instance of the said grave irregularities. The company authorized the issue of debentures to the amount of £25,000 to the said Horatio Bottomley, in return for which he agreed to obtain and deliver to the company debentures of the Guernsey company [John Bull, Guernsey] for the same amount, but such an exchange has never been carried out, and the company was on 31 December 1912 liable to pay off debentures of the Guernsey company of the amount of £6,980, as well as of the said new issue, of which debentures of the value of about £8,000 have now passed into the hands of third persons. The company received no consideration for the issue of the said debentures to the said Horatio Bottomley.
>
> The company is being carried on principally for the *private advantage and benefit of the said Horatio Bottomley* (who

> now has complete control of the directors) and not for the benefit of shareholders, and ought to be wound up. If the company be wound up on this petition, there will be a large surplus for the shareholders.

However, Horatio had another lucky escape: the petition was dismissed, and a motion to appoint a Receiver for *John Bull* was withdrawn after it had been announced that a new business arrangement had been made between Odhams Press and *John Bull*.

John Bull held another sweepstake on the 1914 Grand National and the readers gave it their enthusiastic support. The first prize was £5,000. Bottomley had every confidence that it would be won by one of the 'stable' because they held the tickets of every fancied horse in the race, but a neglected outsider named Sunloch jumped home an easy winner and ruined his plans. The lucky ticket was held by Abraham Tibbs, an electrical engineer from Blackwood, Monmouthshire, who appeared next day with his solicitor at the *John Bull* offices. Horatio did his utmost to try and persuade Tibbs to take half of his prize in 'specially recommended shares', but the Welshman insisted on having five thousand pounds in cash. He even refused to make a small contribution to the *John Bull* Human Documents Fund for the relief of distress. How Horatio must have cursed Tibbs when he walked out of the office with all that cash! Curiously enough, the money proved fatal to Abraham Tibbs. He bought an expensive car in Wales and started drinking, and died two years later without a penny in the world.

In the spring Bottomley ran an extremely popular sweep on the F.A. Cup. The Swiss operations were handled by Smallman and Terry at Geneva, while Houston took charge of the British side. Houston had an excellent organization with agents all over England, Scotland and Wales and twenty-four distributing centres. However, one of his agents at Plymouth was closely questioned by a detective in April, so he immediately called off the entire British operation and informed Bottomley. Six weeks later Houston and his two assistants were summoned to appear at Plymouth Assizes 'to show cause why they should not be committed to prison as rogues and vagabonds for aiding and abetting a lottery'.

On the advice of his counsel Houston pleaded guilty and cited that he had been relying on counsel's opinion. Mr Justice

Coleridge, taking the case, said, 'But for what your counsel has told me on the legal advice you took I should send you to prison. I wish I had before me those who are responsible for this scheme.'

Henry Houston was far too loyal to betray 'H.B.' The case resulted in his being fined £100 and ordered to pay costs of £370. Bottomley should certainly have settled the bill considering he was making a fortune from his sweeps, but he behaved abominably and only sent Houston a cheque for £50 towards his expenses. Consequently Houston was unable to pay his costs and was forced to go bankrupt later in the year. However, Julius Elias of Odhams turned up at Carey Street and settled the debt for him.

John Bull announced that their next sweep would be on the 1914 Derby and there would be £50,000 in prizes. All money was to be sent to Smallman and Terry in Geneva in order to evade the British law against lotteries. This firm had offices in a narrow street in Geneva; when mountains of mail started arriving for them every day the Swiss police grew suspicious and established themselves in premises on the opposite side of the road that overlooked the sweepstake headquarters. Smallman and Terry, anxious about their position, wired to Bottomley to come to Geneva at once.

Horatio called at Smallman and Terry's offices in a car at dead of night and loaded it with sacks of cash and tickets which he took to his hotel. Next morning he chartered a boat and filled it from stem to stern with sweepstake coupons. Then he rowed out to a point three miles from the shore, which he ingeniously pretended was outside territorial waters. And in this location, far from the madding crowd, he made the draw for the 1914 Derby.

The race was won by Durbar II, and *John Bull* reported that the first prize of £25,000 had been won with ticket O.Q.206390 held by a Madame Glukad, 'the blind lady of Toulouse'. Readers were regaled with a heart-warming story about this sweet little old lady, and the following week they heard that Madame Glukad had been inundated with offers of marriage and was so embarrassed by them that she had been forced to leave Toulouse. This was not gospel truth: the lady was certainly blind, but her real name was Helen Gluckman and she was a sister of Saul Cooper, who last appeared at Geneva helping Horatio to count his loot from the remnant sale of tickets. *John Bull* published a photo of a cheque for £25,000 endorsed by Madame Glukad, but all the blind lady got for her winning ticket was £250—the balance of the prize money went into a Bottomley banking account and Saul Cooper took his cut. Sweepstakes had become just as profitable as Westralian gold mines for Horatio. His next venture in *John Bull* was an Omnibus Sweepstake on three races: the Royal Hunt Cup and the Stewards Cup in the summer and the Doncaster St Leger in the autumn.

'A few more sweeps like the Derby one and I'll be able to pay off all my debts and get back to the House of Commons,' he told Houston.

At the end of July he took Peggy Primrose and a big party to Ostend to see his horses run at the Wellington Hippodrome. Racing at Ostend was much more congenial for him than in England while he was still a bankrupt. He and his party stayed at a hotel at Mariakerke; his trainer, Jimmy Hare, and his racing team stayed near them in two flats. Henry Houston was in Germany on his honeymoon when Bottomley wired him: COME AT ONCE. AM STRANDED. YOU CAN RETURN TONIGHT.

Houston set off and did not arrive at Mariakerke till late at night. He was annoyed to find that Horatio had retired to bed after a successful day at the races and he had to wait till the morning to see him. Then it transpired that 'H.B.' had broken up his honeymoon and brought him all this way just to inquire how the new Omnibus Sweep was getting on in his absence. Bottomley had treated him very badly a few months previously, and the wonder was that Houston served him so well for so long. Perhaps it was because Horatio could be so charming to his key men that they were prepared to put up with his lapses.

While Bottomley was preoccupied in August with his sweeps and his Ostend racing, the Great Powers were about to start the First World War. The immediate cause was the shooting of Archduke Franz Ferdinand, heir to the Hapsburg throne, at Sarajevo on 28 June, by a nineteen-year-old Bosnian Serb, Gavrilo Princip. Serbia had been annexed by Austria-Hungary, although the treaty had never been ratified. Austria did nothing about Franz Ferdinand's assassination for three weeks: then, on the advice of Germany, her dominant ally, she sent Serbia a stiff ultimatum. The Serbs rejected it, encouraged by their ally Russia. Russia then ordered part mobilization, while Germany pushed the vacillating Austrians into war against Serbia. At the end of July Germany threatened to declare war on Russia unless she cancelled all mobilization, but Czar Nicholas II did not take the warning seriously and ignored it. Germany then ordered full mobilization and prepared to invade neutral Belgium in order to go through her territory and secure a swift victory against France, her traditional enemy.

The tragedy of the war from Britain's point of view was that Asquith, the Prime Minister, sat on the fence till the eleventh hour instead of making it clear to Germany from the outset that Britain would not allow her to violate Belgium's neutrality. If only he had done so the First World War might never have started. Neither Germany, Russia, Austria–Hungary nor France wanted a major war; they were all rattling the sabre with the idea of fighting a short war and gaining an easy victory.

At nine o'clock on the morning of 4 August Sir Edward Grey, the British Foreign Minister, sent an ultimatum telling Germany to withdraw from Belgian soil by midnight.* But German soldiers had already invaded Belgium at 8.30 a.m. After the ultimatum had been ignored, Britain joined France and Russia in the long, murderous and costly war against Germany and her allies.

These world-shaking events changed the lives of millions of people. However, the first effect of the war upon Horatio Bottomley was an announcement that all racing at Ostend was cancelled.

'That's not fair,' he blustered. 'We'll have to do something about this. I'll go down and see the Stewards myself!'

He was such a good patron at Ostend, and lost so many francs to the bookies, that the Stewards always tried to humour him if possible. But Belgium was at war—the Boches were already on their soil—and Bottomley had to take a back seat. He offered to sell his horses to the Belgian Government for the war-effort, but they were not interested.

He cursed his luck; like many people, he had never expected Britain to get involved in a major European war. If only he had

* Britain's last major conflict had been the Crimean War in 1854, when there was an interval of *two months* between her ultimatum and the outbreak of hostilities.

anticipated it he would have scrapped the current issue of *John Bull*, in which his main article was entitled: TO HELL WITH SERBIA. *Why Should Britain Shed Her Blood To Save A Nation of Assassins?* And now Britain had entered the war as the ally of France and Russia to help them protect 'little Serbia' against the Austrians and the Germans. He was appalled as he remembered the shocking sentiments he had expressed in his article—'Serbia must be wiped out', 'Let Serbia be removed from the map of Europe'.

How the devil could he get out of this mess? He resolved that *John Bull* must jump on the patriotic bandwagon and hoped that its Serbian gaffe would soon be forgotten. Although his racehorses were only worth £400 he sent them back to England in a specially chartered boat, while he returned home in the first available Channel steamer. If jet planes had been invented in 1914, Horatio would certainly have hired one.

III

THE LOST OPPORTUNITY

12 England's Recruiting Sergeant

This war is going to be my opportunity.
BOTTOMLEY, to Henry Houston, August 1914

Bottomley was in such a hurry to see that *John Bull* got on the right side of the British public that he went straight from Victoria Station to the office and worked like a beaver to change the paper from top to bottom. On 15 August *John Bull* appeared with a brand new cover and asked its readers: 'Do you recognize him NOW?' John Bull had been transformed from a countryman into a sailor with 'H.M.S. *Victory*' on his capband. The former Byron quotation had been discarded in favour of patriotic lines from Shakespeare:

Come the three corners of the world in arms,
And we shall shock them: nought shall make us rue,
If England to itself do rest but true.

And the leading article was headed: *The Dawn of England's Greatest Glory. The Day Has Come. Now For The Golden Eventide.*

> ... Let every Briton, therefore, gird on his armour. It is not necessary to be a soldier, but it *is* necessary to be a MAN.

To mark the occasion Bottomley addressed Candid Communications to His Majesty King George V, to Mr Asquith, to

Winston Churchill, First Lord of the Admiralty, and to Lord Kitchener of Khartoum, who had just been appointed Secretary of State for War. Bottomley was fifty-four and had a feeling in his bones that the war was going to be his great opportunity. He told Houston, 'Whatever I have been in the past, and whatever my faults, I am going to draw a line at 4 August 1914, and start afresh. I shall play the game, cut all my old associates, and wipe out everything pre-1914.'

He arranged to bring Eliza home from her villa in the South of France. She was very glad to be back in England and living in security at The Dicker, and it was a treat not to have any workmen about the place. Horatio hoped that having his wife in residence again might help him to turn over a new leaf and liquidate his harem, but that proved impossible because he had fallen deeply in love with Peggy Primrose.

Seymour Hicks, the actor–manager, invited Bottomley to make a recruiting speech at the London Opera House, Kingsway, on 14 September and billed the meeting as '*John Bull*'s Great Patriotic Rally for Recruiting'. Five thousand people filled the opera house and fifteen thousand waited outside to try and get tickets. Seymour Hicks congratulated Bottomley on drawing far more people to a meeting than two Cabinet Ministers had done recently. Bottomley delivered what was to become known as his 'Prince of Peace' speech:

> It may be—I do not know and I do not profess to understand—that this is the great audit of the Universe, that the Supreme Being has ordered the nations of the earth to decide who is to lead in the van of human progress.
>
> If the British Empire resolves to fight the battle cleanly, to look upon it as something more than an ordinary war, we shall one day realize that it has not been in vain, and we, the British Empire, as the chosen leaders of the world, shall travel along the road of human destiny and progress, at the end of which we shall see the patient figure of the Prince of Peace pointing the Star of Bethlehem which leads us on to God.

He spoke about Germany in violently abusive language, prophesying that the war would be over by Christmas, and stated his 'terms' for Germany: they would have to hand over their warships to Great Britain, partition the German Empire into the small States that existed in 1886, and dethrone the Kaiser. Then he appealed to every man capable of bearing arms to join the colours and help to hasten the glorious time of peace. He was followed by the senior recruiting officer of the 1st Lifeguards, who invited any young men present to step up on to the stage and enrol for service. Recruiting officers stood by to sign on recruits at tables covered with Union Jacks.

Delighted at the success of his first patriotic meeting, Horatio told Tommy Cox, 'Professional politicians are useless for this purpose. I'm going to be the unofficial Recruiting Agent of the British Empire.' Charles B. Cochran, the theatre impresario, invited him to appear on 14 January 1915 at a Great War Rally at the Albert Hall which Henry Houston organized. Cochran expected a big crowd, but never imagined that thousands of people would wait in the road for hours on the offchance of getting a seat. The *Daily Mail* described the scene inside the Albert Hall:

> The platform was 'patriotic' in the most complete sense. Occupying its wide space, with the brilliant uniform of the Irish Guards in their midst, was a great body of soldiers representing the Legion of Frontiersmen, the R.A.M.C. (Royal Army Medical Corps), the Civilian Force Ambulance, and about a hundred men of the newly formed Sportsmen's and Footballers' Battalions. There were also sailors, special constables, Chelsea Pensioners and Boy Scouts.

A band played soldiers' favourite songs and Charles Coburn gave his well known rendering of 'Two Lovely Black Eyes'. Then Constance Collier, the actress, recited Bottomley's war poem 'Why Is the Red Blood Flowing?' The opening verses ran:

> Why is the red blood flowing—why do the women weep?
> Why have our dear, long-lost brothers gone to their long last sleep?
> Come, comrade, come—consider: let's look things in the face,
> For this is more than a war, mate—it's a call to the human race.
> Listen! Don't you hear it—ringing through the land—
> Prepare and be ye ready—my Audit is at hand!

JOHN BULL

Vol. XVI. No 419 SATURDAY, JUNE 13, 1914. ONE PENNY

[Registered at the G.P.O. as a Newspaper.]

483912

For meaning of this No. see page ii of Cover.

The world is a bundle of hay;
Mankind are the asses who pull;
Each tugs it a different way,
And the greatest of all is John Bull

—BYRON

Edited by
HORATIO BOTTOMLEY.

CLOSES
JUNE 16

£300

ROYAL
HUNT
CUP
CONTEST

SEE PAGE 36

John Bull in peace

JOHN BULL

Vol. XVII. No. 428 | SATURDAY, AUGUST 15, 1914 | ONE PENNY

[Registered at the G.P.O. as a New-paper.]

479076

For meaning of this No. see page ii. of Cover.

Come the three corners of the world in arms,
And we shall shock them: nought shall make us rue,
If England to itself do rest but true.

Edited by
HORATIO BOTTOMLEY.

John Bull at war

How do your books to mine stand—are all the entries made?
Is anything unsettled—are all the first debts paid?
The Audit will be searching, and this will be the test—
What have we done for England—have we given of our best?
And when the Audit's finished, what are we going to do?
And you, behind the counter, and you—and you—and you?...

These first two verses will suffice to give a general impression of his poem. It had a topical appeal, but was doggerel in imitation of Rudyard Kipling. Bottomley once admitted that he based it on the metrical style of 'After the Ball Was Over'.

Although he was supposed to speak at 7.30 it took him over an hour to get past the crowds milling outside the Albert Hall. Charles Coburn entertained the audience till his arrival by singing music hall numbers and ended up with 'Two Lovely Black Eyes' in ten different languages. Bottomley did not appear till nine o'clock and received a thundering welcome.

'This is not a war in the ordinary sense, but a holy crusade against the devilries of militarism that have been the canker of Germany for forty years,' he began. 'We are going through with it right to the end, whatever the sacrifice called for.'

He warned the audience to beware of discord at home in wartime and appealed to them to 'Stand shoulder to shoulder as part of a great and mighty Empire, united and indivisible'.

He gave a message to soldiers and sailors and their wives and families who had confided their troubles to him through *John Bull*. 'When the time comes I will not hesitate . . . to insist upon the trial by court martial of every man who has taken advantage of his country's troubles to line his filthy pockets with gold at the expense of the State.' He also undertook to investigate all alleged grievances of servicemen and bring them to the notice of the Government and the authorities with a view to getting them remedied.

'Have we fully grasped the meaning of the great titanic struggle on which we are engaged?' he asked, and told the audience later, 'We are not going to come triumphantly out of the struggle without a mighty and stupendous effort.'

Then he spoke about the recruiting problem. 'I wonder that a nation which at a moment's notice can raise four or five hundred millions of money should haggle or falter over a paltry few shillings a week to the only men who matter in a time of national crisis!' He declared that the war was a life-and-death struggle between the Anglo-Saxon race and the barbarous and base Teutonic race. 'This is a mighty struggle, a Marathon of the gods of battle.'

His last words were addressed to the young men. 'I ask all young men if they do not really feel that there is a call for them, can they not hear their comrades calling them from the trenches, and from the hospitals, from the decks of those sea dogs that are guarding our shores? If they do not hear that call, they are unworthy to claim the name of Englishman.'

After his Albert Hall triumph he wrote to Asquith offering his services as Chief Recruiting Officer. The Prime Minister and his Cabinet quite appreciated that Bottomley was an asset to the war-effort, but felt it was out of the question to give him an official post because of his disreputable past. Asquith therefore replied diplomatically: 'Thank you for your kind offer, but I shall not avail myself of it at the moment. You are doing better work where you are.'

Being a super-optimist, Bottomley took this letter to mean not only that the Government approved of his recruiting speeches and *John Bull*, but also that they would find him an official post later. Since he had now become a big box-office attraction, Seymour Hicks engaged him to appear in his patriotic musical show *England Expects* at the London Opera House. Phyllis Dare, who starred in the show with Isobel Elsom, sang the new recruiting song:

We don't want to lose you,
But we think you ought to go,
For your King and your country
They both need you so.

The audience always demanded an encore from Phyllis Dare. In the interval Bottomley appeared with a huge Union Jack in the background and made his 'Prince of Peace' speech, and then urged young men in the audience to join up. Under the influence of his persuasive words, some enlisted on the spot.

Bottomley's successful personal appearance in a theatre gave the impresario Charles B. Cochran an idea for a show of his which was doing very badly at the Empire, Leicester Square. He engaged Bottomley to appear as a special turn at £100 a performance for three weeks. Horatio walked on to the stage after the band had introduced him with a few patriotic chords; in the background he had a chorus of extras dressed up as wounded soldiers and hospital nurses. The 'military' tableau stood on planks and trestles with a girl dressed as Britannia perched precariously on top. Bottomley's turn at the Empire had a magic effect on the takings, which went up £1,000 in his first week.

His fame as a war orator spread through Britain; everyone was clamouring to get him to speak at recruiting meetings. Accompanied by Houston, he went up to Liverpool and Warrington and spoke on the stage at music halls; supported by his chorus of wounded soldiers and hospital nurses, he repeated his success and travelled on to Hull, where a thousand men joined up after hearing him speak. In less than a year Horatio Bottomley became the most popular speaker in the country. His language was commonplace and down to earth, his ideas were jingoistic and not original, and he always stressed that God was on Britain's side. But everyone who heard his speeches succumbed to his personal magnetism which made his words come to life; his twinkling blue eyes and ready wit all contributed to the wonderful performance.

'When are you going to do your bit?' asked a heckler at one of his meetings.

'Would to God it was my privilege to shoulder a rifle and take my place beside the brave boys in the trenches,' he replied. 'But you have only to look at me to see that I am suffering from two complaints. My medical man calls them *anno domini* and *embonpoint.* The first means that I was born too soon and the second that my chest measurement has gone in the wrong place.'*

He accepted an invitation from the Winter Gardens at Bournemouth to give two patriotic lectures in a day and discreetly arranged that he should receive a large percentage of the 'gate'. On the train down to Bournemouth he and Houston roughed out a scenario for a mock trial of the Kaiser to be conducted by Bottomley; he would prosecute the Kaiser and the German nation for the wilful murder of civilization.

'I'll give them the first part of the indictment in the afternoon speech and tell them to come back in the evening for the final speeches and the summing-up,' said Horatio.

The trial format worked beautifully: Bottomley produced such a strong indictment of the Kaiser and the Germans in the afternoon that the Winter Garden was packed in the evening to hear his summing-up. At the end of the mock trial he said:

* Houston.

> Ladies and gentlemen, I want you to pull yourselves together and keep your peckers up. I want to assure you that within six weeks of today we shall have the Huns on the run. We shall drive them out of France, out of Flanders, out of Belgium, across the Rhine back into their own territory.
>
> There we shall give them a taste of their own medicine. Bear in mind, I speak of that which I know. Tomorrow it will be officially denied, but take it from me that if Bottomley says so, it is so!

His forecast was wildly optimistic and totally wrong, but he knew the public had a short memory. He was highly delighted to receive £200 for his two 'lectures' at Bournemouth. He and Houston went on to Torquay where he also gave two lectures in a day; this time his share increased to £212. Quick money like this was something he could never resist. All the good resolutions he had made at the beginning of the war were being thrown out of the window.

'This opens up a new source of revenue,' he said to Houston. 'You must set to work in earnest, Henry, and get me booked up three days a week all over the country.'

That was the beginning of Bottomley's patriotic lectures; from the winter of 1915 he gave a total of 340 lectures in three years. Though he remained in great demand for recruiting meetings, he spoke at only twenty during the same period, refusing to take any fee for them because he hated to think he might be sending young men to their death. Houston gave an admirable account of this phase in his book. Bottomley drew twenty-five pounds from *John Bull* for each patriotic lecture, and always brought in the paper's name to justify it, and he discreetly took between 65 and 85 per cent of the gross takings at his lectures. Houston generally booked him up for three days a week; it was a formidable programme for a man of his age. Houston wrote:

> The expenditure of nervous and physical energy involved in the lecture tour was enormous. Every night when I got him away from a meeting to a hotel I had to strip him and give him a thorough towelling. He was invariably saturated right through to his morning coat with perspiration.

Houston had to act as a deputy unpaid valet and help Bottomley to get undressed: owing to his enormous girth he could no longer take his boots off by himself and even needed a helping hand with his shirt and trousers. When Bottomley gave lectures in halls all over Britain he cynically varied his speech according to the size of the 'gate'. While the local chairman was introducing him on the stage in a long-winded speech he would be calculating the size of the audience. Seats generally cost four shillings, three shillings, two shillings and a shilling, and he soon became an expert at estimating how much his share of the house would be worth.

If it was under £75 he would appeal to the audience to rally round the throne of the Empire King, hereditary president of the British Empire, and would end by saying: 'Remember the words of that grand old anthem which says, "Confound their politics. God Save the King"'—and the band would strike up the National Anthem.

A £75 audience deserved something rather more inspiring and they were given this finale:

> When this great nation emerges from its period of trial—as please God it will—we shall stand erect shoulder to shoulder before the world, and declare with one voice that Britain is the 'Land of Hope and Glory' . . . [Cue for the band to come in and continue] 'Mother of the Free'—[and so on until] 'God Who made us mighty shall make us mightier yet'

and the audience invariably joined in the chorus.

An audience around the £100 mark was entitled to a slightly superior oration, of which this is a sample:

> When this tragedy is over we shall be able to look the whole world in the face and say that this country, this England, has come out of this ghastly conflict with its name unsullied, its escutcheon clean; an example and precept for all mankind to follow. . . .

However, if Bottomley calculated that the audience would bring him in over £100 he pulled out all the stops and gave them the best piece in his repertoire—the renowned 'Prince of Peace' speech. Although this speech seems dated and phoney today, we must bear in mind that Bottomley delivered it like a great actor. Audiences hearing it for the first time used to hang on his words and women in the audience were often moved to tears. He knew exactly how to use with emotional force his wonderful voice, which ranged like a grand organ from a vast volume of sound to the *vox angelica*, while an impressive hush fell upon the audience.

When Horatio had firmly established himself as a popular lecturer he began to take Peggy Primrose on his tours. Henry Houston thought this was most indiscreet, and felt he had to broach the delicate subject.

'You must realize that you're a public man, H.B. This is really very bad for your reputation,' he said.

Horatio was very proud of being seen with Peggy Primrose and did nothing. When Houston remonstrated with him again about Peggy Primrose he said, 'You don't like her, Henry!'

'It doesn't matter in the slightest whether I like her or not,' replied Houston. 'My concern is with you. However fond you are of her, and she of you, I don't think you're helping your public career by being seen with her.'

'Very well, I'll think it over,' said Bottomley.

Their train arrived at a London terminus and he went off with Peggy Primrose for the week-end, arranging to meet Houston at Waterloo the following week to set off on another series of patriotic lectures. To Houston's astonishment he arrived at Waterloo with another girl from the harem on his arm.

'Maggie's coming along with us, Henry. She finds that London is so lonely without me.'

Houston gave it up, realizing, just as Julius Elias had done, that nobody in the world could control Bottomley once he had set his mind on a thing. This total lack of self-discipline was a fatal flaw in his character.

13 Tommy's Bible

We all read John Bull. . . . *We think a lot of Mr Bottomley in the Army.*

SOLDIER, at Bottomley's Y.M.C.A. Lecture, Aldershot, 1915

By 1915 Bottomley had adopted a vicious anti-German policy in *John Bull*: he had a gift of knowing what the public wanted and his paper was reflecting the aggressive mood of the British people at war. He made a point of referring to our principal enemies as 'Germhuns' and his feature articles all harped on the same theme:

Germany Must Be Wiped Off The Map Of Europe

No Mercy For The Berlin Butcher

NEVER AGAIN! Not A Vestige Of The German Empire To Be Left

Lock Up All Germans, Confiscate Their Property

Every week he published lists of people who had changed their German-sounding names into English ones. He wanted all captured German sailors to be hanged or left to drown, and gave his readers some advice for when the war ended:

> If by chance you should discover one day in a restaurant that you are being served by a German waiter, you will throw the soup in his foul face; if you find yourself sitting at the side of a German clerk, you will spill the inkpot over his vile head.

He started a 'Jack and Tommy' column for men in the services which became immensely popular. Any serviceman who had a grievance was asked to 'write to *John Bull* about it'. Soldiers and sailors jumped at his offer and hundreds of letters flowed into the office every day. Bottomley and the staff worked extremely hard to try and obtain a satisfactory answer for each case, and this side of his activities must be placed to his credit. According to King's Regulations serving men were not supposed to communicate with the Press, but the authorities took a sensible view of *John Bull* and turned a blind eye to its postbag because it was an ideal outlet for men who wished to make a complaint.

John Bull appealed to its readers to send them five shillings to pay for 'Jack and Tommy comfort parcels' which would be forwarded to the Front and to the Grand Fleet. There was a magnificent response. Tommy Cox ran the operation and persuaded Bovril, Lyons, Liptons, Black Cat cigarettes and other big firms to contribute their products free to this good cause; so all *John Bull* had to do was to pay the postage, in return for which they obtained the goodwill of thousands of servicemen. The paper also sponsored 'Our War Sufferers Fund' for widows and other victims of the war. Its circulation rose steadily: *John Bull* had established itself as the favourite of the Forces.

Bottomley continued to be extremely optimistic about the Allies' chances of winning the war in the first year and his views were broadcast in *John Bull* and in his patriotic lectures. At the beginning of 1915 he wrote an article entitled 'Why I Believe In The Prospect Of Early Peace'. At this period Lord Northcliffe was the colossus of Fleet Street since his papers controlled half the circulation of London.* The Northcliffe Press completely contradicted Bottomley and warned their readers to brace themselves to face a long and most unpleasant war. Bottomley, believing that pessimism was very bad for the nation's morale, wrote to Lord Northcliffe complaining and called him a Dismal Jimmie. Northcliffe replied:

DEAR BOTTOMLEY

Don't be too sure that I am not right. We are in for a very bad time. My people in Germany tell me that the Germans have not yet started the war, and if you go on preaching

* In 1915 Northcliffe owned the *Daily Mail*, *The Times*, the *Daily Mirror*, the *Evening News*, the *Observer* and the *Weekly Dispatch*.

> optimism as you are at present, you may find one day that the British public will not thank you for it.

Lord Northcliffe and his brother, Lord Rothermere, were about to launch an illustrated Sunday paper to be called the *Sunday Pictorial*. As Bottomley had become a public idol through the impact of *John Bull* and his recruiting speeches, they wanted him to write for their new paper. But Horatio and the Harmsworths were on bad terms because he was annoyed that his political meetings were hardly ever reported in their Press. It was therefore arranged that Randal Charlton of the *Daily Mirror* would ask Charles B. Cochran to act as the go-between in negotiations with Bottomley. Cochran was most surprised when Charlton asked him if Bottomley would write articles for the *Sunday Pictorial* at £100 each.

After Charlton had explained the position Cochran said, 'Bottomley always needs £1,000, never £100. Give me a cheque for £1,000 and I'll get as many articles from him as possible.'

The deal was approved by Mr Lima, Lord Rothermere's business-manager, and Cochran got in touch with Bottomley and outlined the proposition. Bottomley accepted on condition that the articles mentioned he was the editor of *John Bull*. A cheque for £1,000 was sent round to Cochran's office in the West End next day. Horatio was on the line to him five minutes later.

'Do you speak French, Cocky?' he asked.

'A little.'

'Then avez-vous touché?'

Cochran took the cheque round to Bottomley's flat; there is little doubt that he had spent half the money already. Later, Randal Charlton called on him at King Street and asked what he would like to write about in his articles.

'I don't mind what it is,' said Horatio. 'I'll write about anything from gee-gees to Jesus!'

Bottomley wrote for the *Sunday Pictorial* in the style of a lay preacher, as if the paper was his pulpit and its readers his congregation. The articles, advertised all over the country with huge posters of Horatio Bottomley, were an immediate success. The first one appeared on 14 March 1915 with the introduction:

> Mr Bottomley is the Editor of *John Bull*. One of the most eloquent and human speakers in Great Britain, he has

> since the war began proved himself a powerful agent for gathering recruits to the colours, and stimulating the patriotism of the country. As a speaker, a journalist, a politician and a lay lawyer, Mr Bottomley is a public character of untiring energy.

In his second article he discussed the 'tremendous issues raised by the War'.

> I believe this to be a veritable Marathon of the Gods—the Gods of battle: and they are fighting for the conquest of the soul of man. . . . On one hand there is the Demon of Despotism and, on the other, the Deity of Destiny. . . .

On Easter Sunday, 4 April, he called his article 'The New Resurrection—How The War Has Served The Human Race'. British soldiers had been fighting in Flanders and France for eight months and there was widespread discontent in Britain about the Government's conduct of the war. Asquith had only given one war survey to the public and had relied on Lord Kitchener, whose prestige was enormous, to give a monthly survey to the House of Lords, which was far from adequate. This silence of the Government led to the tremendous power of Lord Northcliffe with his dominant Press, and of Bottomley with his gift of recruiting men and the influence he wielded through *John Bull* and the *Sunday Pictorial*.

Winston Churchill, First Lord of the Admiralty, chafed at the way the Army had got bogged down in the trenches, suffering enormous casualties in order to gain a few hundred yards of territory. He proposed sending an expedition to the Dardanelles, instead of sending more armies to 'chew barbed wire in Flanders', to open an 'Eastern' front against Germany. If it was successful, an Army force could take Constantinople and greatly assist Britain's Russian allies. Unfortunately, Churchill was opposed by Kitchener, who had become a dictator at the War Office. The expedition set off to the Dardanelles in March with insufficient troops to mount large-scale landings. A strong force arrived later under Sir Ian Hamilton, but Kitchener procrastinated and Asquith took no action. When the British attacked on 25 April the Turks were well entrenched and the assault was repulsed with heavy losses.

Meanwhile the Allies had been forced on to the defensive in

Flanders and France, so that April was an extremely critical month for Britain. Shipwrights on the Clyde threatened to strike, which would have been disastrous to the war-effort. Lloyd George and Winston Churchill asked Bottomley to go up to Scotland and have a talk to the shipwrights to try and persuade them into a reasonable frame of mind. Bottomley went up to the Clyde and after he had spoken to the shipwrights as man to man they agreed to call off the strike.

Later, he was asked by the Government to visit munition workers in various parts of the country and gave them pep-talks which helped to raise their production figures. Cabinet Ministers also sent Bottomley to give talks to the coal-miners and the railway workers. Bottomley's missions were invariably successful, but it was made clear to him that he was working for the Government in an unofficial capacity.

On 4 May his *Sunday Pictorial* article was written after the American liner *Lusitania* had been sunk by German submarines with the loss of 1,500 passengers and crew. The United States were still neutral and Germany's barbarous action shocked the world.

> *Is War War? Then Hit Back*
>
> *If Germans Want 'Frightfulness' Let Them Have It*
>
> The devil must be burnt with his own coals. But will the politicians block the way? Let me tell them plainly, one and all, that at the moment *they* are not wanted. The Man in the Street—the Man in the Trenches—the Man in the Camp—has no use for them. He has implicit faith in Kitchener and in Fisher* and, rightly or wrongly, he has an idea that the great men are being hampered by Ministerial hesitancy and control.
>
> As story after story of German atrocities comes through from the seat of war he wants to know how much longer we are 'going to take it lying down' . . .
>
> And now comes the news of the *Lusitania* massacre. I want every German now in Britain to get away sharp—never mind how long he has been 'naturalized'. You cannot naturalize an unnatural freak—a human freak. *But you can exterminate it.*

* Lord Fisher, the First Sea Lord, who had been brought back to office in 1914.

Asquith's Liberal Government came under heavy fire from the Press at the beginning of May; unfortunately the Prime Minister was a man of moderation, too steeped in *laissez-faire* ideas to be capable of running a great war. Apart from the Dardanelles disaster, the Government was blamed by Sir John French, the commander of the British Army, for not providing sufficient ammunition in the western sector. . . . Asquith informed King George V on 17 May that 'after consultation with Lloyd George and Bonar Law [leader of the Unionist opposition] I have concluded that for the successful prosecution of the war the Government must be reconstructed on a broad and non-party basis'. Asquith remained Prime Minister and tightened up the administration, yet it became obvious that he was the wrong man to lead Britain in wartime.

Bottomley's first series of articles for the *Sunday Pictorial* was so popular that he was asked to write for them regularly. Being the last person to underrate his own value, Bottomley demanded £150 an article in future, a tremendous fee in those days. Lord Rothermere gave his blessing to the new contract and Bottomley continued writing for the *Pictorial* until after the war. He began his new series in June with an article entitled 'If I were Kitchener' which is worth quoting as one of his most enlightened contributions.

If I Were Kitchener

The Training and Treatment Our New Armies Should Receive

The New Army is a very exceptional thing and I think I should put some of the forces under the command of existing non-commissioned and warrant officers of experience, giving the men so promoted a special rate of pay.

I would see that everything was done to make my new men contented, loyal, and willing, and to prevent any of them declaring—as many now do—that they are 'fed up' before leaving England. I would annul the present stringent rule forbidding correspondence between regiment and War Office. I would invite one weekly letter from all men of each unit who had legitimate grievances to ventilate, and such complaints would be carefully considered and adjusted.

I would impress upon my Commanding and Company Officers that they should not impose arbitrary, harsh and

> unconscionable sentences for trivial offences. . . . I would abolish the trussing of men and the chaining of them to trees or wagons or gun wheels. The degrading sight does not make for recruiting.
>
> I would at any cost see that the dependents of my soldiers obtained their allowances promptly and fully.

The next Sunday he wrote a chauvinistic and morale-boosting article entitled 'Why I Am An Optimist'.

> I confess that it makes me ill to meet so many of my countrymen with long faces. . . . For Heaven's sake, let us buck up. . . . Imagine the British Empire being wiped out by the base and brutal half-bred Teuton. . . .
>
> Talk about being despondent and low-spirited—we ought to be so full of elation that we'd dread to go into St Paul's for fear of pushing the dome off with our heads! We've shown the world that hearts of oak still grow on British soil. So, when the next sad-faced son of sorrow comes wailing to you about what may happen next week or next month, slap him on the back and tell him of fights in the air and fights by sea. . . . Tell him of the splendid pluck of our men, the dauntless patience and fortitude of our women.

His *Sunday Pictorial* articles and the success of *John Bull* were most heartening for Horatio, but he was deep in the red until his patriotic lectures started. He had so many expensive commitments that he said he needed £1,000 a week to keep his head above water. During the second half of 1914 his finances had been at such a low ebb that he could not even pay his household staff. John Kerr, his racing manager, met Reuben Bigland at the beginning of the war and told him such a tale of woe about Bottomley's position that the good-natured Bigland opened his wallet and gave him fifty pounds in notes for Horatio.

When Reuben Bigland read Bottomley's highly paid articles in the *Sunday Pictorial* in 1915, and then heard about his recruiting meetings, he knew that he must be flourishing again and wrote him a polite letter asking for the repayment of his fifty pounds. He got no reply and, although he wrote again several times, all his letters were ignored. Bottomley's ingratitude made Bigland very angry.

'One of these days I'll teach Bottomley a lesson,' he said prophetically to a friend in Birmingham.

Willie Lotinga, *John Bull*'s former racing correspondent, had even more cause to be angry with Bottomley. In 1912 Lotinga had sold him his racing paper, *Lotinga's Weekly*, and agreed to take part of the price in *John Bull* shares valued at two pounds each. But in 1914 they had a difference of opinion about a man called Diamond, who promoted Swiss lotteries, and Lotinga bought his paper back from Bottomley. It was only then that he discovered that his *John Bull* shares were only worth ten shillings. He had a tremendous row with Bottomley and told him, 'You can diddle whom you like so long as you don't diddle me. I want my money!' As *John Bull* shares were only worth a quarter of the price Bottomley had put on them, it meant that Lotinga had been swindled out of £4,200. Although Lotinga wrote to him and threatened to sue him, Horatio refused to pay a farthing.

Reuben Bigland, after brooding for a long time about Bottomley's debt, decided he would show him up in a paper to be called *Answers to John Bull*. He took an office in Fleet Street, without thinking of the difficulties that lay ahead of him. Since he was not a professional journalist, he found that nobody in London would print his paper, and nobody would advertise in it. His friends all told him he was a fool.

'You're wasting your time trying to attack Bottomley,' they said. 'He's much too powerful and clever for an ordinary man like you.'

This was the origin of Reuben Bigland's obsession that Bottomley was playing Goliath to his David. He was feeling very despondent when he happened to meet Willie Lotinga in a Holborn tea shop. He knew Lotinga was furious with Bottomley over the *John Bull* shares and they were soon discussing their mutual enemy.

'Are you game to put on your machines at Birmingham something I myself have written about Bottomley?' asked Lotinga. 'You can name your own price for the work and I'll give you an extra two hundred pounds for the risk you are taking.'

'It will be a labour of love,' replied Bigland.

Lotinga had written a hard-hitting pamphlet about Bottomley, raking up his murky past and giving examples of his swindles. His aim was to distribute it all over the country in order to goad Bottomley into issuing a writ; if there was a case

Lotinga would go into court and expose him for swindling him out of four thousand pounds with *John Bull* shares.

Bigland returned to Birmingham and printed Lotinga's pamphlet at his Far Wood Press. Soon after Bottomley began his patriotic lectures Lotinga's pamphlet was distributed all over England. When Horatio read it he was most upset by the statement that he was the reputed father of several illegitimate children, while the other allegations were so unsavoury that he wanted to stop it in any case. Four paragraphs will suffice to show that he had reason to be worried.

Just to recall a few of Bottomley's swindling companies, I name the "Hansard Union," the "Joint Stock Institute," the "West Australian Finance Corporation," the "Associated Financial Corporation," the "Joint Stock Trust and Finance Corporation, Ltd.," "John Bull," *Guernsey*, the "John Bull" Investment Trust and Agency," and the present "John Bull." His present Co-director even convicts Bottomley in a sworn Affidavit.

I need now only mention a *few* of his victims—usually very old or very young men—with "round" figures as the amounts of which he robbed them. Thomas Hill (£80,000), James Platt (£50,000), R. S. Masters (£83,000), Joseph G. Smith (£70,000), George Parker (£20,000), the juvenile brothers Vincent and Reginald Eyre (over £100,000), R. Allen (£40,000), and quite recently young St. John Willans (£50,000).

Surrounded by, and associated with, criminals and others of his own kidney as "hirelings" to "cloak" all his doings, living as he has always done upon what he robs from an ignorant public (and, of late years, has misappropriated from the "John Bull" shareholders) truly it is pantomimic that this outrageous thief and humbug should put himself up to tell *everybody* else how *they* are to be honest and moral! He uses his artifice and weapon, the "John Bull" paper, upon the helpless who can't "hit back," whilst these outspoken acts stamp him ostensibly as a man of honour, a righteous citizen, incapable of wrong. What a "cloak" to his doings! Luckily I can "hit back"—and dare oppose Bottomley.

He is the reputed father of many illegitimate children—and is, even at this moment, running a sham "Bank," whose "business" embraces that of a welshing bookmaker in one name, a racing paper and tipster's telegrams in another, and a Company fraud in a third false styling—an absolute hotbed of fraud is the "John Bull" Bank, Old Jewry, E.C.! And all the dishonest schemes are advertised and recommended by "John Bull" and each "dummy" principal refers to the other and receives a high reference.

However, Bottomley ignored Lotinga's pamphlet for a few months. Reuben Bigland was advised that the only way to hit Horatio was to make him sound ridiculous, so he printed a pamphlet entitled *What Horatio Bottomley Has Done For His Country and the Wounded Soldiers*, which consisted of twenty-four blank pages. It was distributed with Lotinga's pamphlet in every town where Bottomley was giving a patriotic lecture, and the two men waited to see how long it would take before Goliath went into action.

In July 1915, the *Sunday Pictorial* had a leader on the subject of Bottomley's crusades.

> Mr Bottomley exercises an enormous influence with his pen and his voice. Are recruits needed? He gets them! Is there a strike to settle? He can pour oil on troubled waters. Is there a cause to plead? He pleads successfully.
>
> Yet his great talents are mostly used 'unofficially'. There

> is much work that Mr Bottomley could do. He is a force in the State. . . . His services should be utilized more and more by the Government.

In August the *Pictorial* wrote that 'Mr Bottomley's evolution into a great leader of men has become one of the surprises of the war'. Even allowing for editorial exaggeration it was true that the war had made Bottomley, despite his disreputable past, into the most powerful demagogue in Britain. His only rival as an orator who could appeal to the masses was David Lloyd George, Asquith's dynamic lieutenant, who had been appointed Minister of Munitions. With the backing of Lord Northcliffe, Lord Beaverbrook, Lord Riddell and other newspaper chiefs Lloyd George was to become Prime Minister a year later.

One man who had no illusions about Bottomley was F. E. Smith. Meeting Bottomley when a new Archbishop of Canterbury was about to be enthroned, he said, 'You ought to go along there, Horatio—he needs a crook.' Bottomley thoroughly appreciated the joke against himself.

14 'Send for Bottomley'

> *I should like to see him in the Cabinet, for we want to get on with the War. . . . Bottomley would do much to bring this about, partly by reason of his almost superhuman talents and indomitable energy and partly owing to his enormous influence on people.*
>
> HENRY DE WINDT (explorer), 1916

Horatio Bottomley boasted that he would always see anybody who came to *John Bull* with a genuine problem. One day in 1915 a pale, long-haired young man was ushered into his office in Long Acre and said he was a conscientious objector because he hated the whole idea of war.*

'What shall I do?' he asked.

'Your duty, of course.'

'But my conscience tells me it is not my duty to take life.'

'Are you sure it is your conscience, my lad, or is it something else? "Conscience doth make cowards of us all." Are you going to let it make such a coward of you that you'll never be able to hold up your head in decent society?' Bottomley said challengingly. While the youth was searching for an answer he continued, 'I beg you to think the whole thing over from the point of view of your country. . . . Think of the blood-stained cliffs of Gallipoli and the little cemeteries in Flanders, and just think of England.'

The young man listened intently to him but said nothing.

'Do you remember the lines which Browning wrote one

* Raymond Blathways, *Horatio Bottomley—the man as he is today* (Odhams, 1916).

night when he was steaming through Trafalgar Bay?'

The youth did not reply.

> Here and here has England helped me,
> How can I help England, say?

'Well, anyway, my boy, it won't be by deserting her in her hour of direst need,' declared Horatio. 'For God's sake, think it all over again!'

As Bottomley wrung his hand, he realized that the young man was in tears. He left the room without saying another word and went to the nearest recruiting office to join up.

Bottomley seemed to have the knack of handling young men; throughout the war the soldiers and sailors acknowledged him as their spokesman and one of his most effective articles in the *Pictorial* illustrates this point:

> *To 'Tommy' and 'Jack'*
>
> *A Chat With The Two Men Who Matter*
>
> Tommy, it's a long way to Tipperary, isn't it? But they haven't taken you the short cut. . . . You have been raked out of your trenches with shot and shell without stint. You have been humbugged a lot about your letters and your parcels—your pay and your leave and the other little things, haven't you? . . .
>
> I have a message for you. We're all ready to start. Victory is nearly at hand. So keep your pecker up, old chap—IT WILL SOON BE OVER. And then what a homecoming you shall have: and this time we won't forget you and yours when the shooting is over.
>
> And now, Jack, my boy a word with you. I don't see or hear much of you in these days, do I? But God knows that you are *there*, *there*, on the steel decks behind the armour-plated cells of your ocean fortress—behind the big guns waiting to emit thunder and lightning and bloody death to all who would challenge the right of Britannia to rule the waves. . . . Well, how are you, old man? Tired of waiting? But it can't be helped. . . . The greatest compliment the enemy can pay you is that they dare not come out and fight.
>
> PREPARE FOR ACTION. Now we are ready. . . .

We will have that fleet out of Kiel Harbour—and we will sink it to the bottom of the sea. . . . It is a pity that Winston Churchill has been superseded.* But our shipyards have not been idle! By your valour you have saved the British Empire . . . and by all our Gods your service shall not go unrewarded. . . .

The Allies had begun a new offensive in the West under General Joffre and Sir John French. They won the battles of Loos and Vimy Ridge at an appalling cost of men's lives—60,000 British and 125,000 French—and had only gained three miles by the end of the year. The British people were horrified to learn that Kitchener needed many more recruits for his New Army. So far Britain had held out against conscription; now the voluntary recruiting problem became a major issue.

The *Sunday Pictorial* asked Bottomley, as England's unofficial recruiting agent, to write an article on this subject and he produced one:

Don't Be 'Fetched'

I say to every unlisted man of eligible age and good health, 'Don't be Fetched.' Don't be a fetched man. . . . I am hopeful that words written in the sincerity of our common brotherhood and read in the calm repose of the Sunday quietude . . . may reach the heart and penetrate the soul of some, at least, of those whose ears have not yet caught the cry for help from their pals in the trenches, for retribution for violated girls and women in Belgium† . . . and have not yet heard the cry from Heaven to step forward and avenge the sacrilege and blasphemy of the Huns in Rheims, in Dinant, in Louvain. . . .

You had better read what the Germans have said as to what they will do if they ever succeed in gaining a footing over here. The most brutal outrages in Belgium will be acts of refinement compared with their reprisals on the British. . . .

Never let it be said that *you* were one of those who

* Winston Churchill had resigned as First Lord of the Admiralty after the failure of the Dardanelles expedition in August.

† It is generally believed now that most of the German atrocities in Belgium and France were invented as Allied propaganda.

> forced Britain into the badge of conscription. The word is abhorrent to all British ideas—and yet it connotes merely the primary duty of citizenship.
>
> We have a Minister of Munitions—why not a 'Minister of Recruiting'? . . . or why not, at least, a Recruiting branch of the Ministry of Munitions—under the control of a Director with adequate staff and machinery? Perhaps Lloyd George will think it over.
>
> Today DUTY calls you and says you 'must': and says it in the name of God. At his side, *and yours*, at this very moment, stands the Recording Angel—book in hand, waiting for your answer. May she write your name?

This kind of article would fall on stony ground today, and in the United States it would probably lead to the newspaper's being publicly burnt. But Bottomley understood the psychology of his public at that time, and some young men were persuaded to join up by his appeal to their sense of patriotism with the addition of his religious message. He must have visualized himself as the ideal Minister of Recruiting, but in October his hopes were dashed once more when Lord Derby was appointed Director of Recruiting.

Bottomley and *John Bull* had become so famous that they were introduced into shows and pantomimes. This pantomime jingle was typical:

> A wire I'll send to a gentleman friend,
> I'll call him Horatio B.
> He's noted today for seeing fair play,
> In a country that claims to be free.
> If you feel in a plight, to his journal you write
> And get reparation in full.
> So you'll all say with me, Good luck to H.B.
> And continued success to *John Bull*.

By the autumn his patriotic lectures and recruiting meetings were monopolizing most of his time and the brunt of editing *John Bull* fell on Charles Palmer, his extremely able assistant. Bottomley used to discuss the next issue with Palmer on Monday before he departed on his travels with Houston.

'Well, Charles, I think we ought to write about so-and-so this week,' Horatio would say.

Charles Palmer was indispensable to him; he not only edited

John Bull in all but name, but even wrote many of the articles supposedly written by Bottomley. He only needed a rough draft of what Bottomley intended to say in order to turn out an article, because he knew his style so well that he could produce a carbon copy of it. Bottomley was also writing weekly for the *Sunday Pictorial* and thus became the most widely read journalist in Britain. But he soon found it beyond his powers to write a full-length article for the *Pictorial* after returning from a series of patriotic lectures, so he began to use 'ghosts'. Charles Palmer was the principal ghost; the others were A. G. Hales and W. G. Pilley, both staff writers on *John Bull*. The ghosts used to leave their copy at Horatio's flat in King Street and he would pick it up on his return to town on a Friday. After reading it through carefully, he generally asked Houston what he thought of it, sometimes calling him in as a fourth ghost because he regarded Houston as a storehouse of facts and data.

Henry Houston related that on one occasion the ghost had done his work so successfully that when Bottomley proceeded to 'sole and heel' the article, as he termed it, he only had to add a few words here and there:

> As I write sitting facing the lovely Sussex downs, my favourite collie by my side, licking my hand and looking up into my eyes, my thoughts turn to the simple country parson of the village.
>
> [*Take in A—written by the ghost*]
>
> The bells of the old village church are ringing, calling the people to prayer. The simple country parson passes by on his way to divine service, and my thoughts turn instinctively to [*take in B—written by the ghost*]
>
> God bless that simple country parson!

That seemed to be a wonderfully easy way to earn £150, but one must point out that he always paid his ghosts a good fee for their services and in wartime the public was willing to read anything with the name of Horatio Bottomley on it. However, on some occasions the *Sunday Pictorial* were not satisfied with Horatio's article and returned it to him, 'hoping that Mr Bottomley will be good enough to bring it up to his usual high standard'. If he failed to do this, the Editor would write a polite note with the same request to Peggy Primrose, who had become the power behind the throne. The paper soon discovered that when they wrote to Peggy Primrose Horatio's article invariably came back up to standard.

One of his most effective articles appeared in February 1916.

> When will Ministers realize that this is a People's War? When will they understand that in the mind of the Man-in-the-Street . . . the politician doesn't count to the extent of a tinker's cuss: that it is only the soldiers and sailors and munition workers who matter—and that the sole duty of Parliament is to see that these gallant gentlemen are provided with all the money they require for the conduct of the war? . . .
>
> Why all this mystery—all this suppression of news? Why talk about the 'Kentish coast' when they mean Margate, Dover or Folkestone—or the 'Eastern Counties' when they mean London? One man in the Cabinet who really understood the heart and mind of the British democracy would be worth three army corps to the cause of the Allies. . . .

This was a blatant attempt by Bottomley to try and start a movement to get himself drafted into the Cabinet. The war had made him the complete demagogue: he even appeared in a propaganda film called *Truth and Justice*. It failed to set the Thames on fire, but brought him into the public eye once again.

At the end of 1915 Sir John French had been replaced at the Front by Sir Douglas Haig, but the Allies still continued to be bogged down in the trenches. The Germans took the offensive at Verdun in February 1916 and advanced deep into France. The French put up a valiant defence and stopped the Germans, but it cost them thousands of men. Haig made a counter-attack at the Battle of the Somme in July, but the British lost over a hundred thousand men.

As the war dragged on into the autumn with deadlock in the trenches Bottomley realized it was going to be long and drawn-out, but felt sure the Government would soon call on his services officially. He had already applied to Sir Edward Carson for a job with the Ministry of Information and Propaganda and been turned down. The Establishment would have nothing to do with him officially because he was disreputable, but he would never admit the truth; indeed, he was convinced he was being passed over because the men at the top were jealous of him.

Lord Northcliffe believed that Britain could never win the war as long as Asquith remained Prime Minister, and that the only man who could save us from disaster was Lloyd George. He therefore started a campaign in his papers for Asquith's removal. Haig's offensive on the Somme collapsed in November with total casualties of 400,000 and the shocked British public concluded that the Government's direction of the war was still as inefficient as ever. A strong movement started for a new Government who would go all out for victory against Germany.

One night the *Evening News* had a poster on the streets saying BOTTOMLEY WANTED. The paper's main letter attacked the Coalition for failing to wage all-out war and said Britain needed a new Government immediately, and Horatio Bottomley should be brought into the Cabinet. It really seemed that Bottomley's hour had struck, but unfortunately England's saviour was temporarily out of circulation.

He and Houston had gone to dinner with two girls the previous night and they had been playing cards when Bottomley suddenly cried out in pain: he had a high fever and had to be put to bed in the girls' flat. He was so ill that he could not move the next day. When Houston told him the *Evening News* had BOTTOMLEY WANTED on their posters he nearly went crazy at the thought of being marooned at this moment of destiny.

'You must get me away from here, Henry. I must get to work at once!' he said.

But it was out of the question; he was too ill even to get out of bed. Houston reported the position to Tommy Cox, who took command of the flat in King Street. Many people had been inquiring for Bottomley; Cox managed to keep up the charade that he was upstairs in bed, desperately ill, and the doctors had given special orders that he was not to see any visitors. Even if the Prime Minister called he would not be admitted!

George Rawson, his manservant, greeted all callers with a solemn expression and told them, 'Mr Bottomley is seriously ill and not to be disturbed *on any account.*'

Bottomley gradually improved and was fit enough to travel on the fourth day. Tommy Cox and one of the 'stable' arrived in a taxi at a West End address in the early hours of the morning. They enveloped Horatio in a big blanket and two fur coats and carried him downstairs, then they bundled him into the taxi and drove off to King Street.

'When and where my country needs me, there will I be,' declared Bottomley as soon as he had recovered. He told a *Daily Mail* reporter that he was quite willing to tour round Britain with Cabinet Ministers and make speeches to keep up the public's morale. 'Numerous suggestions have been made, but you will be quite in order in stating that I am willing to go round the country and visit towns where politicians are to speak, and confront them if the public so desire it. I will go to their meetings and question them or I will speak the following night and answer their speeches.'

But to his great disappointment the Government never accepted his offer and the summons to Downing Street never came. Asquith was destroyed after a hostile leader in *The Times* on 4 December had told him to go; a fortnight later the Unionists agreed to serve under Lloyd George and he became the new Prime Minister. Lloyd George, like Bottomley, had sprung from the lower classes, and boasted that he understood the people and they were behind him. He was undoubtedly 'the indispensable man' for England in the First World War and took a leaf out of Bottomley's book by putting businessmen in charge of all the main departments of state. There were three Press Lords in his new Cabinet, but Horatio Bottomley was left out in the cold. Nevertheless, he had a huge following among the working classes and the servicemen, and the sycophantic members of his stable regarded him as a kind of superman. Consequently his head had been turned and, convinced that he was a man of destiny, he never gave up hope of being summoned to high office one day.

In December he introduced the League of the Man in the Street, under the sponsorship of *John Bull*, at a big meeting at the Queen's Hall, London. Tommy Cox had hired a well-drilled claque to give Bottomley a hearty welcome and his speech protesting against the operation of the Government's Central Control Board of Liquor Traffic was loudly applauded.

'When I entered the hall tonight and heard the musical honours with which you welcomed me, I was reminded of the old days . . . during which I was what was called a Parliamentary candidate,' he began. 'I am here at the bar of public opinion as counsel for the man in the street; as an unlicensed lawyer who knows as much about the law as anyone [*laughter and cheers*], as one who has gone through every court in the kingdom except one [*more laughter*]—though as a respectable married man I need hardly mention it! I want to tell the Government—because they do not know it—that there is no necessity for this sort of liquor legislation.'

The Government had put restrictions on drinking hours in Britain because the working classes were getting drunk so frequently that production of several of the vital war industries had gone down. Bottomley thought it was a disgraceful measure because it limited one of the Englishman's main pleasures in life. He sincerely held this point of view, but it was a fact that the brewers paid him a large subsidy for his campaign on their behalf. In December Bottomley started a Business Government Party and undertook to finance any candidates at by-elections who were in sympathy with the ideas of his Party. It was the nearest he could get to making his influence felt in Parliament until he was in a position to pay off his debts, thus qualifying to become an M.P. again.

The combined income from his journalism and patriotic lectures had helped to restore his finances. On Christmas Eve he revived the traditional party at King Street for his stable and his numerous friends. The bar opened at eleven o'clock with wine and champagne and every member of his staff received a fine turkey and a Christmas present. Whatever faults Horatio might have, nobody in his stable would listen to a word of criticism against the 'Guv'nor'.

He was also an extremely popular figure in his Sussex village. Since The Dicker still had the only telephone there, the War Office phoned Bottomley to inform him that the Vicar's son had been wounded in action. Horatio passed the message to the Vicar and insisted that he and his family should stay at The Dicker for the rest of the war. He had always been on the best of terms with the Vicar and some years previously had presented the village church with a rare Bible and a lectern. But as a matter of fact he had never once set foot in it, because he was an atheist like Charles Bradlaugh.

His butler, Louis Flower, had been called up into the Army. He always spent his leave at The Dicker with Bottomley and the family and it was an unwritten law that he should wear khaki when he served dinner at night. Bottomley was an expert at public relations; although he was too old to do his bit, he believed in having as much khaki as possible in his home while Britain was at war.

15 Bottomley Under Fire

> *Just to recall a few of Bottomley's swindling Companies, I name the Hansard Union, the Joint Stock Trust and Finance Corporation . . . and the present* John Bull.
>
> WILLIAM LOTINGA, *Against John Bull*, 1915

During 1916 Bottomley had been making an enormous income from his patriotic lectures and journalism. The *Sunday Pictorial* now paid him £150 an article, so that he was earning £7,800 a year from this source alone, and they also gave him generous bonuses. Nevertheless, he was spending money nearly as fast as it came in.

He once took Peggy Primrose out to a little Soho restaurant where their bill only came to eighteen shillings, but he insisted on tipping the waiter a pound. Sometimes he turned up at her flat at Bedford Court Mansions with his pockets bulging with sovereigns and would say, 'Don't let's go out to dinner, darling. Let's have fun and cook it here.' He was very fond of sausages and left Peggy to cook them, while he took over the cabbage and mash. He was a shocking cook and invariably burned the vegetables, but he insisted on trying his hand at them and they used to laugh at his efforts.

During the war Peggy Primrose's flat became a running bar for half the theatre people in London. Three of the regulars were George Robey, Harry Tate and Toni Edgar Bruce, who owned the Prince of Wales Theatre. Bottomley's bill for wines and spirits ran into hundreds of pounds even in those days. But he never worried about money: his great concern was to try and live down his past and he hated the public to be reminded of his pre-war swindles. Willie Lotinga's pamphlet was still being distributed in every town he lectured in, together with Reuben Bigland's pamphlet, *What Horatio Bottomley Has Done for His Country and the Wounded Soldiers*. Bigland followed this up by writing Bottomley an Open Letter which annoyed him more than he cared to admit. I quote part of it because of its bearing on later events.

> I, a poor uneducated species of humanity, in turn a crossing-sweeper, bootblack and match-seller, am urged by some mystic power to cross swords with the great and only Horatio Bottomley.
>
> I just want to unmask you before the world, to cure you of your dangerous vanity, and, for your own good, I want your congregation* to know the difference between your words and your actions. . . .
>
> The time may come when you would give all you think you have for the chance that is slipping from you for ever—*the chance of doing some good for your country*, if it is only by letting the huge profits of your lectures go to help our wounded heroes instead of into your pocket. I know you *must* have money for the life you lead, but let me advise you not to take a penny from your 'patriotic' lectures, because no first-class patriot wishes to be paid.

Reuben Bigland, the printer from Birmingham, was a very strange man. In the beginning he had a tremendous admiration for Bottomley as a popular politician and journalist. Being a petty crook himself, he respected Horatio for his expertise in this field when he got to know him better. But he finally turned against Bottomley, not for being a crook, but because he was a hypocrite.

However, Willie Lotinga's pamphlet had become a great embarrassment to Bottomley. Amongst other allegations, Lotinga accused him of swindling the public through his crooked companies; of robbing old men and very young ones of substantial sums; and of running a sham bank. It was also alleged that he was the reputed father of several illegitimate children. Bottomley at length decided to apply for an injunction

* A reference to Bottomley's 'lay congregation', the millions of readers of his articles in the *Sunday Pictorial*.

to stop Lotinga's pamphlet, but before the case came into court he found there was an insuperable difficulty: in order to disprove Lotinga's allegations he would have to disclose the names of several of his mistresses who were supposed to have had children by him. Horatio was extremely sensitive on this point. The case was bound to be reported in the Press and he thought it would really ruin his reputation if they published the names of the women in his harem. Therefore, with great reluctance, he cancelled the injunction.

However, he had to do something to counter the effect of Lotinga's pamphlet, so he issued a pamphlet of his own entitled *Who is Mr Bottomley?* which Houston had distributed in every town where he gave a patriotic lecture. Bottomley's pamphlet claimed that he wielded a greater influence and commanded a bigger following than any other public man in England, and said he edited *John Bull*, the great journal 'which has revolutionized the political thought of the nation'.

'So much for Bottomley in his journalistic capacity,' it continued. 'But that is but a portion of his marvellous activities: he is the finest orator in the kingdom: he is the first lay lawyer in the land; the best recruiter; a fine sportsman; a great financier, and a fearless and independent politician.' Some of these claims must rank amongst the most inaccurate statements of the decade.

But *Who is Mr Bottomley?* failed to stop the rot, and Willie Lotinga's pamphlet continued to undermine his prestige with the public. The only solution was to try to come to terms with Lotinga. He called in his friend Thomas Henry Dey, a well-known bookmaker, and persuaded him to act as peacemaker in the dispute. Lotinga agreed to destroy all his pamphlets and proofs and documents on condition that Bottomley paid back £4,200 owing to him in connection with his *John Bull* shares. Horatio accepted these terms and gave Lotinga a cheque for £4,200, although he had to borrow most of it from money-lenders at an exorbitant rate of interest. Thus peace was concluded between them, but Lotinga never spoke to him again for the rest of his life.

In May Horatio decided to bury the hatchet with Reuben Bigland. They arranged to meet at twelve at the Queen's Hotel, Birmingham, where Bottomley was staying after giving a patriotic lecture at a music hall. Bigland produced an amusing version of their meeting in his book about Bottomley. He was in such a hurry that he was on the platform at 11.40 to meet the train from London. Bottomley arrived with Henry Houston and greeted him: 'Well, Reuben the Daring!'

> I instantly replied, 'Well, Bottomley the Brave!'
>
> Thus we mutually chipped each other and eventually made our way into the hotel. Bottomley came down to business right away by asking me a question: 'Bigland, I am determined to come to a settlement with you. What do you want?'
>
> 'I lent you fifty pounds,' I responded, 'and I don't want one penny more or less than the amount due to me.'
>
> He turned round to Houston and said, 'Henry, this is a man who ought to be in our stable. Give him a cheque for fifty pounds.'
>
> I replied, 'I lent you cash and in cash I will be repaid.'
>
> It was arranged that I should call at Bottomley's flat in King Street to be paid in cash the following week. He then displayed the subtlety of which he is a past master. He said casually, 'Bigland, you have done me a serious injury by your articles, not only upon my public but also my private life. Do you realize you have damaged me in the eyes of my lady friends?'
>
> 'Mr Bottomley, I am gallant enough to apologize to any lady whom I have injured,' I said.

Bigland immediately wrote out an apology for any distress he had caused Bottomley. The following Monday he called at King Street and received his fifty pounds in cash. Bottomley opened a bottle of champagne and made him very welcome and proposed they should work together in future. Bigland said he would be delighted to join the stable and they shook hands and made up their quarrel.

Between 1916 and the end of the war Bottomley had some huge betting losses and was hard up on several occasions. He often asked Bigland for a loan and was never refused; in the course of two years Bigland lent him £10,000 free of interest. Reuben Bigland conducted their business in a most gentlemanly fashion, and whenever Bottomley required money he paid it into the John Bull bank, which was under his sole control.

In 1917 Bottomley volunteered to go and visit the Front to

help boost morale in the Army; he thought this mission might force the Government's hand and lead to an official recognition of his war services. After the War Office had accepted his offer he called on Mr Lima, Lord Rothermere's business manager, and persuaded the *Sunday Pictorial* to pay £1,000 towards his expenses as he would be writing articles about his experiences in their newspaper.

He then went to see Julius Elias and obtained a three-figure sum from *John Bull* towards his expenses. Houston accompanied him on the tour and, since they were given travelling-warrants and entertained by the Army the whole time, Horatio made a very handsome profit. Nobody can deny that Bottomley worked hard for Britain in the First World War, but whenever the opportunity arose he made a point of seeing that it paid him a dividend. The troops received him with tremendous enthusiasm and the tour was a great success. The only jarring note occurred when he visited the Officers' Mess.

'Well, Mr Bottomley, will you have a spot?' asked a general.

'What do you mean by a spot?'

'Oh, vermouth, sherry, whisky, that sort of thing.'

'I never drink anything but the driest champagne,' said Horatio pompously.

'I'm sorry to hear that, for we've no champagne here,' said his host.

Bottomley had overtaxed his health with his patriotic lectures and recruiting meetings and journalistic and political activities, and had got into the habit of relying on champagne to sustain him. He depended on it just like a drug, and no other drink had the same effect on him. He pined for it the whole time he was at the Front, and officers who had expected him to be the life and soul of the party were greatly disappointed; he was listless and at a low ebb in the Mess. His first article appeared in the *Sunday Pictorial* on 16 September.

> *My Visit to The Front*
>
> *What I Have Seen With The Boys In France*
>
> . . . Today has been spent at a huge Base Hospital—and the memory of it will dwell in my soul as long as life endures. . . . Did I speak of the transcendent glory of the war? Well, I have seen of it today as I have witnessed the fortitude, the resignation of the suffering and the sacrifice

> of these dear boys. Did I speak of the devilish iniquity? God in Heaven, what have I seen of that, too. I have been through ward after ward; I have been in the operating theatres; I have been in the mortuary—and I have stood, spellbound, in the Hospital Cemetery, with its little crosses pointing to Heaven, each with the name of the sleeping hero resting beneath its shadow, and each surrounded by flowers and evergreens. . . .

On the following Sunday he gave readers his impressions of the trenches:

> In the trenches—with the boys who are actually fighting: with guns roaming all round and above you, with air machines—both our own and the enemy's—over your head and with German lines not 200 yards in front of you.
>
> . . . The tragedy of the trenches—where every phase of the human dream is encountered: One moment, the pandemonium of hell—followed by the silence of the tomb: the ecstasy of martial triumph—then the cold hand of Death . . . and I could not but marvel at the satire upon our civilization which directed *all this energy and enterprise and capital to the destruction of life and property instead of into channels for the happiness and welfare of mankind.*

Bottomley was too intelligent not to realise the futility of war in spite of the jingoism in his patriotic lectures and his newspaper articles. While he was walking within sight of the German lines with General Sir William Robertson, he was told to get down on his stomach at once.

'Not me!' protested Bottomley. 'D'you think I want to give them a target as big as the Bank of England?'

When a colonel took him out on a tour behind the lines Horatio, wearing his tin helmet, was soon perspiring heavily. The colonel whispered, 'Shell hole on the right,' and he passed on the message.

A mile further on the colonel whispered, 'Barbed wire.' Bottomley again passed on the message to the others. Two miles on the colonel whispered, 'Dead horse,' and Horatio passed on the message. A mile later, when he felt ready to drop, he gasped, 'How far away are the Germans?'

'About forty miles.'

'Then why, why on earth are you whispering?'

'I'm not whispering, Mr Bottomley—I am suffering from laryngitis.'

Bottomley insisted they should return to headquarters at once by the quickest route.

'On the Somme Battlefield' appeared in the *Pictorial* on 30 September:

> But who of you has stood on ground covered with battle debris, rifles, helmets, spades, bayonets—and newly dug graves—with search and burial parties still at work—on ground where but a few minutes previously great armies were fighting to the death, with all the demoniacal implements of war? Such has been my experience in Flanders.
>
> . . . Over many graves stands a cross bearing a simple, sad inscription—just *A British Soldier* . . . somehow these particular graves appealed to me more than any of the others. *A British Soldier* . . . poor, dear boy, long ago probably reported missing; anxious, loving wife or mother or sweetheart, still hoping against hope—and here he sleeps in the bosom of glorious France, a simple 'British Soldier'.

In December Bottomley was invited to visit the Grand Fleet, under the command of Admiral Sir David Beatty at Scapa Flow. Both the *Sunday Pictorial* and *John Bull* contributed to his expenses and Houston again accompanied him. This time he made sure of his champagne as he and Houston brought several cases of it with their baggage. His Sunday article of 9 December is quoted for its entertainment value:

> *With the Grand Fleet*
>
> I am somewhere in the Northern Seas—ugh, those seas! I think I must change my first name: it isn't fair to Nelson that I should retain it! . . . The whole scene is vibrant with expectancy. . . . Exactly where I am and what I am seeing I must not say. . . .
>
> My most vivid recollection will always be that of my experience down a submarine. . . . I wondered how on earth I was going to climb on to it, for it is quite an error

> to speak of a submarine's deck—you simply stand on the top of a spheroid, clutching to a rope, or, here and there, a bit of rail. But I found that a little canvas and cork strap was hung to the side whilst I, by means of a kind of acrobatic exercise, with its assistance landed myself upon the slippery back of the fish. . . .
>
> When the Commander conducted me to another part of the vessel and, raising a lid, directed me to disappear down a chute of just about the same circumference as myself, I began to think of Home, Sweet Home and to realize, as never before, the truth of the words of that song. . . .

At that time Mr H. Freaks was a rating serving aboard H.M.S. *Galatea*, a light cruiser of the Grand Fleet. He remembers Bottomley speaking to hundreds of ratings and officers in the New Dry Dock at Rosyth. Bottomley made a magnificent 'patriotic' speech which acted like a tonic on the morale of everyone who heard it. 'For quite a time if anyone had said a word against the great Horatio Bottomley he would have got a "rough-house" as they thought so much of him,' Mr Freaks said.*

Horatio was at the top of his form during the visit to the Grand Fleet, and Houston put it down to the fact that the ward-room where they were entertained had a plentiful supply of champagne. Their last night was a most enjoyable occasion and next morning Bottomley decided he had better 'stoke the engine' at breakfast. He began with porridge, but before he could tackle the sausages the ship moved off suddenly and he vanished and was violently sick. When he and Houston were put ashore at Thurso at 9.30 he looked a perfect wreck.

'My God, I do feel ill, Henry. Where can we get a glass of wine?' he asked.

They went in to the nearest hotel and Horatio called the manager. 'I'm Bottomley!' he declared, as if this was the equivalent of 'Open Sesame'.

'Yes, sir, what would you like for breakfast?' said the manager.

'No, old man, I'm ill. I must have a bottle of champagne,' replied Horatio.

'I daren't sell one before time, sir.'

* Letter to author.

'Then *give* me one, I'm Bottomley!'

He looked so forlorn that the manager gave him a bottle of champagne. In those days there was really magic in the name of Bottomley.

In 1918 Henry Houston, who had been tremendously valuable to Bottomley on his patriotic lectures and tours, was seconded to Lord Rhondda at the Ministry of Food. Bottomley made an appointment to see his Lordship at the Ministry to ask for war work and felt that the interview had passed off successfully. 'I think Rhondda is going to offer me a post,' he told Houston in his office afterwards. However, nothing came of it. Disappointed and piqued, Bottomley wrote to Lord Rhondda requesting Houston's release from the Ministry as he required him for work of importance to the war effort. What he really meant was he wanted Houston to return in order to assist him with his highly profitable patriotic lectures.

'Mr Houston's services are too valuable to be dispensed with,' replied Rhondda.

This put Bottomley in a rage, and he told Charles Palmer that *John Bull* would run a series of articles attacking the Ministry of Food for inefficiency. The articles, written in a hurry, were ill informed and most unfair to Rhondda's Ministry. When Houston criticized 'H.B.' for publishing them he stormed out of the office.

In 1917 the United States had come into the war on the side of the Allies, which made a great difference to the final outcome. The general opinion was that it was only a matter of time before Germany was defeated and Horatio entirely agreed with it. But if he was going to make his political come-back it was important to present himself in a favourable light. A fresh attack had been just made on him in a pamphlet entitled *Horatio Bottomley Exposed*, copied from an article by Clarence Henry Norman. Like Lotinga's pamphlet, it was distributed in every town where Bottomley held a meeting. This savage exposure of Bottomley, far better written than the others, began:

> Mr Horatio Bottomley is a person who has never ceased to claim that he is the best interpreter of the mind and morals of the ordinary hard-working decent 'British citizen'.

It then dragged up five law cases in which Horatio had been exposed as a swindler—in particular the pathetic case of old

Masters, the retired Indian Civil Servant, whom Bottomley swindled out of a fortune. It ended:

> With that we leave Mr Horatio Bottomley, only reminding our readers that nothing could be more conclusive proof of the rottenness of British democratic and political life than the fact that such a man is consulted by the rulers of this country, leads Press campaigns, and is hearkened to by hundreds of well-meaning dupes in his endeavours to drum off the public stage any agency which stands for national security and working-class freedom.

Bottomley complained that he found copies of the pamphlet everywhere he went and that his business friends and private acquaintances were being bombarded with it. He therefore consulted Reuben Bigland.

'Norman's scandalous pamphlet is circulating wherever I go, Reuben, and I must stop it. If I bring an action for libel and win it, other people will be prevented from repeating these statements. Do you think you could find a printer whom I could sue?' Bottomley asked. 'I'll make it worth his while.'

In the Midlands Reuben Bigland found an old, down-at-heel printer named John Greaney who was only too pleased to print six copies of Norman's pamphlet and earn a bonus of fifty pounds. Bigland happened to know that he was an ex-convict, but it did not seem to matter under the circumstances. As soon as Greaney had printed the pamphlet Bottomley sued him for libel.

The case was tried before Mr Justice Darling and a special jury in the King's Bench Division on 20 July 1918. Greaney offered his apologies to Bottomley for printing and publishing the pamphlet, but did not appear in court. Thus the only question for the court to decide was the amount of damages to be awarded to Bottomley. The latter, in his most eloquent vein, gave the court his 'innocent' version of the five law cases which Norman had cited in his pamphlet. Mr Cecil Hayes, counsel for Greaney, said at one point in the proceedings, 'I do not like to interrupt Mr Bottomley.'

DARLING, J. It is your business to interrupt Mr Bottomley unless it is something which really calls for my interference, which has not happened yet.

HAYES — Mr Bottomley is so interesting that one is loath to interrupt him.

DARLING, J. — It is not your interest but your client's interest that you have to consider.

Although Horatio protested that he did not ask for vindictive damages against Greaney, he made one of his most effective speeches to the jury.

BOTTOMLEY — I do not think little men because they are little men financially should be encouraged to hurl libels at other men trusting to their magnanimity not to make them pay for it. I do not disguise from you that what I want in this case is the public warning to other people that their pamphlets must cease. . . .

I ask you to look at the case of a reckless printer copying something which he now admits to be libellous and untrue, making no inquiry whatever as to its truth, and hurling it at me in the hope that I would extend to him the same immunity as I did to the others.*

There must be a point at which this sort of thing stops and without exaggerating the damages I have suffered, but putting to you the right of a public man to immunity from dishing up this dirty old stuff of years and years ago for no serious purpose at all, and to make such public work as I am doing less effective than one would wish it to be, I do ask you to give me such a verdict as would be a deterrent to other people and to remove the handicap under which I have worked for the past few years. With these words I leave the action in your hands.

After Mr Justice Darling had summed up entirely in Bottomley's favour the jury decided to award damages of £500 against Greaney. The latter was waiting with Bigland outside the court,

* This was the fourth time Norman's article had been copied in a pamphlet and thousands of copies had previously been printed.

having taken fright when he heard Bottomley attack him with such power. Greaney received a double bonus of a hundred pounds from Bigland and departed.

The Greaney libel case had been reported fully in all the national papers, and after his decisive triumph Bottomley felt that his reputation was safe at last.

16 The Victory Bond Club

At the end of the war Bottomley had the public by the ears, the Government by the hand and his past by the throat.

'TENAX', *The Gentle Art of Exploiting Gullibility*

'For purely personal reasons I am compelled to work outside Parliament,' lamented Bottomley in *John Bull* in the summer of 1918. Although he was not eligible to stand for Parliament because he was still a bankrupt with total debts of £233,000, he was sure that once they had been settled he could regain his old seat at South Hackney. He expected that the war would probably be over before Christmas and believed that as soon as Britain had won Lloyd George, the great opportunist, would call a General Election, hoping to be returned as the Victory Premier. Bottomley's problem, therefore, was how to make nearly a quarter of a million in the short space of six months, or, better still, how to make a smaller sum if he could arrange to get his debts reduced, as he generally did.

The year 1918 had again begun badly for the Allies: in March the Germans under Ludendorff had launched their final offensive in France with striking success. They had driven three great wedges in the Allied lines, but in doing this they had overstretched themselves. The Allies were reinforced by fresh British troops and the new armies from America. In July Marshal Foch, the supreme commander, defeated the Germans at the second Battle of the Marne. In August the tanks, the new weapon, were exploited by the British in a surprise attack which overwhelmed the German forward divisions, and twenty-two thousand prisoners were taken.

'August 8 was the black day of the German army in the history of the war,' said Ludendorff. 'It put the decline of our fighting force beyond all doubt. . . . The war must be ended.'

Germany's allies—Bulgaria, Turkey and Austria—surrendered in the next two months, and when revolution broke out in Germany in November her delegates had to accept the drastic terms of the Armistice. At eleven o'clock on 11 November, the First World War came to an end.

Earlier in the year Bottomley had been summoned to an interview with Lloyd George at 10 Downing Street at which Lord Rhondda and Sir Edward Carson were also present. They really sent for him because the Premier wanted him to correct various inaccurate statements in *John Bull* articles on food distribution. Horatio tactfully agreed to their suggestions, but also leaked to the Press that he had been offered a post in the Cabinet, and this was never officially denied. Bottomley still saw himself as the country's born leader and assumed that as soon as he returned to Parliament he would be brought into the Cabinet. He told a newspaper reporter in 1918: 'It is the plain, unvarnished, non-university man, the man with no frills, no family tradition, no sixth-form spirit, he is the man to get things done.'

In other words, 'Send for Bottomley, the man of Destiny who never went to Eton or Oxford, but was educated in the University of Life and is all the better for it.' Curiously enough, Lloyd George had the ideal background for Bottomley's new type of Prime Minister, having come from yeoman Welsh stock and left school at fourteen and started in a solicitor's office after his mother had been left penniless.

Mrs Vera Lakin was sitting in the lounge of the Royal Albion Hotel, Brighton, one afternoon in 1918 when her father spotted Bottomley in a corner. He said to her *sotto voce*, 'There's our next Prime Minister!'

Somehow Horatio's keen ears caught the magic words and he rose and gave Mrs Lakin and her father a little bow of acknowledgement. . . .

During the war it was considered the duty of a good citizen to stimulate the patriotic public's interest in buying War Bonds, and Bottomley was an expert in this good cause. A few days after the Goverment had issued new War Savings Certificates he announced his War Stock Combination scheme in *John Bull.*

> Invest money with Bottomley, who will purchase Government war loan securities and out of the interest which will accrue from the large mass of war stock purchased by Bottomley, a fund will be created which can be distributed among the War Stock Combination stockholders as prizes. . . .

The Government had issued War Savings Certificates in denominations of 15*s.* 6*d.* and each certificate would be worth £1 tax free after five years. Bottomley aimed to get £77,500 subscribed and to put it into saving certificates, so that in five years it would appreciate to £100,000. At least this was the way in which he stated the scheme would be run. *John Bull* readers responded magnificently to his appeal and during October he actually received a total of over £80,000. But he had overlooked one simple fact: that you could only buy £500 War Savings Certificates in the same name. He therefore used part of the funds subscribed to the War Stock Combination to purchase War Stock—and we shall hear a great deal about this holding later—and arranged to have the first year's prizes drawn on the 23rd of the month.

'Unlucky' subscribers who did not win a prize—and their number was legion—were given the chance of investing in another Bottomley scheme called the War Stock Consolation Scheme. Subscribers were able to participate in it at the cost of 15*s.* 6*d.* for a £1 share. The scheme, which was supposed to be limited to a total fund of £50,000, was heavily oversubscribed. Bottomley then announced that he would raise the stake to £1, so every subscriber had to pay an extra 4*s.* 6*d.* for his ticket. It was estimated that in this way Horatio finally netted a total of £93,736.

Prizes for the War Stock Combination scheme and for the War Stock Consolation were drawn in 1918. The winning numbers of both funds were published in *John Bull*, but *not* the names of the winners. Bottomley was working exactly the same racket as he had done with his racing sweepstakes before the war.

When the war ended Bottomley worked day and night to settle up his old debts in order to get his bankruptcy annulled. First of all the Restoration Syndicate, a 'dummy' Bottomley company, persuaded most shareholders of the John Bull Investment Trust and Agency to sell their shares in 'this derelict undertaking' for sixpence each. Thus 41,800 shares were accounted for and Bottomley's liabilities to this concern reduced to £34,250. Most of these debts were purchased by three of his other dummy companies, the Northern Territory Syndicate, the Mining Commercial and General Trust, Ltd (Director, Tommy Cox), and the South African Petroleum Exploration, Ltd (Director, Tommy Cox). Bottomley also had unsecured creditors with claims of £41,860 whom he had to pay in full. His political friends paid part of this for him. He settled the outstanding balance by using money which had been subscribed to the War Stock Combination scheme: £25,000 in cash and £9,000 in War Stock. The Official Receiver accepted Bottomley's extremely involved explanation of his financial position without asking awkward questions; it appears that he had been instructed that Bottomley should be treated leniently on account of his valuable war services.

Thus, when Lloyd George called a General Election for 14 December, Bottomley was just in time to be nominated as an Independent candidate for his old seat at South Hackney.

When Bottomley fought South Hackney he was thoroughly exhausted by his efforts to run the Bond Clubs and get his debts cleared off, and was also feeling the effects of all his heavy drinking during the last years of the war. Tommy Cox and Henry Houston found him a most troublesome candidate to handle: he failed to turn up at meetings, made childish suggestions for election stunts, and was quite incapable of working as hard as he did before 1914. However, Cox and Houston, assisted by the People's Perkins and other members of the stable, ran an effective campaign for him. They had a twelve-foot poster of Bottomley—the biggest one ever made at that time—and underneath it the slogan: BOTTOMLEY, BRAINS AND BUSINESS. His opponent, Arthur Henri, never stood a chance, and South Hackney welcomed Bottomley back with open arms. When the votes were counted it was announced that he had got in easily:

Horatio Bottomley	11,145
Arthur Henri	2,830
Majority	8,315

There was a rumour that Parliament would not be summoned until the Peace Treaty had been signed at Versailles, which was obviously going to take several months. Bottomley, in bombastic mood, challenged the Government through the columns of *John Bull*.

> Unless Mr Lloyd George—who I am not certain is coming back—calls Parliament together a few days after 14 December 1918, I shall take a taxi-cab to Buckingham Palace and have a few words with His Majesty.

When it was announced that he had won South Hackney by a thumping majority he gave an interview to the *Weekly Dispatch*:

> Having been elected again to Parliament by an amazing majority . . . I am now preparing to proceed to Westminster to run the show. . . . All Britain knew that I was aching to be returned for South Hackney as the unofficial Prime Minister and the unofficial Prime Minister I am going to be. I have, up my sleeve, some very big things and I shall get busy on them as soon as Parliament opens. . . . You can be assured that before the session has advanced a week everyone will know I am there.
>
> I shall be watching the Government's every move and will support them whenever they are acting in the interests of our soldiers, sailors and citizens.

In 1919 the Government issued Victory Bonds at £5 each, which made them too expensive for most working-class and retired people. This suited Horatio down to the ground: *John Bull* announced in July that he was running a Victory Bond Club which would be the ideal medium for patriotic small investors. They were offered a fifth of a Victory Bond for £1, and a chance of making their fortune. It sounded a wonderful ideas as outlined in his circular:

> Send me your £1, or as much as you can, and I will buy bonds, *and hand them over to trustees*, and each year we will draw for the accruing interest. Your capital will remain intact, or at any time, if you wish it, *you may receive it back in full.*

> A new road to fortune, £1 gives you the opportunity of winning £20,000.

The italics serve to emphasize the extremely vulnerable clauses in Bottomley's prospectus which were to prove his undoing. The prospectus had been drawn up in a hurry because Horatio, convinced that he had found a great money-spinner, was too impatient to have it vetted by an expert. The patriotic readers of *John Bull* fell hook, line and sinker for the Victory Bond Club and heavy applications for tickets started immediately. Subscribers all thought Bottomley had been most generous in making no charge for his expenses so that all the money could be used to provide big prizes for the winners.

Henry Houston, who was still at the Ministry of Food, visited the Victory Club's headquarters at 26 King Street one day. He was shocked to find that Bottomley had left such obvious loopholes in the terms of the Victory Bond Club and told him, 'It's madness to allow nothing for your expenses!' Already £10,000 had been spent on Press advertising, £13,000 had gone on printing the tickets and Bottomley also had to pay a staff of twelve clerks to handle the distribution of the tickets. Bottomley's business friends warned him that he ran a great risk by promising subscribers that they could have their capital returned to them any time they asked for it.

Horatio laughed at their forebodings as the money poured into his flat in King Street. It was a fantastic success—even in his wildest dreams he had never expected anything like it! Ex-servicemen, naval and military officers, pensioners, doctors, clergymen, maiden ladies, widows, domestic servants, school-masters, stockbrokers, solicitors and even bank managers sent him their pound notes or fivers or tenners or postal orders or cheques. Every day an army of people, most of them ex-servicemen, queued up the whole length of King Street and waited with their money to buy tickets. At the height of the Victory Club boom Bottomley was receiving cash at the rate of £100,000 a day.

'Isn't it wonderful, Henry? Just like the old days!' he said to Houston with dancing eyes. 'We have received twenty thousand registered letters today!'

'I suppose you are really going to buy the bonds?' Houston asked.

'Oh, I'm not going to buy them now,' Bottomley replied in

his happy-go-lucky way. 'They're sure to go down in price and I'll be able to buy them cheaper in the open market later on.'

Another point that Bottomley had overlooked was that the interest on the Victory Bonds, which was meant to provide the club's prizes, was subject to income tax. But in the first flush of his success he was in a complete state of euphoria. . . .

The first hint of trouble came from his staff of clerks who were working overtime in chaotic conditions trying to cope with the rush for tickets. Ex-servicemen, engaged pell-mell by Bottomley without any references, they were absolute amateurs at this kind of work. So many people were applying for tickets by post or in person that it had become impossible to keep up with their demands. Horatio, a hopeless organizer, had no system and no control whatsoever over his clerks. He would feverishly help them to open the subscribers' letters and watch them getting snowed under with postal orders and cash, trying to match each contribution to the correct amount of Victory Bond tickets. After a while he could not bear to watch the growing muddle any longer and would retire to a small inner room and swig a glass of champagne. He ought to have engaged twice the number of clerks and made sure that they had proper references for the job.

As the rush of applications kept growing, he decided that the blue Bond Club tickets should be revised so that they simply read:

> This is to certify that the bearer is the holder of one share of £1 in the above club and is entitled to one chance in the annual draw.

Each certificate, of course, bore a number. But he had made another big mistake: it was absurdly easy to forge tickets on the same common blue paper, and forged tickets were soon being sold in pubs all over London. Some subscribers paid for their tickets with dud cheques, and by the time these had 'bounced' the tickets had already been sent off. The overworked clerks found it impossible to keep up with the huge daily post containing applications for tickets and got many days behind with their task. One or two light-fingered types helped themselves to the cash and never sent out any tickets at all.

Thousands of subscribers started writing in to demand the return of their capital, which they were entitled to do under the rules of the Victory Bond Club; there was also a long queue of applicants in King Street: £50,000 was paid out during the club's first month and Bottomley stated that he had paid out a total of £150,000 by the end of 1919. Owing to the total lack of system in issuing Bond Club tickets, many subscribers were overpaid by the clerks when they applied for the return of their capital, while others wrote in two or three times for their money and got away with it.

In August Bottomley bought £500,000 War Bonds for the club at a cost of £387,000; at that time his bank receipts from the Victory Bond Club and other schemes stood at £687,000. But in September he yielded to an insane impulse to try and become a newspaper tycoon and compete with Lord Northcliffe, and paid £41,500 for the *National News* and the *Sunday Evening Telegraph*, both of which were losing money. What on earth possessed him to take this step when he had no free capital and the Bond Club and his other schemes were running into trouble? One can only ascribe it to his vanity and his gambling instinct; he must have assumed that under his management the two papers would catch on as *John Bull* had done and make enormous profits.

Being unable to pay for the *National News* and the *Sunday Evening Telegraph* out of his own pocket presented no problem to Horatio, since he had sole control of £500,000 War Bonds and there was still a big balance in the Victory Bond Club banking account. Although his prospectus had stated that the funds would be handed over to trustees, he had been unable to find any responsible people to undertake this duty. He had even asked the Public Trustee to do so, but that individual had replied that 'the lottery aspect of the scheme makes it impossible for a Government Department to recognize it'. He therefore obtained £41,500 to buy the two newspapers by arranging a bank loan through a firm of solicitors; their bank took £100,000 War Bonds as security.

The Victory Bond Club situation grew steadily worse during the autumn. The masses of people who were demanding their money back were not only Bond Club subscribers because Bottomley had been handing out Victory Bond tickets to anybody who had complained of being duped in his previous money-raising schemes, such as the John Bull Loan Club, the Derby Sweep of 1915, the War Stock Combination and the War Stock Consolation scheme.

The British public had begun to sense that the Victory Bond Club was a colossal swindle. Discontented subscribers in the provinces, whose letters to Bottomley had been ignored, formed themselves into committees and took legal advice. Many sent deputations to the House of Commons to interview Bottomley, and whenever he addressed meetings in London or the provinces he found himself confronted by Bond Club subscribers clamouring for their money back; he had to take a cash reserve in order to pay out subscribers in the audience. The Victory Bond Club had got out of control and he was incapable of coping with it on his own. To make matters worse, the two newspapers he had bought were both making a loss and he was afraid they were white elephants.

Reuben Bigland urged him to publish the *names* of the prize-winners in the War Stock Combination and the War Stock Consolation funds, but he was unable to comply with the request for obvious reasons. He and Bigland had started to quarrel again in connection with a chemical product which, it was claimed, would turn water into petrol. Bigland had asked Horatio to back it and was furious because he refused to put up a penny. I shall return to this feud in the next chapter.

Horatio had set his heart on trying to make Peggy Primrose into a theatrical star and, ignoring his increasing difficulties with the Bond Clubs, he financed another show for her in 1919. He had first tried to launch her in July 1918, in a spy melodrama called *The Hidden Hand* at the Strand. Unfortunately London had a surfeit of spy plays at that time, and this was only a run-of-the-mill effort, but apart from that Peggy Primrose was amateurish in her role. 'Though seemingly rather overweighted in making her first appearance as a heroine of drama, Peggy Primrose played with unaffected simplicity of style,' the *Stage* reported. The play had run four months and had lost money.

In December 1919, Horatio took a lease of the St Martin's Theatre and it was announced that Peggy Primrose had gone into management and that her first starring vehicle would be *The Dear Little Lady*. The big scene in this offering was a 'daring' bedroom encounter between a strong, silent hero and a sweet young thing (Peggy Primrose) who spent the night together in a totally innocent fashion. Tried out at the Palace Pier, Brighton, it was cut by the censor because too many intimate feminine garments had been exhibited on the stage. When produced at the St Martin's it got lukewarm notices. Poor Peggy Primrose was informed that 'she plays agreeably and coquettishly enough . . . but lacks strength in the semi-serious closing scene'.

Horatio seemed to be a hopeless judge of a popular play and never managed to make up for his dreadful mistake in turning down *Charley's Aunt* in the nineties. And the truth was that Peggy Primrose had neither the talent nor the experience needed to become a successful leading lady. *The Dear Little Lady* came off in a few weeks and was an expensive flop; this show and his lease of St Martin's cost Bottomley over £10,000.

On New Year's Eve, Henry Houston had a phone call from Horatio. He had not seen 'H.B.' much during the year because he was very annoyed that he had only just paid up a long-standing debt.

Horatio sounded most cordial on the telephone. 'Houston, we have always seen the old year out together and I can't let this year pass without seeing you. . . . Come and have breakfast with me tomorrow.'

Houston, like many other people, found it hard to resist the soft, purring voice of 'H.B.' when he turned on his charm and he accepted the invitation. They had an early breakfast together at King Street next morning and afterwards Bottomley disclosed his real reason for getting in touch with Houston.

'I want you to take over the Victory Bond Club, Henry. You have no idea what a mess I'm in.'

'I have a pretty good one.'

'The organization was too much for me, Henry. We couldn't open the envelopes fast enough! I had to engage a scalliwag staff, and all is hopeless confusion.'

Bottomley groaned at the memory of what had been going on at King Street for the past few months. 'I had no control over the thing, and I found myself being robbed right and left,' he complained.

They went down together at eight o'clock to the huge board-room. There were stacks of correspondence four or five feet high all over the room, with three main piles headed:

People who sent cheques; no tickets received

People who sent postal orders; no tickets received

People who stopped their cheques; query tickets sent?

Houston read a few sample letters and sighed with despair. The chaos was indescribable—how on earth could it ever be put right?

'Houston, you're a born organizer—come and take it on!' Bottomley urged.

Henry Houston, who had seen enough of the shambles to realize that some clerks had been lining their pockets with cash from the subscribers and not sending them any tickets, said he would only take over the organization on condition that certain clerks were sacked at once.

'I can't accept the responsibility unless these men are out of the way, H.B.'

After Horatio had accepted his terms Houston took charge of the Victory Bond Club although he realized things had gone too far and that he could only try and stop all the office confusion in future. He estimated that the club had lost almost £50,000 owing to the combination of hopeless muddle, forged tickets and thieving clerks.

The First World War had been a great opportunity for Bottomley to redeem his reputation and to put his feckless finances in order. One might have expected him to be solvent by the end of the war, thanks to his huge earnings from journalism and the patriotic lecture tours, yet he still owed large sums to bookmakers, money-lenders, and other concerns. However, the war had brought out some of his best qualities: he had played an important part in keeping up the morale of the British people and had helped thousands of servicemen and their wives and dependants in many ways through the medium of *John Bull*. On the other hand, his large earnings from the patriotic lectures had gone straight into his pocket and he never took Reuben Bigland's advice to give away some of the proceeds for the benefit of wounded soldiers and sailors.

The war had failed to change his character and he was still absolutely incapable of self-discipline. If he wanted to put five thousand pounds on a horse or buy a newspaper for forty thousand he would go ahead and do it without ever considering if he could afford it. His vanity and his ambition drove him to get back to the House of Commons at all costs, and his vicious circle of debts meant that he had no chance of paying them off to get his bankruptcy annulled unless he could find a way of getting rich quick. Hence the War Stock Combination scheme, the War Stock Consolation scheme and the Victory Bond Club, which were to lead to his downfall.

He had already dipped into the subscribers' funds twice—first to help him pay off his debts to the Official Receiver and then to buy two newspapers. After that he never had a ghost of a chance of putting his accounts straight and was on a collision course heading for disaster.

JULY 12TH 1919. JOHN BULL.

AN ALTERNATIVE INVESTMENT.

JOHN BULL :—"If you can't afford that, Jack, have a quid or so in this."

(See page 8.)

IV

THE ROAD TO RUIN

17 Bigland Challenges Goliath

I heard a voice from Heaven saying unto me, Confess! . . . The spirit of William Lotinga is urging me on to unmask England's Greatest Living Humbug, the man that takes the name of the Lord to cover up his terrible sins.

BIGLAND, telegram to Bottomley, November 1920

To understand the relationship between Horatio Bottomley and Reuben Bigland one must realize that Bigland had a touch of the buffoon in his character which made his actions unpredictable; this helps to explain why Bottomley never took him seriously. Their second quarrel began when Bigland impulsively put up some money for a new invention brought over to this country by an American who claimed it would revolutionize the cost of motoring: it was a chemical powder capable of transforming water into petrol at an estimated cost of 5*d.* per gallon. Without properly investigating the truth of the American's claims he had paid £4,000 to Andrew Smith, the inventor's representative, for an option on the British rights and also given the hard-up inventor £500 on account. Bigland then started looking for a wealthy backer to pay £60,000 for the British rights of the invention. His friend Richard Wooton, the racing trainer, arranged for him to give a demonstration at a Newmarket stable on Cesarewitch Day, October 1919.

Wooton persuaded a number of wealthy racing men to assemble at Pratt's stable in the afternoon to see the marvellous chemical powder in action. After filling a pail of fresh water from the pump yard, the inventor stripped right down to his trousers to show there was no deception. Then he took three bottles out of a little black bag and poured the contents into the water, and proved it had been turned into petrol by burning various objects in it. Everybody applauded, and Bigland clapped loudest of all. Finally, the inventor poured the mixture into the petrol tank of Pratt's car. Bigland, who was in the seventh heaven, ran to the car and drove off at full speed. This was a fatal mistake because all the racing men left to go and watch the Cesarewitch.

When Reuben Bigland drove back he found himself alone in the stable yard with the horses and realized the demonstration had been a fiasco. However, he went up to town in the evening and saw Bottomley in the hope that he would put up the money for the invention. But Horatio had been overindulging in champagne in an effort to forget his Bond Club troubles and was in no condition to consider a business proposition.

'Sorry, Reuben, but I can't discuss it tonight. Look, old chap, call as early as you like in the morning—we'll go into it together.'*

'If you take me on tomorrow with this scheme, I'll be the best man you ever had in your stable,' said Bigland enthusiastically.

Reuben Bigland felt confident that Bottomley, who must have been coining money with his Bond Clubs, would back the invention. He was so excited about his prospects that he got up early next morning and called at King Street at seven. He found Horatio in bed working on one of his schemes. Bigland outlined his plans for marketing the invention and produced his agreement with the American inventor and his option on the British rights. Horatio made no comment, he merely read out a scathing account in the *Daily Express* of Bigland's demonstration at Newmarket.

'My dear Reuben, this is a swindle.'

Bigland swore he was wrong and shouted that the invention was absolutely genuine and the chemical powder would only cost fivepence a gallon.

'Don't you believe it, old chap.'

'But, Horatio, the man is not born of woman who could swindle both you and myself!'

Bottomley shook his head and said he wouldn't put up a penny. (He had privately checked up on the invention and found it would cost one pound a gallon to manufacture the

* Bigland, *Bottomley*.

powder and that any chemist could make it.) Bigland, infuriated by his refusal, lost control and ranted at Bottomley for his ingratitude.

'You have used me all the time, Horatio! I lent you money whenever you wanted it and helped to clear your name, and the first time I ask you for help you turn me down! You call this friendship, Horatio? You have taken a million pounds of the people's money and when I leave this room I shall make it my business to see the club members have fair play.'

Horatio, amused at Bigland's outburst, started laughing at him. 'Why don't you go and see Elias and ask him to back your invention?' he suggested. He had summoned his manservant, George Rawson, to show Bigland out. As Bigland left the bedroom he turned round dramatically and said, 'From this moment I shall be your enemy!'

Bigland called on Jimmy White, the financier, and later on Elias and on two other financiers to try and interest them in his chemical powder; but nothing came of it. As Bottomley had discovered, the concentrated preparation would cost a pound a gallon and not fivepence. Nevertheless, Bigland still felt that Bottomley had treated him abominably. 'I formed the fixed determination that he must be exposed,' he said.

But how? He found the legal fraternity were afraid of Bottomley because of his unorthodox but highly successful methods in court. Most solicitors advised their clients to leave him alone and some people called him the Houdini of the Courts. Reuben Bigland, who held some Victory Bond Club tickets, put an advertisement in the *Daily Mail* asking subscribers to contact him, but did not get a single reply. He then wrote to Lloyd George and Cabinet Ministers about Bottomley's frauds, but they all ignored his letters.

Henry Houston had agreed to take over the management of the Victory Bond Club at the end of 1919, but even this born organizer found it impossible to bring order out of chaos at 26 King Street. After his first week he reported to Bottomley on the shocking state of affairs.

'I think I have found a way out of our dilemma,' Horatio told him.

On 19 January 1920, Bottomley called a meeting of Victory Bond Club subscribers at the Cannon Street Hotel, the scene of many of his former financial triumphs. He explained plausibly that, through no fault of his own, but because of the overwhelming popularity of the club, there had been a most appalling muddle in checking the tickets at King Street. However, subscribers could rest assured that the club had £500,000 War Bonds as their capital.*

As he wanted to avoid the muddle with the club tickets growing any worse, he had therefore decided to initiate the Thrift Prize Bond Club which would be run on the same lines as the Victory Bond Club, but subscribers would buy French Credit National Bonds with prizes to be provided out of the interest on them. He invited Victory Bond Club subscribers to switch into the Thrift Prize Bond Club on the basis of £10 of Victory Bonds for £15 of French Credit National Bonds; all they had to do was to pay the difference of £5. Many subscribers, worried about the Victory Bond Club muddle, were rash enough to accept his offer and threw good money after bad. The big catch in it was that you could buy a French Bond for £9 while Bottomley was charging subscribers £15 for it. An article in *Truth* pointed this out and advised people to steer clear of Bottomley's schemes. *Truth* had already warned the public about the Victory Bond Club in the following words:

> People are handing out their money to the unfettered control of the promoter of a so-called club, having neither a committee or any rules, nor indeed any sort of legal constitution or existence.

Bottomley sued *Truth* for libel, but they ignored his writ, took no notice of the ones he issued later, and continued their attacks on him. In a fit of temper he got in touch with the leading wholesale newspaper distribution agents and threatened to make trouble unless they stopped all copies of *Truth* which contained gross libels on him. But the agents refused to be intimidated and continued to sell *Truth*.

Fifty thousand Victory Bond Club subscribers paid an extra £5 or a multiple of that sum to join the Thrift Prize Bond Club, which gave Horatio's finances a new lease of life. In Paris he bought French Bonds at £9, for which subscribers had paid £15, thus making a handsome profit on each one. The Thrift Prize Bond Club had its headquarters in Paris at Messrs Cunliffe Russell & Co., stock- and sharebrokers, while Bottom-

* This was a lie. He had already cashed £100,000 of the Club's War Bonds when he bought two newspapers in September 1919.

ley installed himself in a large luxury suite at the Grand Hotel. *Truth* made another attack on him on 7 July.

The Bond Clubs

> Letters are still reaching me with reference to the Victory Bond Club and the Thrift Prize Bond Club, those twin products of Mr Bottomley's artfulness in circumventing . . . the Lottery Acts. . . .
>
> Like the Victory Bond Club, the Thrift Bond Club does not appear to have any definite and legal constitution—indeed, I should think that both concerns, although styled clubs, are really unregistered companies, or what are known in the Companies Act as illegal associations. However, one thing is made clear. The £500,000 which the public are asked to put up is to be 'under the personal control of the president, who shall determine the time, method and amount of the club's investments'.
>
> I hardly know which to admire most—the courage of the president who undertakes this responsibility single-handed, or the courage of those who accept what seems to be so unbusinesslike an arrangement.

Ugly rumours began to circulate all over the country about the 'Swindling Bond Clubs'. Bottomley decided to abandon his 1920 Derby Sweepstake when the police threatened to confiscate all correspondence because it was a lottery. In September he sent out a circular to Bond Club subscribers and used the hostility of the police towards him as an excuse for moving the Victory Bond Club offices from London to Paris, 'where they understand these things better'. He was again attacked by *Truth* on 13 October.

Mr Bottomley's Clubs

> With regard to the Thrift Prize Bond Club's circulars . . . many copies reach me . . . some of them with inquiries whether I recommend the scheme. To them I can only reply in the negative. A proposition which involves the placing of an uncertified fund for half a million sterling under the private control of one individual, whoever he may be, strikes me as fundamentally unsatisfactory. Judging from my correspondence it is a method of business

> which has not worked satisfactorily in the previous case of the Victory Bond Club.
>
> It does not appear that the members have received any notice [of the closing down] or of the drawing of prizes which should have been held in September, or indeed any recent communication of any kind in regard to an undertaking in which they invested several hundred thousand pounds.
>
> No doubt Mr Bottomley has great demands upon his time, but surely a businessman should not undertake business which he is too busy to conduct properly.

It was impossible for Bottomley to justify his one-man management of the Bond Clubs. *Truth* kept up their attacks on his highly vulnerable position, and their criticisms were so accurate and their language so venomous that he kept issuing writs which they kept consigning to the waste-paper basket. Although the Thrift Prize Bond Club had brought some sorely needed cash into his coffers, it soon began to disappear. His staff bill in Paris alone amounted to £200 a week and in addition he had big private expenses and heavy losses to meet on his two newspapers, the *National News* and the *Sunday Evening Telegraph*.

In November Bottomley went up to Wellington, Shropshire, to support General Townshend, who was standing as the Business Government candidate at the Wrekin by-election. The anniversary of the end of the First World War, 11 November, was being observed in Britain as Cenotaph Day. The *Daily Mirror* commissioned Bottomley to write an article giving his impressions of the burial of the Unknown Warrior in Westminster Abbey, and he began it:

> And I heard a voice from Heaven saying unto me, 'Write'. . . . It was during that awful silence—when the world stood still—that I heard that voice from Heaven, telling me to write. . . .

Reuben Bigland, back in Birmingham, had begun to feel it was beyond his powers to expose Bottomley, or Goliath as he called him. Then he read Bottomley's article in the *Daily Mirror*, and it made his blood boil to think of his hypocrisy in writing for the masses as if he was a lay preacher.

William Lotinga, the racing correspondent, had just died in the great flu epidemic of 1919 and in his will had told his sons, Jack and Ivor, to beware of Bottomley: 'I hope that neither of my sons will ever meet or have anything to do with Horatio Bottomley or will ever read *John Bull.*'

Lotinga's death and the article in the *Mirror* inspired Bigland to send a telegram to Bottomley:

> AND I HEARD A VOICE FROM HEAVEN SAYING UNTO ME 'CONFESS'. . . . THE SPIRIT OF WILLIAM LOTINGA IS URGING ME ON TO UNMASK ENGLAND'S GREATEST LIVING HUMBUG, THE MAN THAT TAKES THE NAME OF THE LORD TO COVER UP HIS TERRIBLE SINS. I SHALL COME TO WELLINGTON, HAND BACK YOUR WAR BOND AND GIVE MYSELF UP TO JUSTICE TO CLEAR MY CONSCIENCE.

Bigland travelled up to Shropshire determined to expose Bottomley and to give him back the two £500 War Bonds he had received from him in a rigged draw for the War Stock Combination scheme in 1918. At Wellington he saw Mr Clarke, a solicitor, and told him he owed Bottomley £1,000 and wanted to settle the debt. Bottomley made an appointment to see them at the Charlton Hotel at 5 p.m. Bigland and the solicitor were shown up to Bottomley's room at the hotel; to their surprise two six-foot toughs were with him and remained in the background throughout the interview.

'I understand you owe me £1,000, Bigland,' said Horatio aggressively. 'If you do, pay me!'

'Do I?' asked Bigland.

'I don't know that you do but if you do, pay me!'

'Very well, if I don't I don't,' said Bigland playfully, and started to leave the room.

Bottomley followed him to the door livid with rage and stormed at him. 'What about giving yourself up to justice!' he demanded fiercely. 'Look here, Reuben, if I have any more of these wires from you, I shall see that justice overtakes you. You understand that?'

Bigland, completely deflated, lost his nerve at the crucial moment and slunk off and took the next train back to Birmingham. Later, he wrote a letter of apology to Horatio. 'I came there to do you a great wrong. I failed. You have won.' Why did Bigland throw in his hand? Partly because Bottomley was a much stronger personality and gave him an inferiority complex and partly because he did not dare to face him with two bruisers in the room.

After reading Reuben Bigland's letter Bottomley imagined he had choked him off for ever. His candidate, General Townshend, won the Wrekin by-election by a big majority and put him in a good mood. But in London he found there was growing agitation about the Bond Clubs and his two newspapers were still losing money. He decided to re-vamp the *National News* into the *Sunday Illustrated* and run it in competition with the *Sunday Pictorial*, for which he had written since 1915. It meant severing his long connection with the *Pictorial* to write a weekly article for the *Sunday Illustrated* instead.

'I'm going to beat Lord Rothermere at his own game or go bankrupt,' he declared.

It was another of his foolish mistakes. He ran the *Sunday Illustrated* on the cheap from small offices in Fleet Street and never took the trouble to give it a test launching. The paper was unattractive, mediocre, and not in the same class as the well produced, extremely lively *Sunday Pictorial*. Horatio's weekly article in the *Illustrated* was dull and lacked interest; he had no professionals to guide him as they had done on the *Pictorial*. His contribution made little difference to the new paper, which never succeeded in appealing to the public.

A great many writs were out against him. J. N. Nabarro, a young solicitor, called at 26 King Street to deliver one personally to the great man and was ushered into the presence by his manservant, George Rawson.

'I am so sorry we had to issue this writ, Mr Bottomley,' he began.

'Not at all,' said Horatio, beaming. 'George, show the young man where we put them.'

Nabarro saw a great stack of writs on a table. George Rawson put his on the top of the pile. . . .

Truth continued its attacks on him, and although he had moved the Bond Clubs to Paris he was still being bombarded with letters from subscribers and people still called at his flat and at *John Bull* to demand their money back. He was most upset when Bond Club subscribers even heckled him at his meetings at South Hackney.

Once more Reuben Bigland returned to the fight against Goliath. He wrote again to Lloyd George and to Cabinet

Ministers, denouncing Bottomley as a swindler who had robbed the public of millions and urging the Government to take action against him. All his letters were ignored again, but he refused to give up.

At this critical phase in his affairs Bottomley received an invitation to speak at the Oxford Union from their brilliant president, a young man named Beverley Nichols. He accepted immediately; he was to follow Winston Churchill at the Union and could not resist the challenge. It was arranged that he would speak on a motion in favour of the independent political party. Beverley Nichols wrote a most entertaining account of Bottomley's visit to Oxford.* Nichols and two friends met Horatio at the station, having got wind of an undergraduate plot to kidnap the 'outrageous Bottomley' and keep him a prisoner at Boar's Hill for the duration of the Union debate. This was how Beverley Nichols described him:

> A grotesque figure. Short and uncommonly broad, he looked almost gigantic in his thick fur coat. Lack-lustre eyes, heavily pouched, glared from a square, sallow face. . . . It was not till he began to talk that the colour mottled his cheeks and the heavy hues on his face were lightened. . . .

Before they went to the Union Horatio entertained the undergraduates with a dazzling display of figures to demonstrate how he managed to avoid paying any income-tax. When the debate began he became nervous; his face grew flushed and hot and he began mopping his forehead and seemed out of his depth amongst the light and airy chatter they indulged in at the Oxford Union. He rose to speak and started with an inept historical reference; there were titters.

Bottomley paused and then rallied: 'Gentlemen: I have not had your advantages. What poor education I have received has been gained in the University of Life.' From then on his speech was a continuous success. Beverley Nichols said, 'Its eloquence was uncanny. For sheer force of oratory I have never heard anyone like him. Compared with him, Asquith was a dry stick —I am talking of the manner, not of the matter.'

A speaker referred contemptuously to Bottomley as a voice crying in the wilderness. 'All my life I have been crying in the wilderness,' replied Bottomley. 'All my life I have battled alone

* *25* (Jonathan Cape, 1926).

fought alone, struggled for causes that other men have described as hopeless. "A voice crying in the wilderness." Yes, gentlemen, I am proud of it!'

He won his motion easily, but was characteristically most disappointed that he had not broken the record for the numbers attending a Union debate.

'Are you sure there was no mistake in the counting?' he asked.

Beverley Nichols greeted him at his hotel next morning. Bottomley looked extremely tired; the lustre had faded from the heavy eyes.

'What would you like for breakfast, Mr Bottomley?'

'A couple of kippers and a nice brandy and soda.'

On 21 June 1921 Scotland Yard received a tip-off that a man was going to a stockbroker's office in the Strand to sell a stolen War Bond. The police went there and arrested a well dressed man who refused to give his name. He was therefore sent to Brixton Prison for seven days and then revealed that he was Reuben Bigland. He wrote to Bottomley asking him to attend when his case was heard at Bow Street and received the following evasive reply:

> SIR
>
> Yours to hand.
>
> Please let me know the name of your solicitor. If you are not represented, please let me know the evidence you require.
>
> Yours truly,
>
> HORATIO BOTTOMLEY

Bigland replied in one sentence: 'All I want is for you to go into the witness box and tell the truth.' Bottomley did not appear at Bow Street when Reuben Bigland was charged, so Bigland subpoenaed him to attend court the following week. The case was heard by Mr Graham Campbell on 2 July. It was established that the 'stolen' Bond had been won by Bigland's niece, Miss Sanders, as a prize in the War Stock Combination. She had handed it over to Bigland by a previous arrangement and naturally enough refused to bring a charge against him. Reuben Bigland was therefore ordered to be discharged.

'I don't want to be discharged,' he protested. 'I want Mr Bottomley to come into the witness-box before I am discharged.'

'I am satisfied that there is not sufficient evidence that the Bond in your possession was stolen or unlawfully obtained, and you are discharged,' said the Magistrate.

Bigland shouted that he was representing twenty-five thousand people and demanded a hearing. However, the case was dismissed and he was freed; the authorities thought he had a screw loose.

So Goliath had foiled Bigland again! But Reuben Bigland refused to give up the struggle; he emulated the late Willie Lotinga and printed a pamphlet exposing Bottomley entitled:

THE DOWNFALL OF HORATIO BOTTOMLEY, M.P.
HIS LATEST AND GREATEST SWINDLE

HOW he gulled POOR Subscribers to invest One Pound Notes in his GREAT VICTORY WAR BOND CLUB.

Reuben Bigland and three friends, all wearing masks, sold pamphlets for a penny each in the big towns of Lancashire, Yorkshire, Leicestershire and Nottinghamshire. Then Bigland drove off in his old Ford to the West Country and distributed them in Bristol, Bath, Exeter and Plymouth. The latter was Lady Astor's constituency and he knew the pamphlets would sell well there; they thought a lot of Lady Astor in Plymouth and disliked Bottomley for the vindictive attacks he had made on her in *John Bull* at the time of her divorce.

The pamphlets sold so well that Bigland printed an extra quarter of a million for London. Masked hawkers sold them all over the West End and were instructed to patrol Bottomley's special haunts, such as the *John Bull* offices in Long Acre, Romano's in the Strand and the area around St James's and Pall Mall which adjoined his flat in King Street.

Horatio was dining at the Eccentric Club in Ryder Street, St James's, on Saturday 21 September when he heard through the windows the hawkers crying out, 'The Downfall of Horatio Bottomley.' A member of the Eccentric taunted him that his sins were finding him out at last. Bottomley lost his temper and strode out of the club.

He went straight to the *Sunday Illustrated* offices and added a postscript to his article for Sunday. He announced that he would not tolerate Reuben Bigland's offensive pamphlet and had decided to prosecute him for criminal libel. Many people in h circle, including well known barristers and solicitors, advised Horatio to change his mind and ignore Bigland's pamphlet, but he refused to listen to their arguments. On Monday morning he went to Bow Street with Sir Ernest Wild, K.C., and applied for a warrant for the arrest of Reuben Bigland.

Bigland sent a wire to Bottomley in his inimitable style:

> CONGRATULATIONS. PLEASE TEMPER JUSTICE WITH MERCY IN YOUR POWERFUL POSITION. HOPE CHARLIE CHAPLIN WON'T BE ANNOYED AT LOSING SOME OF THE LIMELIGHT. WHAT A PLAY! SELLING PAMPHLETS. YOURS SINCERELY REUBEN BIGLAND OF BIRMINGHAM, THE MAN WHO DARED TO CALL YOU A COMMON SWINDLER.

Bigland telephoned the Birmingham police that he would give himself up at eleven o'clock the following Monday morning. He was arrested on 3 October.

'I am glad you have come,' he told the police. 'In the interests of justice and the poor people I desire light to be brought on the Victory Bond Club swindle.'

18 Bigland on Trial (1)

I've been sitting on a barrel of gunpowder for thirty years and it might go up at any moment.
HORATIO BOTTOMLEY, to Ernest Hooley, 1920

Julius Elias, Henry Houston, Tommy Cox and other associates of Bottomley felt it was a great mistake for him to prosecute Reuben Bigland and they all urged him to call off the case.

'But I can do nothing in the way of business until this pamphlet is out of the way,' Bottomley argued.

Bond Club subscribers were calling at the flat in King Street at all hours of the day to demand their money back. Bigland's pamphlet had wrecked his chances of borrowing money to cover his losses on the *Sunday Illustrated*; his other paper, the *Sunday Evening Telegraph*, was on the point of closing down. His friends warned him that criminal libel was a funny business.

'You're quite right. No man ought to bring an action for criminal libel unless he is as spotless as the Angel Gabriel—and even then there is the danger that Peter will rake up something from the past,' quipped Horatio.

Besides the criminal libel he had added two charges of blackmail against Bigland. The first alleged that Bigland had tried to blackmail him for £60,000 to back his invention in October 1919; the second that Bigland came up to Shropshire during the Wrekin by-election in 1920 and tried to incite three men to blackmail him.

Henry Houston, well aware that his future livelihood depended on Bottomley, was so worried about the imminent prosecution that he had a secret meeting with Reuben Bigland on his own initiative. Bigland declared he had only attacked Bottomley in order to force him to pay out the little people who had been swindled in his Bond Clubs. Houston promised to see that these people were paid the £12,000 owing to them if Bigland would agree to call off the case. Carter and Bell, the solicitors, were acting for Bigland's defence, and Edward Bell advised him to consider Houston's proposal.

However, they failed to reach an agreement before the Police Court proceedings. Reuben Bigland was therefore charged at Bow Street before Sir Chartres Biron on 8 October 1921. He was defended by Arthur Comyns Carr, a bold and tenacious junior counsel, a man who was never overawed by a judge or more eminent opponents. He was an extremely skilful cross-examiner as Bottomley was about to find out. Bottomley was represented by Sir Ernest Wild, K.C. For several weeks Sir Chartres Biron, the magistrate, had been pestered by Bond Club subscribers applying to him for advice on how to get their money back, which prejudiced him against Bottomley from the start.

The charges against Bigland were that he published a defamatory libel and, secondly, that he had tried to extort money at the Wrekin by-election by threatening to publish or to abstain from publishing and printing his pamphlet against Bottomley. Sir Ernest Wild, prosecuting, stated that this was the culmination of a long series of efforts by Bigland to extort money from Bottomley. He quoted from Bigland's pamphlet, of which the most damning sections were:

> Horatio Bottomley became the possessor of nearly one million pounds of the poorer people's money; with no trustees to co-operate and watch the interest of the widows and the demobbed soldiers. Money is a great temptation to some people to have possession of. But to Horatio Bottomley it is, and always has been, that possession is 99 points. He knows the great art of spoofing and wriggling. Those who have given Mr Bottomley their £1 notes have only got in exchange a piece of common blue paper.
>
> The British Government have allowed one of the greatest crooks ever born of woman to issue as £1 shares nearly one million of these pieces of common blue paper, thus permitting this editor of a well known paper to assume the right to hold this huge sum alone, with no trustees, no auditors,

> and a secretary only in name, and no one to say yea or nay if he cares to draw £10,000 to have a flutter at Ostend on his horse Aynsley, or on a roulette table at the Casino. . . .

'There is not a word of truth in any statement that has been made by the defendant with regard to the Victory Bond Clubs,' said Wild. 'Mr Bottomley will swear that he has never made a penny out of this matter. . . . He is already £35,000 out of pocket owing to buying the Club's Victory Bonds at £85 and being forced to sell them at £73 in order to pay clamouring subscribers; owing to Bigland's pamphlet there has been a run on the club.'

He stated that £450,000 had been subscribed to the Victory Bond Club and £350,000 had already been returned. 'Given time, Mr Bottomley will certainly repay every penny of the outstanding £100,000, even though it means a further loss to be borne from his own pocket.'

Sir Ernest Wild outlined the history of Bigland's attempts to extort money, culminating in October 1919 when 'he forced his way into Bottomley's bedroom at King Street at seven in the morning and demanded £60,000 from Bottomley to finance his water-into-petrol invention'.

Bottomley went into the witness-box for his examination-in-chief. He denied going to Birmingham in 1916 to pay Bigland fifty pounds he had borrowed from him, stating that he went there to deal with Bigland's allegations that the *John Bull* Bullets competition had been rigged. He then described Bigland's visit to his bedroom at seven in the morning in 1919 to ask him to back his invention. He had refused to put up any money, being convinced that it was a hoax, but Bigland stood over him and shouted, 'Come into your bank and hand me £60,000 Victory Bonds.'

BOTTOMLEY Bigland pointed meaningly at a bundle of copies of his pamphlet, *Answers to John Bull*. 'If you don't do it,' he said, 'I will smother the country with these documents and will never leave you until I bring you down into the gutter.' [*Breaking off, to Mr Comyns Carr, defending counsel*] Oh yes, Mr Carr, this is not a smiling matter.

SIR C. BIRON You must not make observations of that kind to counsel. You do not create a favourable impression by that sort of action.

The magistrate was determined to keep him in order in court, unlike the many magistrates and judges who had been extraordinarily lenient to him in the past.

WILD [*to Bottomley*] Did you ever make any money out of the Victory Bond Club at all?

BOTTOMLEY Never, and never intended to do so.

Afterwards Sir Chartres Biron asked Bottomley how many people had subscribed to the Victory Bond Club.

BOTTOMLEY I cannot give you the exact figure.

SIR C. BIRON Surely you must have a record of the number of subscribers?

BOTTOMLEY We have a record in the books of the bank of every penny received. This is rather like cross-examination from the bench.

SIR C. BIRON It is not cross-examination. It is my duty to put questions to get an understanding of what the facts are. . . . I am asking you if you have a list of subscribers.

Sir Ernest Wild apologized to the magistrate for Bottomley's remark.

SIR C. BIRON I think you had better try, Sir Ernest, to keep Mr Bottomley reasonably in order.

BOTTOMLEY It is a very trying position. I have quite enough to do to fight Mr Bigland.

Evidently Bottomley was totally unprepared for the magistrate's hostile attitude. In his past cases he had always taken the initiative and often 'broken the rules', but this time he was forced on to the defensive from the start. Sir Chartres Biron continued to ask searching questions about the financial transactions of the Bond Clubs.

BOTTOMLEY [*to the magistrate*] I was advised by my counsel that all I could or would be expected to do here would be to give a general denial of the libels and that no question of justification would be gone into at this court.

WILD I shall take an opinion of that and go to the High Court if necessary.

SIR C. BIRON There is no question of justification. If he gives evidence he is entitled to be cross-examined about it. I don't want to discuss it at this stage —we will wait until the time comes.

Later, Bottomley was cross-examined by Comyns Carr. This examination lasted over a period of four days: it was so exacting and aggressive that it must have made Horatio vow never to face Comyns Carr again if he could possibly avoid it.

COMYNS CARR Did Mr Bigland during the years 1916–17–18 lend you substantial sums of money at your request?

BOTTOMLEY No. . .

Later, Comyns Carr asked if Bottomley had made money out of patriotic lectures during the war.

BOTTOMLEY Not a penny. If there was any money left after the expenses had been paid I always handed it over to the *John Bull* fund for soldiers and sailors.

SIR C. BIRON Do I understand that if there was any money left over it was always paid to you?

BOTTOMLEY Yes, if there was. There was very little.

In the course of the cross-examination Comyns Carr referred to Bottomley's patriotic lectures as 'a music-hall turn'. Sir Ernest Wild rose to make an objection. The magistrate asked him not to interrupt.

WILD [*furious*] I will either interrupt or leave the court. First of all, you will not allow my client to make any objection and suggest it would be done through his counsel.

SIR C. BIRON Your remedy is in cross-examination.

WILD You distinctly said that if any objection should be taken it should be done through counsel. . . . I am here to protect Mr Bottomley and if you will not allow me to make any observations I am of no use here. If you continue in that course of conduct I shall leave the court.

SIR C. BIRON No, I have not said that.

WILD Am I entitled to raise any objection to any point of cross-examination?

SIR C. BIRON Of course you are, and I shall always listen to any submission you wish to make.

WILD I wished to make a submission in regard to Mr Bottomley being described as a music-hall turn. And now you say 'sit down'.

By the third day of the proceedings Sir Ernest Wild, Bottomley's counsel, was at daggers drawn with the magistrate. This was most unfortunate for Horatio since Sir Chartres Biron had been biased against him from the start. Later, Bottomley stated in cross-examination that all the books of the War Stock Combination had been removed to Paris in January, at the same time as the Victory Club books were sent there. He assured Comyns Carr that they would be back in time for Bigland's trial at the Old Bailey.

COMYNS CARR Was that the only reason for removing them to Paris?

BOTTOMLEY Absolutely. If you can suggest another reason I will answer it.

COMYNS CARR I am suggesting to you that the reason for taking all these documents to Paris was to prevent the subscribers or anyone getting hold of them?

BOTTOMLEY Why did the subscribers want to get hold of them?

COMYNS CARR Would you mind answering my question first?

BOTTOMLEY The answer is most certainly not; nor has any subscriber ever yet asked to get hold of them.

COMYNS CARR Have any of the books or papers relating to the Victory Bond Club or the War Stock Combination crossed the Channel in the last few weeks?

BOTTOMLEY Not to my knowledge. . . . I know that . . . whenever I cross the Channel I am always informed by Home Office officials that I am being watched, just as a Scotland Yard man called at the Paris office on Saturday.

SIR C. BIRON You have no right to make such observations.

BOTTOMLEY I have every right to defend the attacks made against my reputation as a public man.

Later, Bottomley admitted in cross-examination that no trustees were ever appointed for the Bond Clubs, although the circular had stated there would be trustees. He said there were legal difficulties about appointing responsible persons as trustees, and he had not appointed auditors because he thought their fees were too high.

COMYNS CARR I am suggesting that from the beginning your intention was that the whole machinery should be under your absolute control and that no one else would be in a position to control it, or to find out how much money there was, or how many subscribers.

BOTTOMLEY Nothing of the kind. Your client's suggestion is that I stole the money, put it on horses and so on—it is a blackmailing suggestion.

Comyns Carr questioned him about the numbers on the War Stock Combination tickets. Bottomley was replying with a long explanation when the magistrate told him to give simple answers and not make speeches.

BOTTOMLEY If I break the law of evidence you have a right

to stop me, but I think I am entitled to say what I did.

SIR C. BIRON You must obey my ruling. [*To Sir Ernest Wild*] Will you please keep your client in order. He doesn't know how to behave himself in court!

Later, Comyns Carr asked Bottomley how many series of the Victory Bond Club tickets had been issued.

BOTTOMLEY I cannot be certain of the numbers.

COMYNS CARR Do you tell the magistrate that, having taken £450,000 of the people's money under your sole management and control, you don't know in what series you issued the tickets to them?

BOTTOMLEY If the magistrate passes that as a proper question and not a speech, my answer is that I don't know how many series there were.

George Rawson, his manservant, and Mrs Rawson, his cook, gave evidence of Bigland's calling at the flat in King Street at seven in the morning. Rawson said that as he was taking up the morning papers to Bottomley he heard him say, 'Don't be absurd. I haven't got such a sum.' Bigland had replied, 'If you don't give it to me I'll scatter the country with these papers.'

Mrs Rawson, the cook, said she overheard Bigland say, 'I want sixty thousand pounds.' Later, he said to Bottomley, 'You've got the funds of the Victory Bond Club.' She saw Bigland pick up two papers from the bed and heard him say, 'If you don't give them to me I'll scatter the country with these.'

The next witness, Julius Elias of Odhams, stated that Bigland called on him later that day in a very angry mood. 'He said, "Mr Bottomley has refused to let me have sixty thousand pounds for my invention and I am determined to bring him down to the ground and have told him so."' Bigland showed him a pamphlet against Bottomley which he intended to broadcast all over the country. Naturally Elias did not want to have the pamphlet circulated, but he refused to give Bigland his personal cheque for £60,000 to stop it.

'On the 10th of this month did you arrange through the witness Houston for Bigland to see you at the Metropole in London?' Comyns Carr asked him.

'Mr Houston asked me to see Mr Bigland and I did so,' replied Elias.

'Did you ask him to withdraw the charges he had made against Mr Bottomley and apologize?'

'I did not ask him to,' said Elias . . .

Later, Elias stated in cross-examination that he told Bigland that if he would admit he had made a mistake and offer Bottomley an apology, and undertake not to issue any more pamphlets, he would do his best to get Bottomley to accept his apology. He gave Bigland a sheet of paper and said, 'A few points I have noted which should be cleared up.' Bigland read them and said he would take proper advice before deciding if he would accept Elias's proposition. He arranged to meet him at the Metropole Hotel the following evening. He never turned up, but phoned Elias and said, 'I have decided I cannot do anything.'

COMYNS CARR What I am suggesting is that it was at *your* suggestion that Houston got Bigland to come and see you?

ELIAS Absolutely not.

COMYNS CARR When you saw him at the Metropole had you got ready written down on a piece of paper questions to be put to Mr Bottomley in cross-examination?

ELIAS I have already said . . .

SIR C. BIRON Just answer the question!

ELIAS Yes.

COMYNS CAR You said 'points'; they were questions!

ELIAS They were in the form of questions.

COMYNS CARR Had you discussed them with Mr Bottomley?

ELIAS No. I just ought to explain.

SIR C. BIRON Just answer the question first. You can explain afterwards.

Elias admitted that he had seen Bottomley before his appointment with Bigland and tried to persuade him to call off the case if Bigland was willing. Bottomley said, 'If it is to be done certain points have to be cleared up,' and gave him the piece of paper. Comyns Carr asked Elias if he had reported to Bottomley that he had failed to persuade Bigland to call off the case. Elias said that Bottomley refused to talk about it.

SIR C. BIRON The evidence is of such a remarkable and extraordinary character that it obviously must lead to a good deal of investigation.

Comyns Carr continued his cross-examination of Elias the following day.

COMYNS CARR In the course of the interview at the Hotel Metropole did you say to Bigland, 'Do this for my sake. I will see to you'?

ELIAS No.

COMYNS CARR Or anything to suggest that he should get some money if he agreed to your proposal?

ELIAS Most emphatically not.

COMYNS CARR Do you know that Mr Houston had told Bigland that he could have ten thousand pounds if he agreed to your suggestion? Had you arranged with Houston to say that to Bigland?

ELIAS Certainly not.

Later, Comyns Carr asked Elias if he knew Mr Hooley. Elias said he did not know Hooley, but had seen him and knew him by repute.

COMYNS CARR But you authorized Mr Hooley on 13 October to offer to the defendant's son, Mr Walter Bigland, that ten thousand pounds would be paid over if Mr Bigland would withdraw these charges against Bottomley?

ELIAS Most emphatically no, and I would like to add that I have never seen Mr Hooley since. The insinuation is that I am in touch with Mr Hooley, but I have only seen him twice in my life.

COMYNS CARR Did you authorize Mr Hooley on 28 October, the day after you gave evidence here, to increase the offer to twenty thousand pounds?

ELIAS I have never been in touch with him, directly or indirectly.

COMYNS CARR I suggest definitely that on 28 October you authorized him to increase his offer to twenty thousand pounds?

ELIAS It is absolutely and entirely untrue, and you know it!

SIR C. BIRON You must not say that and counsel is entitled to put the question.

Sir Ernest Wild re-examined Julius Elias, but his cross-examination by Comyns Carr had been so deadly that he was no longer convincing. Elias lacked Bottomley's long experience in telling plausible lies and half-truths, and had been so shaken by Comyns Carr that he had lost his temper and been rebuked by the magistrate.

Wild then called three men as witnesses to Bigland's attempt to extort money from Bottomley at the Wrekin by-election in 1920.

The first was John Harrison—otherwise known as the People's Perkins. He said he met Bigland in the Market Square at Wellington and Bigland said, 'You're just the man I want to see. I'm going to distribute pamphlets at the meeting showing up old Bottomley properly. . . . He'd rather pay fifty thousand pounds than lose the election for General Townshend.'

COMYNS CARR [*cross-examining*] I have to suggest that you have never spoken to Bigland in your life?

HARRISON Oh yes, more than once. I spoke to him in Birmingham eight or nine years ago.

The second witness, George Swinfield Wells, a political lecturer for the Bottomley Parliamentary Group, said Bigland had approached him in a pub to try and blackmail Bottomley.

Bigland offered him a share of the money but he refused to have anything to do with such a contemptible suggestion.

COMYNS CARR [*cross-examining*] I suggest that you never had a conversation with Bigland in your life?

SWINFIELD WELLS That would not be true.

The third witness, Thomas Phillips, a concert agent who had been helping General Townshend in his election campaign, said Bigland had met him and threatened to flood the place with anti-Bottomley pamphlets unless Bottomley bought him off.

COMYNS CARR I suggest you have never spoken to Mr Bigland in your life?

PHILLIPS I have. I remember the incident well as it was a threat to General Townshend.

Sir Chartres Biron adjourned the case for a few days in view of the new evidence about the meeting between Bigland and Elias.

On 8 November Henry Houston was recalled for the defence. He stated that Bottomley and Bigland had periodical rows and then made friends again. He wanted to try and persuade them to bury the hatchet on this occasion. Bigland had agreed to meet Elias at the Metropole Hotel at three in the afternoon. Houston waited outside the hotel while they had their discussion. Afterwards, Bigland said, 'I have agreed to nothing. I want some advice as to whether, if I apologize, the magistrate will accept my apology, or whether he will send me for trial, in which case my defence has gone.'

Later, Comyns Carr asked Houston if, after the interview with Bigland on 10 October, he had called at his hotel twice to try and see him.

HOUSTON Yes.

COMYNS CARR Did you meet him in Cranbourne Street on 14 October?

HOUSTON Yes.

COMYNS CARR Did you realize this was after he had been charged with blackmailing Mr Bottomley?

HOUSTON It did not occur to me.

COMYNS CARR Even after the charge had been made you were still friendly with him? Did you believe the charge? [*To Magistrate*] I am going to ask the witness what he said. [*To Houston*] Did you say, 'I went down on my knees to the old man not to charge you with blackmail, as I knew you would not do such a thing'?

HOUSTON Yes.

SIR C. BIRON Then you did not believe the blackmail charge at that time?

HOUSTON I did ask Mr Bottomley not to proceed.

SIR C. BIRON Yes. You did not believe it.

Houston's admission that he could not believe Bigland could be guilty of blackmail was extremely damaging to Bottomley's first charge of blackmail.

Sir Ernest Wild re-examined Houston, but it was of no avail: Houston had given most valuable testimony for Bigland's defence. This concluded the case for the prosecution. . . .

Sir Chartres Biron decided to commit Bigland on a charge of publishing a common libel. Comyns Carr stated that Bigland would welcome the opportunity of justifying the allegations made in his pamphlet. Regarding the charge that Bigland had tried to extort £60,000 from Bottomley, Comyns Carr contended that there was a great deal of difference between the verbal evidence and the documentary evidence. He quoted letters written by Bigland to Elias which did not contain the slightest hint of trying to blackmail Bottomley for £60,000; Bigland was simply angry with Bottomley for his ingratitude.

COMYNS CARR It appears from the evidence that the scheme for putting questions for Bigland to ask Mr Bottomley was hatched by Mr Elias and Mr Bottomley before Mr Houston came on the scene. Mr Bottomley has stated that he did not authorize Mr Elias to interview Mr Bigland on

> his behalf. I don't like to use harsh expressions, but having regard to the evidence given by his own witness [*Houston*] there is a decided economy of frankness about these answers which Mr Bottomley gave to me in cross-examination.
>
> I venture to suggest that, looking at that incident alone, it shows that Mr Bottomley's evidence is not to be believed, and that he had deliberately set out to deceive you with regard to a very vital and important matter. The whole of the evidence at this point is of a tainted character. It reeks of midnight oil and careful preparation.
>
> I submit that there has been an attempt to use the procedure of your court, not for the bona fide purpose of vindicating justice, but for the purpose, and with the aid of large sums of money . . . and of intimidation, of inciting the defendant to withdraw his attacks and make it appear to the general public as if he were satisfied that there had been no foundation for his charges. . . .
>
> The charge of blackmail has really been brought into the case for the purpose of trying to draw a red herring across the real issues which Bigland desires to have tried.

'Now that I have all the facts before me, I should like to have an opportunity of going through the depositions,' said Sir Chartres Biron. 'I shall announce my decision at eleven o'clock tomorrow morning.'

Sir Ernest Wild was most indignant at the insinuation that the magistrate might decide that the prosecution lacked enough evidence to submit a case against Bigland on which a jury would convict.

On 9 November, Sir Chartres Biron made a long statement in court. He began with Bottomley's charge that Bigland had tried to blackmail him in October 1919. 'The first thing that strikes me about that charge is that it is a stale charge,' said the magistrate. No proceedings were taken by Bottomley for two years and it depended almost entirely on his personal evidence.

'All the facts appear to me to point to the probability that their interview was more in the nature of what Mr Houston suggested in his evidence, and that Bigland . . . thinking that he had some claim on Mr Bottomley for services rendered quarrelled with Mr Bottomley because he wouldn't give him the money.'

The magistrate was very severe on Julius Elias and Henry Houston—and also Bottomley—for trying to 'come to terms' with Bigland after the case had started in court.

'I say at once that all those responsible for the conduct of those negotiations are worthy of, and deserve, the greatest possible blame. It is something very like a conspiracy to defeat the ends of justice.'

He then castigated Bottomley for lying on oath when he denied that he had arranged for Elias to suggest that Bigland should put certain written questions to him in cross-examination. 'He knew that he had written out the very questions in his own handwriting and that Mr Elias had taken them to Bigland,' said Sir Chartres Biron.

'In the face of these facts, after carefully considering the case, and with a true sense of what I am saying, I am unable to believe Mr Bottomley on his oath. I don't believe this blackmail prosecution is an honest and bona fide prosecution. . . . Therefore, upon the charge of threatening to publish libel on Mr Bottomley with a view to extorting money I shall dismiss Bigland.'

However, he decided to commit Bigland for trial at the Shropshire Assizes on a charge of inciting three people to publish libels against Bottomley with a view to extorting money from him.

Bigland made a statement from the dock. He swore that he had never spoken to any one of the prosecution's three witnesses at the Wrekin by-election. He concluded by saying, 'I am determined to expose the wrongs of the thousands of people, most of them poor and ignorant, who have been duped for years by Mr Bottomley, by means of his succession of sweepstakes and lotteries every one of which, I say, has been fraudulently conducted.'

Horatio Bottomley must have left Bow Street with profound regret that he had ever decided to prosecute Reuben Bigland; yet he refused to admit it to his friends and associates. He took

Peggy Primrose out to dinner at Romano's and drowned his sorrows in several bottles of Dry Pommery. He had lost the round to Bigland and had faced a counsel—Comyns Carr—whose cross-examination had put the fear of God into him. But years of adulation from the people, and the gallons of champagne he had imbibed, had made Horatio an incurable optimist who would clutch at any straw. Now he was banking on Bigland's trial for blackmail being tried at the Shropshire Assizes before the Old Bailey trial for libel, and if only Bigland could be convicted of blackmail he would be discredited when he came to face his trial at the Old Bailey. However, his luck was out: Bigland's trial for libel was fixed for hearing at the Old Bailey on 23 January 1922, while the blackmail case did not come on at Shropshire Assizes till February.

In December the Odhams brothers decided to sever their connection with Bottomley and he was retired. Since his contract as editor of *John Bull* ran for life it was arranged to pay him £25,000 compensation. In the shareholders' report they paid tribute to him: 'The loss of a journalist of unique power, a man with gifts of speech and pen fitted to influence great masses of people, has had to be met.'

In the meantime Edward Bell, the solicitor, had been working to try and obtain the evidence he needed for Bigland's defence of his libel at the Old Bailey. Receivers had been called in for the Bond Clubs, and on 10 November he made an appointment to inspect the remaining books and papers still at Bottomley's flat in King Street. When he arrived there Tommy Cox was in charge of operations, his object being to make sure that Bell did not get a sight of a single document. Edward Bell was shown to a room upstairs where the Bond Club Receiver's solicitor and Bottomley's solicitor were sitting together at a long table. Opposite them were various clerks and solicitors and Bell recognized the Bond Clubs' Receiver.

'I have come to inspect the books,' said Edward Bell.

'I represent the plaintiffs,' said the Receiver's solicitor. 'We produce these books to nobody without a consent or agreement, or anything of that kind. I do not know by what authority these books are produced.'

'I have been called here,' said Mr Bottomley's solicitor. 'I have given no authority for the production without an order.'

'Have you got the books?' asked Bell.

The reply was extremely evasive.

'Then you refuse to produce the books,' said Bell, annoyed.

The atmosphere became reminiscent of a comic opera by Gilbert and Sullivan. Everybody spoke at once then during a pause the Receiver's solicitor asked Bell, 'By what authority do you ask the Receiver to produce these books?'

'Under the authority of the subpoena served upon him, and his undertaking, and your letter making this appointment which I now produce,' said Bell.

'The subpoena is dead!' cried the Receiver's solicitor amid general laughter.

Edward Bell said to the Bond Clubs' Receiver, 'I warn you, you have no right to allow these books to remain here. They ought to be in your personal possession and control.'

'Do not answer!' advised the Receiver's solicitor. There was more laughter.

'The meeting closes with the usual vote of thanks,' said the solicitor and everybody roared with laughter.*

Bell left King Street in a huff. Horatio had managed to get a friendly solicitor appointed as Receiver for his Bond Clubs with the result that Bell never obtained a single document from him. Edward Bell then wrote to *Truth* magazine to ask if they would lend him any copies of the Bond Club circulars in their possession, or any letters from Bottomley's victims which they might have in the office. *Truth* replied that as the matter was a criminal prosecution they did not think they were justified in complying with his request. He therefore wrote to the Official Receiver asking for permission to study the Victory Bond papers in his keeping. But he never got a single document because the Receivers of the Bond Club funds had been proposed by Reginald Bate, a solicitor who was as well disposed towards Bottomley as any man in London.

By December Edward Bell began to get desperate: Bigland's libel case was coming up on 23 January. As a last resort he appealed to the three banks in which Bottomley had opened accounts for the Victory Bond Club and his other schemes. The banks gave him permission to see them on 4 January, after he had obtained court orders entitling him to inspect the accounts of the Victory Bond Club and its allied undertakings. Edward Bell and Bigland's other legal advisers went meticulously through every item in the three sets of statements; tracing the complicated financial transactions of Horatio was rather like

* 'Tenax'.

fitting together the pieces of a jigsaw puzzle, but they soon became aware of very large enigmatic withdrawals out of the Victory Club account. By the 23rd they were in a position to produce an accurate account of how Bottomley had manipulated the various *John Bull* funds for his own financial needs.

In his Christmas message to readers of the *Sunday Illustrated* Bottomley had said: 'Woe to him who sits on a pinnacle . . . for verily he shall become a target for mud-throwers.' And in the New Year he told his readers: 'For the third time in my life I am challenging a judicial inquiry into my whole commercial record.' He referred of course to the Hansard Union trial and the Joint Stock Trust trial, from both of which he had been acquitted against all the odds.

Reuben Bigland was tried at the Old Bailey on 23 January before Lord Justice Coleridge for publishing criminally a libellous pamphlet against Bottomley. The latter was represented by Sir Edward Marshall Hall, Bigland was again defended by Arthur Comyns Carr. Bigland had produced seventy-eight witnesses and had filed a plea of justification of the libel containing fifty-seven specific allegations of fact. He pleaded Not Guilty to the indictment and stated that he wished to read his plea of justification.

'The practice is to read the plea after the jury have been sworn,' Lord Coleridge told him.

Marshall Hall asked for the case to be adjourned to enable Bottomley to secure the attendance of certain witnesses vital to the proper presentation of the case before the jury.

'Is this agreed to?' asked Lord Coleridge.

'No, my Lord, by no means,' replied Comyns Carr.

Marshall Hall did his utmost to secure an adjournment of the case because Bottomley desperately wanted to get it postponed as long as possible, knowing that Bigland could justify his libel. 'The difficulty is that I and my friends think it is vital that all the accounts connected with these great undertakings, involving getting on for a million pounds, should not only be investigated, but be properly audited and put before the court,' Marshall Hall submitted.

He told the court that in November everything connected with the matter had been handed over to the Receivers. The prosecution were waiting for copies of the account in order to rebut the charges made against Mr Bottomley by Bigland, who claimed that the Bond Clubs and other affiliated undertakings were fraudulent. 'Even up to the last moment I had hoped that we might be able to get that account, but we have not.' . . . Marshall Hall thought Mr Comyns Carr would have welcomed the production of the books, instead of opposing the application for adjournment.

'If the case is adjourned until a report of these accounts can be properly put before the court . . . I would be prepared to stand or fall by the properly audited and certified report.'

'I oppose the application and ask his Lordship to go on with the trial,' said Comyns Carr. 'The defendant is here at great expense with a large amount of witnesses and a great number of documents to justify his plea. I am ready immediately to proceed to prove his plea of justification.'

Comyns Carr stressed that Bigland had been committed for trial on another charge on 13 February and the present case was due to be tried first. An application for adjourning this case made at the eleventh hour ought not to prejudice his position. He also thought it was highly desirable in the public interest that they should be enlightened about the Bond Clubs and Mr Bottomley's other schemes as soon as possible.

He demolished the prosecution's pretence that they had been hampered because they were waiting for the Receivers to present an account.

'Mr Bottomley has had ample time to prepare the accounts of his own books, and the suggestion that the accounts could not be prepared until the unfortunate people who have been deprived of their money have sent in their claims is only capable of one interpretation. If it is true, it means that the books have been kept in such a contemptible manner that they do not contain any proper record of the clubs' business, in which case they would not help the court at all.

'My accountants and I have inspected the bank accounts of the Victory Bond Club and the other organizations,' continued Comyns Carr. 'They are good enough for me, and I am prepared to go on trial and to invite the jury to judge from them . . . whether very large sums indeed belonging to this organization have been appropriated by Mr Bottomley. . . .'

MARSHALL HALL If his Lordship will agree to an adjournment I will not stand in the way in regard to the costs. . . . As to the case which is coming before the Shropshire Assizes, that is entirely outside this matter. The charges at the Shropshire Assizes are entirely independent of this case. . . .

COMYNS CARR — I absolutely dissent from that.

MARSHALL HALL — As far as I know Mr Bottomley will not even be called in the Shropshire case. Whatever the result of this case, the charges at the Shropshire Assizes will have to be tried.

COMYNS CARR — [*to Lord Coleridge*] My Lord, so closely are the charges at the Shropshire Assizes interrelated that . . . at the Police Court the charges in this case and those at the Shropshire Assizes were taken on one set of depositions, and Mr Bottomley gave a great deal of evidence relating to the Shropshire case.

Lord Coleridge then questioned Comyns Carr on certain points. 'I am willing to proceed with the trial and to prove the plea of justification,' said Comyns Carr.

'I don't think I can refuse this demand,' declared Lord Coleridge.

The charge against Bigland was then read and the jury sworn.

MARSHALL HALL — The prisoner has pleaded Not Guilty. I am not going to assist him by giving him the opportunity to read the fifty-seven counts of his plea. I therefore propose to offer no evidence on the general count. The jury must, of course, find the prisoner Not Guilty.

COLERIDGE, L.J. — [*addressing the jury*] The prosecution intimate that they offer no evidence against the prisoner. Therefore it is your duty to acquit him. Will you kindly do so?

The jury returned a formal verdict of Not Guilty. Bigland was ordered to be discharged. Lord Coleridge ordered that Bottomley should pay the costs of the trial at the Old Bailey and in the Police Court.

Next day *The Times* launched a broadside on Bottomley.

The Bigland Trial

> General surprise was expressed yesterday when it became known that Mr Bottomley had decided to offer no evidence at the Central Criminal Court in his prosecution of Mr Reuben Bigland for an alleged criminal libel in a pamphlet on the Victory Bond Club and similar investment schemes. . . . The words which gave rise to the prosecution were chosen without delicacy. They charged Mr Bottomley with being a swindler, with having gulled persons to invest money, and with being 'one of the greatest crooks ever born'. The reply of the prosecution was a failure to call evidence at the last moment. The public activities of Mr Bottomley make it incumbent on him to meet the moral indictment of his honour which is implied in the abrupt ending of this trial. . . . He owes it to the great numbers of the public who put their trust in him; he owes it to his constituents; he owes it to Parliament. He is astute enough to be aware that the collapse of the prosecution will not be set down to his credit, and that his decision not to call witnesses and his omission to produce accounts will not satisfy public opinion about the duties and obligations of a member of the House of Commons.

Horatio made an attempt to justify his position in his reply to the *Times* leader. In the course of his long letter he said:

> I agree with you that it is incumbent on me 'to meet the moral indictment of my honour which is implied in the abrupt ending of this trial' . . . and I owe this duty 'to the great numbers of the public who put their trust in me, to my constituents, and to Parliament'. Rest assured that I shall not fail to appreciate the unanswerable duty which devolves upon me upon all these points. . . .
>
> I am prepared to stand or fall by the accounts [of the Bond Clubs and other schemes] but that is a very different thing from consenting to have cartloads of legally privileged sewerage thrown at me for several weeks, covering a period of twenty years, comprised in the defendant's plea of justification. . . .

Reuben Bigland inserted notices in various newspapers, appealing for people to send him funds for his defence at the

Shropshire Assizes. Bottomley attempted to defend himself in an article in the *Sunday Illustrated* on 29 January entitled 'The Secret History of the Bigland Case. Why I allowed the Defendant To Go'. It was an unconvincing piece, considering that it came from the pen of a master of plausibility; the best he could do was to promise his readers that when Bigland's trial for blackmail took place in February he would have no difficulty in vindicating himself before the public. Bottomley's article was ruled contempt of court. He, Odhams Press and Sunday Publications were each fined £1,000. Bigland, who was also in contempt of court, was fined £10 for appealing for funds for his trial in the Press.

Bottomley had lost great face with the British public: *he* was really on trial, and not Bigland, and the Shropshire Assizes would present him with his last chance to disprove the accusation that he was 'one of the greatest crooks ever born'.

19 Bigland on Trial (2)

> *Bigland's story has been supported by documents and not contradicted in one single particular. . . . The man who could have contradicted the defendant on a hundred points has used every kind of artifice to keep himself out of the witness-box.*
>
> MR JUSTICE DARLING, at Bigland's prosecution by Bottomley at Shropshire Assizes, February 1922

Reuben Bigland was charged at Shropshire Assizes on 18 February 1922 before Mr Justice Darling on three charges of inciting three people to extort money from Bottomley during the Wrekin by-election. Comyns Carr again defended Bigland, assisted by Mr F. T. Vachell. Cecil Whiteley, K.C., led for the prosecution, assisted by Mr Ronald Powell. The charge was that Bigland approached the three men—Phillips, Swinfield Wells and Harrison—a few days before the poll at Wellington on 20 November 1920.

Cecil Whiteley, opening the case, said that Bigland's defence at the Bow Street proceedings had been that he never spoke to the witnesses.

'If that were true it means that each of the witnesses has deliberately invented the whole thing. The question for the jury to decide is whether they believe the witnesses or not. . . . Mr Bottomley can give no relevant evidence with regard to the indictment, and the prosecution do not intend to put him in the box.'

Thomas Phillips, a concert agent, gave evidence of what Bigland had said to him at the Wrekin by-election.

COMYNS CARR [*cross-examining*] Do you remember my suggestion to you at the Police Court that you have never seen Mr Bigland in your life?

PHILLIPS It was an infamous suggestion.

COMYNS CARR Never mind about that—answer: do you remember?

PHILLIPS Yes. . . . I regarded his threat of flooding the division with pamphlets against Mr Bottomley as very damaging to the interests of General Townshend, the candidate.

Phillips admitted he did not attach much importance to the interview with Bigland till he mentioned it to Bottomley and was told that Bigland had been pestering him.

'I cannot remember specifically what I said to Mr Bottomley,' admitted Phillips.

'It is a funny thing that your evidence has agreed word for word with what you said at Bow Street about what Mr Bigland said at the interview to which you attach no importance—and yet you cannot remember what Mr Bigland said which caused you to attach importance to it!' Comyns Carr remarked.

Phillips said he had not mentioned that Bigland was trying to extort money from Mr Bottomley to Mr Houston, the election agent.

COMYNS CARR Surely that is the important part of it?

WHITELEY [*for the prosecution, to Phillips*] The suggestion is that none of the conversation took place between you and Bigland. What do you say to that?

PHILLIPS Ridiculous, of course.

George Swinfield Wells, a political lecturer, gave evidence of being approached by Bigland to try and extort money from Bottomley.

COMYNS CARR [*cross-examining*] You thought the circulation of pamphlets attacking Bottomley during the election could do a great deal of harm?

S. WELLS Yes.

COMYNS CARR Did you repeat the conversation to the election agent?

S. WELLS I did not come into personal contact with him.

COMYNS CARR Is the election agent so sacred that you couldn't speak to him?

S. WELLS I always regarded the election agent with a good deal of reverence because he was a most important person in winning an election. [*Laughter*]

COMYNS CARR That was all the more reason why you should have reported it? In the Army you never go straight to the Colonel. You deal with your immediate superior. [*Laughter*]

The next witness was John Harrison, the People's Perkins, who said he had reported to Houston that Bigland was in Wellington in November 1920 'breathing blood and fire against Mr Bottomley'. He said to Bigland, 'If you bring your Birmingham chopper mob to my meetings, the Shropshire people will know how to deal with them.'

COMYNS CARR [*cross-examining*] Did you mention it to your speakers, Captain Jeffries and the Reverend Waldron?

HARRISON No. It would have been bad policy to tell them that their meetings might have been interrupted.

DARLING, J. I gather that if you had told Captain Jeffries that the chopper mob was coming from Birmingham he would have run away. [*Laughter*]

COMYNS CARR I suggest that if this really had happened, it would have been your duty to have warned Captain Jeffries and Mr Waldron as to what was likely to occur.

HARRISON There was only one man in my team I would have taken into my confidence. He couldn't speak, but he was very good with his hands. [*Laughter*]

Cecil Whiteley announced that this ended the case for the prosecution.

Comyns Carr was most anxious—as, of course, was his client—to do everything in his power to make Bottomley go into the witness-box, being confident that he could expose him as an arch-swindler under cross-examination.

He submitted that the prosecution case should not have closed until the evidence of the other witnesses called at Bow Street had been called. . . . It would be impossible to have a fair trial unless the evidence on the depositions was before the jury.

'This is a prosecution that involves a man's liberty, not a game of chess,' he declared.

'I have the depositions before me,' said Mr Justice Darling. 'If I am satisfied that it is necessary for the truth of the inquiry to call Mr Bottomley, Mr Houston and Mr Elias, I will do so unhesitatingly. If they are not called for the prosecution they expose themselves to the comment which I have no doubt will be made.'

'It is not suggested that either of the three witnesses were present at the indictment and therefore there is no necessity to call them,' argued Cecil Whiteley, trying to gloss over his weak position.

When Horatio Bottomley returned to his hotel at Shrewsbury after the first day of the trial he told Houston he was very confident of winning the case.

'After today's evidence Bigland is good for eighteen months.'

'Don't be too sure, H.B., there's many a slip, you know.'

While Bottomley was counting his chickens, Reuben Bigland at his hotel was in the depths of depression about the case. As he went in to dinner with his son Walter and a friend, he said gloomily, 'This may be the last for some time.' Bottomley had appeared frequently before Mr Justice Darling and hitherto had always won his cases. Bigland feared that the judge was antagonistic to him and also thought that Bottomley's three perjured witnesses sounded convincing. Reuben was so worried about the outcome that he could not touch a thing at dinner.

'There's only one way for me to secure an acquittal,' he told the other two. 'I must go into the witness-box tomorrow!'

After dinner, although it was late, the three men went to see Comyns Carr. Bigland told him that he had thought things over and had made up his mind to go into the box.

'You'll get a terrible cross-examination from Cecil Whiteley,' Carr warned him.

'Mr Carr, counsel is not yet born who can cause me any trouble if you will only put me in the witness-box, because I have only to speak the truth,' Bigland replied.

In the end Comyns Carr agreed to this course and Bigland returned to his hotel. Julius Elias, who was also staying there, saw him go off to the Assizes next morning and called out to him, 'Good luck, Bigland, good luck! And I mean it!'

There is an enigma about Elias's relations with Bottomley; it is possible that he had only co-operated with Bottomley in some dubious transactions in order to try and protect the good name of *John Bull*, which was an Odhams paper. But after Odhams had severed connection with Bottomley in 1921 the whole situation had changed. Elias felt Bottomley had made a fatal mistake in bringing this case and probably admired Bigland for having the courage to stand up to him.

At the Assizes Comyns Carr outlined the case for the defence. He contended that it was absolute lunacy to suppose that Bigland, who was represented as a cunning blackmailer, would go to three perfect strangers for the purpose of inciting them to blackmail. 'It is the last thing a blackmailer would do!'

He called Reuben Bigland as the first witness for the defence. He asked Bigland what he meant when he sent Bottomley a telegram to Wellington saying, 'I will hand you your £1,000 Bonds to clear my conscience.'

BIGLAND I was mixed up in money matters with Bottomley, and this, to my shame and sorrow, was one of the things I had done which was not straight. In 1918 he persuaded me to balance up an account by being a party to a swindle in what was termed the War Stock Combination. . . .

Bottomley said, 'For the money I owe you [£500] and for services rendered you shall have third prize in the War Stock Combination.' . . . The third prize was £1,000. I agreed to my shame and it was said I had better get a nominee.

COMYNS CARR What were the services you had rendered?

BIGLAND They were for bribing a man named John Greaney, whom Bottomley framed in a case at the Law Courts, which was heard before your Lordship [Darling] and which was a bogus case, the same as this is today. Bottomley agreed with Greaney that he should print a scurrilous pamphlet about him, and Greaney was to be the defendant. It was a pamphlet dealing with law cases in which Mr Bottomley had been concerned. The pamphlet generally was written by a man named Norman. . . . Bottomley said he wanted to get a verdict in the Law Courts to frighten everyone else from doing such a thing. Greaney was merely the figurehead.

DARLING, J. You mean Greaney agreed to lose the action?

BIGLAND Yes, he agreed to put up a nominal defence, so that really Bottomley would only have to address the jury as to damages. [*Laughter*] Bottomley got a verdict for £500 and costs, but really he paid £100 and costs to Mr Greaney.

DARLING, J. I suppose I summed up in his favour, didn't I? [*Laughter*]

BIGLAND . . . Bottomley did not carry out his proper plans. In his beautiful eloquence he addressed the jury in such a style that Greaney was very distressed, and I had to take him out in the passage. [*Laughter*] Later, Bottomley handed me £100 which I gave to Greaney.

Bigland said that another service rendered to Bottomley was in connection with an action brought by a man named Barratt in 1917 against *John Bull*. The paper had offered £1,000 if anyone could prove their 'Bullets' competition was crooked. Barratt claimed he could do this because he had a declaration of fraud from a man named Duos, a former employee of *John Bull*. Duos was paid £200 by Elias to stay out of court and Bigland acted as the go-between. Later, Bottomley and Elias paid Barratt £750 to drop the case.

BIGLAND In September 1918 Bottomley handed me a ticket, saying, 'Here is your £1,000 prize for the War Stock Combination.' . . . My niece was my nominee. I wrote a letter, which she signed, and the prize was sent on. It was simply a plot between Bottomley and myself. No names were published of the winners of the draw.

After reading Bottomley's article in the *Daily Mirror* ['I heard a voice from Heaven and it said, "Write"']—I made up my mind to clear my conscience. I went to Wellington to deliver myself up to justice and hand back the £1,000 War Bonds . . . When I told Mr Bottomley he said, 'I want no £1,000. You owe me nothing.'

Comyns Carr questioned him about his visit to Wellington.

BIGLAND Neither Bottomley nor anybody else stated that I had made any proposal to extort money from him.

Later, Bigland related how he arranged to be arrested 'in unlawful possession of a £500 War Bond' in order to try and get Bottomley to go into the witness-box at Bow Street.

BIGLAND I was discharged at the Police Court against my will.

DARLING, J. You have had no sort of luck. [*Laughter*]

Comyns Carr questioned Bigland closely about the many vicissitudes of his friendship with Bottomley.

BIGLAND I have not at any time attempted to extort money from Bottomley by using my knowledge about him. My only object was to get the people in the Victory Bond Club and the War Stock Combination their just rights.

Bottomley, listening intently in court, must have received one of the greatest shocks of his life when Bigland got up in court and exposed some of his crooked rackets. At last he realized how seriously he had underrated Bigland, the man he was going to 'squash like a fly'. He dared not risk going into the witness-box and facing Comyns Carr again, preferring to gamble on the possibility that his counsel, Cecil Whiteley, would be able to discredit Bigland in cross-examination.

WHITELEY [*cross-examining*] You admit here in the witness box that for some years you have been a willing party to fraud?

BIGLAND I admit I have been a willing party to a fraud with Bottomley to my shame and sorrow.

WHITELEY A fraud relating to a prize your niece won; a fraud relating to the Greaney action and the Duos matter?

BIGLAND Well, not exactly a fraud, but assisting Bottomley's request to do these bad things.

WHITELEY Misleading the court and his Lordship when he tried the case of Greaney—a bogus and collusive action from beginning to end?

BIGLAND Absolutely.

WHITELEY When did your conscience first smite you?

BIGLAND It was always there, but it didn't come to a head. I believe it first came to a head when I read in the *Daily Mirror* his article commencing 'I heard a voice from Heaven say "Write"'.

WHITELEY Then you appreciated you had been mixed up with a fraudulent person?

BIGLAND I appreciated that I had been mixed up with England's greatest humbug and hypocrite.

WHITELEY And which was prominent in your mind—the punishment of England's greatest hypocrite, or the making of a confession in regard to your own misdeeds?

BIGLAND To clear my conscience *and* expose Bottomley. I got locked up to clear my conscience and I have tried to make reparation, but the two £500 Bonds have gone in the expense of the law. I wrote to the Prime Minister and a number of other people wishing to put forward the whole story with regard to these charges I make.

While Cecil Whiteley was questioning Bigland, Bottomley was sitting with his counsel at the solicitors' table and making audible remarks. Comyns Carr interrupted to protest at Bottomley's behaviour.

COMYNS CARR I have been enduring Mr Bottomley's behaviour in this court for a long time, but now I must protest at the way he is endeavouring to prejudice the jury by making audible remarks when he has not the courage to go into the witness-box and make a statement on oath.

DARLING, J. I have seen Mr Bottomley nodding and so on. That must stop! He is not technically a party in these proceedings, and he must not express consent or dissent to what counsel is saying. Mr Bottomley is here merely as a witness. I see he is instructing Mr Whiteley, but it must be done quietly and unobtrusively.

Bigland, re-examined by Comyns Carr, confirmed that he had had an offer of £20,000 from Mr Hooley.

DARLING, J. What was it for?

BIGLAND I was to stand in the dock, fold my arms, and let Mr Bottomley win the case.

WHITELEY [*cross-examining*] What I am suggesting is that, far from Mr Bottomley offering you £20,000, you were writing to Mr Hooley to get the money out of him?

BIGLAND No.

Whiteley had done his best to try and shake Bigland's sensational and damning evidence, but to no avail. The issue was a foregone conclusion, and Bottomley's outrageous behaviour in court can only have prejudiced Mr Justice Darling and the jury against him.

The second witness for the defence was Henry Houston, who had been at the Charlton Hotel, Wellington, when Bigland came to see Bottomley there on 20 November 1920. Houston stated that he had never heard it mentioned that Bigland had tried to extort money from Bottomley.

The Rev. Arthur Waldron, who had been helping General Townshend at the Wrekin by-election, said he knew nothing about Bigland trying to extort money from Bottomley. Richard Clarke, who followed, was the Wellington solicitor who had been present at the interview between Bottomley and Bigland at the Charlton Hotel. He stated that Bigland had said that he owed Bottomley £1,000 but Bottomley said he was not aware of it. Bigland left the hotel without saying any more and there the matter ended.

COMYNS CARR [*addressing the jury*] Mr Bottomley is a general who delivers the attack against Mr Bigland from a place behind the line. He dare not go into the witness-box and face cross-examination. He wants to clear his character by the indirect means of bringing this charge against Mr Bigland. Mr Bottomley's character is one which could do with a coat of whitewash now and again and this is an ingenious method of whitewashing.

Comyns Carr referred to the recent correspondence between Mr Hooley and Bigland, offering Bigland inducements to drop the case. Mr Bottomley realized Mr Bigland would carry out his threat to expose him in public, so he got his private secretary to write to Mr Hooley to say that he (Bottomley) would provide a sea voyage for the benefit of Bigland's health. 'Whose health would have benefited most if Bigland had gone on that sea voyage—Mr Bigland's or Mr Bottomley's?' asked Comyns Carr.

Mr Justice Darling then summed up.

DARLING, J. Mr Bigland has given his explanation of why he was in Wellington and he does not pretend it was with a friendship towards Mr Bottomley that he went there. He asserts that he went there to throw back money which he was

> ashamed to have received under disgraceful circumstances, and from that time to expose Mr Bottomley as 'the greatest humbug in England'.
>
> Mr Carr has done all he can to drive Mr Bottomley into the witness-box, while Mr Whiteley has used every legitimate means to keep Mr Bottomley out. In the Greaney case . . . there was brought about a gross and wicked miscarriage of justice. . . . The stories also of the £1,000 Bonds and the Duos incident were to be part of Bigland's plea of justification at the Central Criminal Court.
>
> When all this has been given in evidence by the defendant, what do you think of Mr Bottomley still remaining silent? It is a wonderful, almost incredible story as told by Bigland and it might have been contradicted in one word by the man who is present and must know whether it is true or not. Bigland's story has been supported by documents and not contradicted in one single particular by the man who could contradict it. Not only that, but the man who could have contradicted the defendant has used every kind of artifice to keep himself out of the witness-box. Not only has he not gone into the witness-box, but he has used all the skill of his counsel to prevent a number of questions being asked which he might have to contradict.

The jury retired at 7.50 p.m. and after only three minutes they returned a verdict of Not Guilty. Bigland was discharged and Bottomley was ordered to pay the costs of the action.

Bigland and his son, Walter Bigland, caught the 8.20 train from Shrewsbury to Birmingham. The evening papers had just come out with the news that he had been acquitted at Shropshire Assizes and he was given a hero's welcome at the station.

It was a very different story for Bottomley; public opinion had turned right against him as a result of the trial. On Monday

20 February, *The Times* had another leader about him which reflected the views of most people in the country.

> *The Second Bigland Trial*
>
> Once again Mr Horatio Bottomley, M.P., has decided not to enter the witness-box and make answer to the charges of gross fraud preferred against him by Mr Bigland. In the case which ended on Saturday, Mr Bigland was indicted on a charge of inciting three persons to extort money from Mr Bottomley and the defendant made accusations which, in spite of his own confession of fraud, the public must think require an immediate reply. . . .
>
> After the trial at the Central Criminal Court we suggested that it was Mr Bottomley's duty as a member of the House of Commons to find an opportunity to allay the comments and, indeed, to dispel the general reflections on his conduct which were on every lip. It was expected that at the Shropshire Assizes he would have welcomed the opportunity. . . .
>
> He has only himself to blame if rumour and gossip seek to play havoc with his name as a public man who has had the confidence of large classes of the people, and who has been described by Mr Justice Sargant as a trustee for the subscribers—many of them poor people—to the Victory Bond Club and similar investment schemes. Whatever may be said in criticism of his accuser, Mr Bottomley must realize that he cannot in honour permit unchallenged the publication of statements that prizes in competitions conducted by him, or his agents, were corruptly awarded and that he used the process of the King's Courts in a collusive suit.

A few days later Bottomley was summoned by the Director of Public Prosecutions to appear at Bow Street on 8 March on a charge of fraudulently converting £5,000 of Victory Bond Club funds to his own use. He wrote a farewell article in the *Sunday Illustrated* on 26 February in which he told his readers that he had decided to drop all his journalistic and political activities in order to concentrate on his own case. He asked his friends to suspend judgment while he took up the gauntlet in defence of his honour, and included one of his favourite Shakespearean quotations:

My honour and my life are one
Take honour from me and my life is done.*

Horatio Bottomley was nearly sixty-two and his health had started to break up; he was on the brink of ruin and yet acted as if he was invincible. He summoned an accountant to The Dicker to go thoroughly into his financial position. After lunch he retired to the stables and the accountant waited patiently for his return. He came back hours later and never spoke a word about his finances for the rest of the day. Right up to the last moment he remained ridiculously optimistic.

'Several members of the Cabinet won't allow me to be prosecuted,' he assured his friends.

On the first day of the Police Court proceedings at Bow Street he made highly complimentary remarks about Travers Humphreys, K.C., who was prosecuting him. The sequel was that Humphreys had a message that Horatio would like to see him alone in a private room for five minutes. Humphreys agreed to see him, but took the precaution of taking his clerk with him as a witness. At their interview Bottomley made two requests to him.

First, would he arrange to have an adjournment at 11.30 every day to enable Bottomley to drink a pint of champagne? Bottomley by this time ate practically nothing and could not get on without champagne, calling it his medicine. Humphreys consented on condition that the magistrate was notified.

The second request concerned the sum of £1,000 which had been transferred from a Victory Bond account at Covent Garden to an account at the same bank in the name of 'a certain lady who has been very good to me'. The lady, of course, was Peggy Primrose. Humphreys chivalrously promised to keep her name out of the proceedings, and instead he would allege that the money had been transferred to Bottomley's private account at this bank.

It was inevitable that Bottomley was committed for trial to the Old Bailey. As soon as the news came out his creditors pounced and sold up his flat in King Street. Nearly every stick of furniture was removed and his beautiful dining-room was soon stripped bare. All the brokers left him was a small bed in his bedroom and, to make matters worse, his telephone was cut off.

* A typical misquotation: the first line should be: 'Mine honour is mine life; both grow in one'.

When his solicitor called to see him, he was sitting at a borrowed card table in a bare room with only two wooden chairs. He greeted him cheerfully and invited him to sit down. At eleven o'clock he opened a bottle of wine and produced two glasses. He was living in a fantasy and behaved just as if he was still sitting in his opulent drawing-room without a care in the world.

20 The Mighty Fallen

> *Your crime is aggravated by your high position, the number and poverty of your victims, by the trust which they reposed in you and which you abused. It is aggravated by the magnitude of your frauds, and by the callous effrontery with which they were committed and sought to be defended.*
>
> MR JUSTICE SALTER, *sentencing Bottomley at the Old Bailey, May 1922*

The trial of Horatio Bottomley opened at the Old Bailey before Mr Justice Salter on 19 May 1922, on a charge of fraudulently converting to his own use sums of money entrusted to him by members of the public for investment in the Victory Bond Club, the War Stock Combination and other funds. Bottomley defended himself and appeared in person. Travers Humphreys, K.C., led for the prosecution and Carter and Bell were solicitors for the Crown. Travers Humphreys was noted for his extreme fairness and his remarkable grasp of figures; he had the great gift of making the most complicated case clear to a jury. He had already appeared in many famous criminal trials, including those of Crippen, the Seddons, Sir Roger Casement and Hobbs (the 'Mr A' case).

Mr Justice Salter was known in the legal world as 'Drysalter' on account of his arid manner. He was a quiet, clear-headed, unemotional lawyer who refused to be hurried or bamboozled in his cases, the very worst kind of a judge for Bottomley. In the past Horatio had scored his triumphs by bluffing and play-acting, but Salter was not at all impressed by forensic tricks.

There were twenty-four counts in the indictment. When Bottomley was asked how he pleaded he replied, 'Most decidedly not guilty.' While conducting his defence he was allowed to sit at the solicitors' table in order to consult his advisers.

'The indictment refers to four separate schemes—the War Stock Combination, the Victory Bond Club, the Thrift Prize Bond Club and the Victory Club Derby Sweepstake 1920,' said Travers Humphreys.

He began by outlining the War Stock Combination scheme. Bottomley had received over £80,000 from subscribers to this fund and he actually bought £80,000 National War Bonds. But he did *not* lodge them with trustees, 'although Mr Bottomley's position in the circumstances was not less than that of a trustee'. The prosecution alleged that he fraudulently converted £10,000 of the securities by giving Mr Howard, a stockbroker, £10,000 National War Bonds to pay off a Stock Exchange debt incurred in 1912.

'That £10,000 he converted to his own use, and no human being could doubt that he did so fraudulently,' declared Travers Humphreys. 'He was a trustee and had no more right to use the money for his own purpose than a solicitor has a right to use his client's money which he is holding as a trustee.

'Bottomley also paid £7,500 of the same security to John Bull Investment Trust. This money was used for his own purposes and benefit directly in violation of his promise, and the undertaking upon which the money had been subscribed.'

The Victory Bond Club was launched in 1919. In July and August Bottomley paid £421,000 for War Bonds with a nominal value of £500,000. On 30 September he needed £41,500 to complete the purchase of two newspapers—the *National News* and the *Sunday Evening Telegraph*. On the security of £100,000 War Bonds Mr A. S. Cohen, a solicitor, arranged for his bank to loan the money to Bottomley. On 23 October the solicitor's bank sold £75,000 Bonds for Bottomley in order to reduce the bank loan and Bottomley received the balance of the money in £1,000 notes: £14,000 of this sum had been traced to various Bottomley accounts. The remaining £30,000 Bonds were put into his private account at Williams Deacon's Bank, while he still had £38,000 of Victory Bond Club funds in cash at the Covent Garden branch of the London City and Midland Bank. The prosecution alleged that he used all this money for his private purposes: £5,000 for the upkeep of his horses at Ostend, £1,000 for the supply of champagne; and £25,000 was traced to his private Northern Territory account.

Travers Humphreys dealt next with the Thrift Prize Bond Club, advertised by Bottomley as 'a unique chance to help our French Allies, and at the same time to win a fortune'. A total of £200,000 received from subscribers went into a French banking account. Eventually the Victory Bond Club was merged with the Thrift Prize Bond Club and all the books were sent to Paris.

In 1920 he drew out from the Victory Bond Club account £5,000 for Mr Elliott, his brother-in-law; over £15,000 to pay for the German submarine *Deutschland* which *John Bull* had exhibited all over the country; £8,180 to purchase some *John Bull* shares; £7,000 for racing expenses; £2,000 for his niece to buy a house; and £1,650 for shares in a hotel at Worthing. On 16 July 1920 he drew out the rest of the War Bonds and deposited them in his private account at the Crédit Lyonnais. All of them were sold to repay club subscribers who were clamouring for their money back; no books of the club were handed over to the Receivers and there was no regular audit. Bottomley was the only trustee.

Travers Humphreys sat down after speaking for four hours. The prosecution called several witnesses who had subscribed to the War Stock Combination and the Victory Bond Club. Bottomley cross-examined them, but failed to shake their evidence. George Howard, a stockbroker, confirmed that Bottomley had settled up his 1912 Stock Exchange debt with a £10,000 National War Bond. Walter James, assistant in the Inspectors' Department at the head office of the London Joint City & Midland Bank, confirmed that £400,000 War Bonds were withdrawn from Bottomley's account and confirmed that he had paid various private sums from this account of the Covent Garden branch on 16 June 1920.

A. S. Cohen, a solicitor, gave evidence that he had arranged a temporary loan for Bottomley of £41,500 for the purchase of the *National News* and the *Sunday Evening Telegraph*. Bottomley gave him £100,000 Victory Bonds as security for the bank and later authorized him to sell £75,000 Bonds which realized £57,800. Mr Cohen had never heard of the Victory Bond Club when Bottomley handed the bonds to him.

C. A. Jalama, a wine-merchant in the Strand, admitted that he had supplied Bottomley with champagne costing £1,050.

BOTTOMLEY [*cross-examining*] Was not the champagne purchased for a small syndicate?

JALAMA I think it was.

BOTTOMLEY I don't want you to think that I drank it all. [*Laughter*]

Charles Owen, a stockbroker, stated that between 1920 and 1921 his firm sold, on written instructions from Bottomley, War Bonds of a total nominal value of £397,000. There was a loss of £37,000 on their purchase price owing to the depression of the market. The prosecution then called witnesses to establish that Bottomley had paid £2,000 for a racing account to Weatherbys; £5,000 to the liquidator of the Joint Stock Trust; and £2,000 to his niece for a new house at Richmond. Charles Urquhart, chartered accountant, gave evidence about the Receivers' investigations on behalf of the Bond Clubs.

BOTTOMLEY [*cross-examining*] Assuming a club of a million members, would you have done the necessary work of keeping their books for £5,000?

URQUHART Yes, I would have done quite well out of it.

BOTTOMLEY And if, before the club was a week old, 50,000 people were clamouring for their money back, because they were out of work or for other reasons, that would require a large staff?

Bottomley opened his defence by claiming that he could call a hundred thousand witnesses who had bought his Victory Bonds and had their money back. This was his method of trying to discredit the prosecution for calling only twenty-two people who had subscribed to the Bond Clubs.

'There are few ordeals more trying than for a man to sit practically silent . . . while all kinds of charges are being hurled at his head by counsel for the prosecution,' he said, addressing the jury. 'So you have the accusation made against me, which, if true, stamps me as a hypocrite of the deepest dye. You may have entertained a high opinion of me and thought that, whatever my faults in days gone by, I have endeavoured to do my duty as a citizen to my King and country.'

Bottomley complained that Travers Humphreys had distorted the facts to make it sound as if all the capital of the Bond Clubs had disappeared. The truth was that £25,000 had been handed in to the Receivers and there had been a loss of £37,000 on the depreciation of the Victory stock which he had been forced to sell to repay the subscribers.

'The only question for the jury is, have I fraudulently dealt with the funds and securities of these clubs?' he contended. 'You have got to find that I had the intention to steal the money of poor devils such as ex-soldiers who subscribed to these clubs. You have got to find that Horatio Bottomley, editor of *John Bull*, the man who wrote and spoke throughout the war with the sole object of inspiring the troops and keeping up the morale of the country, went out to the front to do his best to cheer up the lads —you have got to find that that man intended to steal their money. God forbid!'

He said that the Victory Bond scheme kept him working day and night. He had engaged a hundred ex-servicemen* at £1 a day to help him and he had personally paid them £15,000.

'If I can prove I was paying out much larger sums than I received, then there is an end to all fraud. That was what was done.'

He said he had approached well known men to act as trustees† but none of them would take on the responsibility. So he was forced to act as sole trustee and manager of the club. 'I hold myself accountable for every penny that came into my hands,' he declared. 'So long as I can do that, there is no fraud.

'I will show the jury not only that I have not had the money belonging to the clubs, but I will show them how much I have spent,' he promised. 'During 1920 and 1921 I received £200,000 in connection with the conversion of my business in journalistic enterprises and other things. Every penny of that money has gone to the clubs.'

He explained to the jury that there was a run on the clubs in the summer of 1921 owing to Bigland's pamphlets, which had flooded the country. 'From that day forward everybody became alarmed; everybody wanted their money back and we simply could not do it.'

* Bottomley had only twelve clerks working at one time on the Victory Bond Club tickets, according to Houston. 'A hundred clerks' was a figment of his imagination.

† It would have been more convincing if he had mentioned at least one of the public men by name. 'He was already so discredited that no man of repute would act as a trustee.' (Sir Chartres Biron.)

'I shall satisfy you, I hope, that so far from robbing these clubs, they spelt my financial ruin.* I hope to satisfy you, if they were the last words to pass my lips, that I am incapable of robbing an ex-soldier,' he stated dramatically.

'If you were to find me guilty on this indictment, it would be a shock to the conscience of the community—a shock to every man who fought for his country! I do not run away . . . and if you thought me guilty, no word would come from me for mercy, although it could not alter the fact that I was innocent. I would not demean myself nor humiliate myself by asking for mercy.'

At this stage Bottomley was trembling with excitement and emotion. 'I wish you could realize what the last three years have been to me,' he told the jury, appealing for their sympathy. 'It is a marvel that I am standing here!'

He burst into tears and continued almost in a whisper: 'I tell you there are times in the silent hours of the night when I think of all I have endeavoured to do to wipe out my sordid past and to justify the confidence of the fighting man, moments when the trouble has been overwhelming.'

Bottomley resumed his seat and wiped away the tears. Continuing his defence, he said he would try to satisfy the jury that he had refunded £384,000 of Victory Bond Club funds, and in addition £86,140 had been paid out of club funds which were transferred to Paris. There were also a sum of £37,000, for the depreciation of the £500,000 Stock, and his total expenses for running the clubs. He claimed that all these items greatly exceeded the amount received from the Victory Bond Club subscribers.

'I am over £50,000 out of pocket in the matter,' he said. 'We have paid many certificates two or three times over. Something like £200,000 came to me in 1921 . . . and I used it to an enormous extent for the purpose of repaying members of the club.'

'I have never endeavoured to make one penny piece, and I swear that I have never had a penny out of it. I swear before God that I have never fraudulently converted a penny of the Club's money,' he concluded.

Bottomley had made a typical emotional appeal to the jury,

* This disarming and sentimental appeal to the jury, which was a complete lie, had also been used by Bottomley at the Hansard and Joint Stock Trust trials.

but somehow it lacked conviction. Then Travers Humphreys began his cross-examination; it was a masterly performance, which gradually demolished the flimsy edifice of Bottomley's defence.

HUMPHREYS When did you make up your mind to use £10,000 of the bonds to pay your debt to Mr Howard?

BOTTOMLEY I had advanced £20,000 to the club and took stock of that value in settlement.

HUMPHREYS Did you tell your subscribers that you had used £10,000 worth of these War Bonds in order to pay your private debts?

BOTTOMLEY No and it would have been an absolute lie had I done so. They were my bonds!

HUMPHREYS They were the bonds of this club?

BOTTOMLEY They were my bonds. I am not going to be tricked into a silly admission. I lent the club £20,000 about the time it was formed and I took War Bonds in payment of that advance.

Later, Bottomley was cross-examined about the annulment of his bankruptcy:

HUMPHREYS You were anxious to get your bankruptcy annulled?

BOTTOMLEY I was, in order to be in time for the election.

HUMPHREYS Therefore you handed over to the Official Receiver £11,000 of these National War Bonds.

BOTTOMLEY Yes.

HUMPHREYS Did that stock belong to you?

BOTTOMLEY Yes, that was the first question the Official Receiver put to me. I told the Official Receiver all about it.

HUMPHREYS What was the total amount due to you at the time from the club?

BOTTOMLEY Altogether about £11,000 at this time.

HUMPHREYS How convenient it was that the club should owe you the amount you required to pay the Official Receiver!

BOTTOMLEY How natural it was!

Bottomley stated that he believed that £50,000 War Bonds were sold in the last quarter of 1919.

HUMPHREYS What did you do with the proceeds?

BOTTOMLEY . . . The proceeds were paid into my private account at the Crédit Lyonnais.

HUMPHREYS Don't you think the Victory Bond Club's bankers would have been the best trustees?

BOTTOMLEY My bankers laughed at the idea of becoming trustees. Much against my will, I was left as sole trustee and without the assistance of auditors.

Bottomley claimed that there was nothing in the Victory Bond Club circular to stop him from paying for stamping, clerks, printing, etcetera, so he drew a cheque for these expenses. He admitted that he withdrew £25,000 from the club accounts because he thought the police were trying to seize the money and the bonds.

HUMPHREYS Was it necessary to spend it after drawing out the money?

BOTTOMLEY I had spent that money over the club and I was entitled to spend it as I liked.

Bottomley stated that in 1919 he had an income of £25,000 a year, but by the middle of 1920 it was £40,000 a year. In addition he had £100,000 capital when the *John Bull* Company was transferred to Odhams. However, Travers Humphreys quoted from an affidavit which Bottomley swore in May 1920, giving his income at about £11,000 a year subject to certain liabilities.

HUMPHREYS In the May 1920 affidavit the figure of £11,000 is hardly Mr Bottomley's figure of £40,000 a year. I take it that the statements of fact in the affidavit are correct?

BOTTOMLEY I think so.

Bottomley was then cross-examined about the meeting he held of members of the Victory Bond Club at the Cannon Street Hotel in January 1920.

HUMPHREYS Did you tell them that £100,000 out of the £500,000 War Bonds had gone?

BOTTOMLEY I told them that I had dealt with £100,000 at 82 [points] . . .

HUMPHREYS There is a statement that the stock should be held by the bankers in the club's name. Yet you transferred the stock to your own private account at the Crédit Lyonnais and sold out by February 1921?

BOTTOMLEY It is quite true that it was all sold out by 1921.

HUMPHREYS Is that practically the same as remaining with the club's bankers?

BOTTOMLEY It couldn't remain there if members were demanding their money back.

Almost every question Humphreys asked had a deadly purpose: to destroy the credibility of Bottomley; it was a remarkable feat to keep Bottomley on the defensive all the time. By hammering home damning facts about Bottomley, Humphreys succeeded in cancelling out his great emotional sway over a jury.

Travers Humphreys cross-examined him about the Victory Bond Club draw which was supposed to take place before a French notary. Bottomley explained that the French authorities would not allow it.

HUMPHREYS Did the draw ever take place?

BOTTOMLEY There was one drawing in London at 26, King Street. It took place on a Saturday afternoon when everything was quiet.

HUMPHREYS Was it before a French notary?

BOTTOMLEY No, he was not represented. . . . We couldn't get anyone. I presided at the draw.

Travers Humphreys produced a cheque dated 23 April 1920, drawn in payment of the prizes totalling £7,000 according to Bottomley.

HUMPHREYS I suggest that part of the proceeds of the cheque went into another person's account which was sometimes used for betting purposes?

BOTTOMLEY It may have been, but everyone was paid.

Bottomley admitted that all the amounts mentioned in the indictment had been drawn for his own purposes, but these amounts were owing to him as he had advanced large sums to the club.

Travers Humphreys remarked that Bottomley, on opening his defence, had alluded to his patriotic services.

HUMPHREYS Were you paid for your patriotic speeches during the war?

BOTTOMLEY Never a farthing for my recruiting meetings, but, later on, as lecturer, I got certain remuneration, nearly every penny of which, if you force me to say it, I gave away to wounded soldiers in towns I went to.

HUMPHREYS Did you make considerable sums through your patriotic lectures at music halls?

BOTTOMLEY They were not 'patriotic' lectures, but lectures on the war. I was a bankrupt at the time and had to get my living.

Travers Humphreys produced correspondence between Bottomley and Farrows Bank, to whom he owed £5,000. In September 1915 he wrote them a letter mentioning his special addresses on the war.

HUMPHREYS [*reading*] 'A large percentage of receipts are paid to me . . . the average receipts for some months past have been between £300 and £400 a week.'

In a later letter to Farrows Bank you wrote: 'My proposal is that your Bank should advance me £3,000 repayable at £200 weekly, taking a first charge upon the lecture receipts referred to in my previous letter.'

So the war did you pretty well, after all?

BOTTOMLEY No, it did not . . . after a time receipts began to fall. Out of these receipts, every time I went to a town I left at a local hospital a substantial portion of my receipts for the wounded soldiers* . . .

On four days a week, day and night, I travelled at my own expense on recruiting, and when cheques were sent in I always returned them. When I spoke of work in the war I was referring to my recruiting meetings and not professional lectures. I think it is rather unfair to introduce this.

Travers Humphreys completed his cross-examination of Bottomley, of which the most damaging feature was probably the debunking of his much-heralded patriotic war work. Horatio was betrayed by his letters to Farrows Bank in which he stated that he was making hundreds a week from his patriotic lectures. We know from Henry Houston that he gave over 340 paid patriotic lectures and under forty recruiting speeches during the war, so he could rarely if ever have made four recruiting speeches a week, as he stated.

The first witness for the defence was Ernest Hill, former manager of the Paris branch of Thomas Cook's, who became manager of the Victory Bond Club in Paris in 1921. Hill's statement showed that he had refunded Victory Bond Club certificates to the value of £473,883, and there were also expenses of £40,000. He concluded that after the two Bond

* Although Bigland had urged Bottomley to give his lecture earnings to the wounded soldiers, there is no record of his doing so; he was lying to counsel.

Clubs had merged they owed Bottomley £19,000. Travers Humphreys opened his cross-examination by handing up an account book to Hill.

HUMPHREYS Were those entries not all made on the same day?

HILL [*to Justice Salter, angrily*] I don't know anything about English courts, my Lord, but counsel would not dare to ask such a question in France!

SALTER, J. It is quite a proper question.

HILL Certainly they were not. Do you wish to insinuate that I am faking the books?

HUMPHREYS I suggest as clearly as possible that entries of Victory Bond payments on one page in that book were written at the same time?

HILL I signed them as I received them.

HUMPHREYS You say you are personally incapable of making a false entry in a book?

HILL Certainly.

Travers Humphreys quoted a letter written by Hill to Thomas Cook, his former employer in Paris, on 14 August 1920.

> A stupid suggestion was made, and I, in a weak moment, agreed to show an incorrect balance so that you should not ask questions. I am ashamed and heartily sorry that I should have stooped so low as to do such a dishonourable act, and I beg you to forgive me.

Hill explained that one of Cook's employees had made out a balance-sheet incorrectly and he signed it and had to 'take the racket'.

SALTER, J. You signed the balance-sheet thinking it correct, and when you found it was not, you allowed your signature to stand, and did not tell your employers?

HILL Precisely.

HUMPHREYS And they discharged you for it?

HILL I fought them in the French courts. . . .

HUMPHREYS I suggest there are thousands of people still waiting for their money, although they have sent in their certificates.

BOTTOMLEY You have no right to make that suggestion.

HILL At the present time, I think there is something like £150,000 due to members, but these accounts are in the hands of the Receivers.

BOTTOMLEY [*re-examining Hill*] It has been suggested that one page in your notebook is a fake, and that the entries were all made at one time. Is there an atom of foundation for that suggestion?

HILL No, it is infamous.

Travers Humphreys had established that Ernest Hill was a weak character who had agreed to 'fiddle the books' at Thomas Cook's and had been sacked, and the implication was that Bottomley engaged him because he knew that in order to keep his job he would carry out instructions even if they were unethical.

Bottomley's next witness was Arthur Newton, an accountant, who said he vouched for the accuracy of Mr Hill's books of the clubs in Paris. Mr Clewett, secretary of a limited company, confirmed that £3,500 had been repaid to his syndicate of small subscribers to the Bond Clubs. Mr Symes, chief accountant of the National Provincial and Union Bank, Piccadilly Branch, confirmed that Bottomley had paid out about £38,000 to small Bond Club subscribers. Mr James, assistant inspector of the London Joint City and Midland Bank, who was recalled, estimated that Bottomley had paid out £76,000 to small subscribers.

H. V. Reed, Bottomley's pay clerk since August 1919, said he had paid out an average of £300 a day when certificates were surrendered and there was a run on the Victory Bond Club. Bottomley had given him £500 a day for this purpose.

Bottomley rose to make his closing speech to the jury on the seventh day of the trial.

'You can't possibly say I am guilty unless, beyond any reasonable doubt, you are satisfied that I "had the intention of stealing moneys and funds from these Clubs",' he declared. 'I cannot emphasize too strongly your prerogative in answering that question. It is the only security for every citizen in this country.'

He assured the jury that he was pleading for his liberty and practically for his life. He alleged that Travers Humphreys was biased against him and quoted Mr Justice Hawkins, who had once said, 'I hate to see animus on the part of Crown counsel.'

He submitted that Mr Hill had paid out £185,000 Victory Bonds in Paris, then there were also the large sums paid out to subscribers in England. 'If you add £37,000 for depreciation of the stock and any reasonable sum for expenses you will find every penny subscribed to these clubs has been accounted for,' he contended.

'£218,000 fraudulently converted by me!' he said scornfully. . . . 'Why did I want to convert fraudulently? . . . In the autumn of 1919 I had £60,000 in cash in my safe and I said I could prove where it came from.'

He tried hard to nullify the effect made by Travers Humphrey when he produced an affidavit stating that Bottomley's income was only 'eleven thousand a year'. According to Horatio this affidavit showed he had already received £30,000 on account from Colonel Grant Mordern and other sums had come to him later. 'So we have the position in 1920—I had about £200,000 of my own money and a vastly increased income owing to journalism and other undertakings.

'Two hundred thousand pounds!' he cried, thumping the table. 'And £218,000 stolen from the clubs!* I must have nearly half a million hidden away somewhere, yet I am hounded by bankruptcy petitions and claims are coming in every day. . .

'You are trying a public man for something dearer than life and . . . there is a phrase in Shakespeare which I will venture to apply to myself:

My honour and my life are one,
Take honour from me and my life is done.†

* There is a desperation about his speech at this point. He was repeating the 'big lie' about his £200,000 to the jury, hoping to bludgeon them into believing it.

† See note, p. 251.

'That is the spirit in which we are meeting face to face,' he continued. 'Friends have been saying to me, "What arrangements have you been making in case everything goes wrong?" My arrangements have been made. Things won't go wrong. If things go wrong, it would be the most appalling error of justice the world has ever known.'

Later, he suggested that the jury might treat his case as a special one. 'You will say: Bottomley may have been reckless, daring and unconventional: he may have treated these clubs as mere children of his own: he may have mixed one thing with another, but he has not stolen this money.

'Why a man with £200,000 of his own and a huge income would want to rob poor soldiers of these clubs passes my understanding. . . . I cannot stand and look you in the face if there is an atom of justification in these charges. I won't want my liberty if I have done such a thing. I don't want my life if I have done such a thing . . . and the sooner my life is wiped out the better I will like it.

'Even if the terrible verdict of Guilty came from your lips tonight, I still believe something would happen to undo it. . . . I will ask you on the evidence to say I have paid on behalf of these clubs more than I received, and that at no time when I drew a penny piece from those accounts was I in need of money. . . .

'The suggestion that I made a good thing out of the war is the most ingenious thing I have ever known,' he said indignantly. 'From the time war broke out I was four days a week travelling all night, and always at my own expense. I recruited more men for the British Army than all the other recruiting interests put together!'

Bottomley referred to the account he had to pay the Official Receiver in 1918 in order to get his bankruptcy annulled.

'Will you believe that I am such a clumsy thief as to take £7,500 worth of stolen Bonds to the high official of the High Courts of Justice and the Board of Trade? As a rule, a man who steals a five-pound note doesn't take it to a policeman to be changed!'*

Speaking with great passion he said: 'I will not trust myself to make an emotional appeal to you. . . . I suggest that I have killed this case. . . . You will never convict me. The jury is not yet born who will convict me of these charges. It is unthinkable!'

* But this is exactly what Horatio Bottomley had done, in his desperation to pay off his debts and get back to Parliament.

Pointing to the sword hanging over the judge's chair, he declared, 'That sword of Justice would drop from its scabbard if you gave a verdict of Guilty against me. I say it with a clear conscience.

'If you were unanimous in convicting me let me say this: I will bear you no ill will. I should know you said it because you thought it was true. But . . . knowing the truth in this matter, without one atom of hesitation, one atom of fear, I shall in due course take my place where thieves and felons and murderers have stood—but where also innocent men have stood—and know—by the Mercy of God and the spirit of justice, you will liberate me from this ordeal.'

Horatio, very moved, sat down after speaking for an hour and a half, and members of the jury were also very moved by his second onslaught on their emotions. However, the Gods seem to have deserted Horatio in his hour of need: he completed his speech on a Friday afternoon and the impact of his words had been lost on the jury by the time his trial was resumed on the following Monday.

Travers Humphreys began his closing speech on the Friday and did not conclude it until after the week-end. Based on facts and logic, it was entirely lacking in 'frills'; it could hardly have been a greater contrast to Bottomley's address to the jury.

HUMPHREYS One of the things you will have to consider is: 'Are you prepared to believe this defendant on his oath when his evidence is entirely uncorroborated, or are you not?' Many of the most vital things that Mr Bottomley has said in his evidence are things which depend on his statement of the facts, and you cannot find either in documents or in the evidence of other witnesses one iota of evidence to corroborate them.

If the defendant, or trustee of these clubs, has used them sometimes without informing the subscribers, done it in violation of the terms on which he has received them, it would be possible to argue whether this was fraudulent conversion. Of course it was! Mr Bottomley so cleverly concealed his movements in regard to the War Stock Combination that the prosecution would never have traced it had it not been

> for the admissions of the defendant [Bigland] during his cross-examination in the Bigland case.
>
> If Mr Bottomley's speech appealed to the jury they will show it by their verdict, but if facts and evidence appeal to them there never was a clearer case of fraudulent misuse of securities. The difference between the prosecution and the defence is that the prosecution have proved their figures, while the defendant has suggested his. We have proved that the trustee* within twelve months of the commencement of his trust—from June 1919 to June 1920—had £101,000 in cash out of the Trust, and that he had £57,000 which he got in cash by using the Allotment Letter. I have pointed out that up to June 1920 the defendant had taken out of the coffers of the Victory Bond Club for his own purposes nearly £100,000, quite apart from the use he made of the Allotment Letter.

'Can you accept Mr Bottomley's statement that he supplied during the period £60,000 for the purposes of the club?' demanded Humphreys. 'It certainly did not come out of the banking accounts. . . . No one doubted that very large sums had been repaid to the subscribers.'

During the week-end Bottomley appeared confident that the jury would acquit him. He went to the Billy Wells versus Frank Goddard boxing match on Saturday afternoon and then drove home to The Dicker. On Sunday he saturated himself with champagne from nine o'clock in the morning. During the day he saw Jimmy Hare, his trainer, and told him he expected to get off on Monday afternoon.

'Are you sure, Guv'nor?' Hare asked.

'Oh, I'll be all right, Jimmy. The telephone will ring about two o'clock to tell you I've been acquitted,' replied Horatio.

On Sunday night he motored up to town and had dinner with Peggy Primrose, who was surprised that he was so confident about his prospects. Yet he must have realized that his

* This refers to Bottomley's trusteeship of the Victory Bond Club.

only hope of being acquitted was in the unlikely event of Mr Justice Salter's summing up in his favour. . . .

After Travers Humphreys had concluded his speech for the prosecution on Monday, Bottomley took his seat in the dock and prepared to listen to Mr Justice Salter summing up.

'The charge is not that the defendant mismanaged his clubs, but that he fraudulently converted to his own use moneys entrusted to him and that he did that on twenty-three different occasions,' Mr Justice Salter began.

The Judge said that in order to establish Bottomley's guilt the prosecution needed to prove three things: 'The first is that he received the money on behalf of others; the next that he in fact converted the sum in question in each case to his own use; and, thirdly, that when he did that he did it dishonestly and fraudulently, knowing at the time that he was doing a dishonest thing. He might well have hoped to repay the money. No errand boy who stole out of the till but hoped, by some lucky chance, to be able to repay it.'

SALTER, J. The onus of proof on these three things is on the prosecution. If, in any of these cases, the prosecution fail to satisfy the jury of these three things, it is the duty of the jury to acquit the defendant. If the prosecution has satisfied them, it is their duty to convict. . . .

What the jury have to determine is, whether or not the defendant fraudulently appropriated to his own use certain sums of money. . . . A trustee might be justified in removing funds to a safe place, but not in putting them in his own pocket. The difference is that the money was owing to Mr Bottomley and therefore he thought he was justified in what he did. The all-important question is this great indebtedness to the defendant on the part of the clubs, or whether he might have thought there was much indebtedness. . . .

Mr Justice Salter resumed his summing up after lunch.

SALTER, J. . . . In Mr Bottomley's evidence he said he had in his bedroom in King Street a chest containing £60,000 in small change and that some of the payments [to club subscribers] had been made out of that chest. . . . The defendant has been at pains to show that he expended large sums in paying people out. . . . But he had £60,000 of money and bonds out of which to pay. . . . The money has all gone, except £23,000 which the Receivers took over, and no one will doubt that the bulk of the money has properly gone in repaying people. . . . The defendant had these large sums of money out of which to pay it all. The question is, Did he pay it out of his own pocket? Where is the evidence, except for his own statement, that he ever put his hand in his pocket to pay out a single person?

BOTTOMLEY [*interrupting*] I told you, my Lord, in evidence—£55,000 *John Bull* shares—

Bottomley mentioned other items, but he was inaudible. He could sense that the summing-up was going against him, and this was a desperate attempt to gain the sympathy of the jury.

'I don't wish to be interrupted,' said the judge sharply. 'If these great sums of money came from the source just referred to by the defendant, where are the documents, where are the receipts? There is such a thing as a stupid muddle in keeping of accounts, but there is such a thing as a clever muddle and an intentional confusion. If the jury think there has been an intentional muddle from the start on the part of the defendant to cover up his traces, they may consider that was an important matter. No trustee or auditors were appointed.'

The judge said he thought Bottomley would have been well advised to have had the clubs' books audited, even though a firm of accountants had quoted him a fee of seven thousand guineas for this work, because he was dealing with nearly £900,000 of other people's money. 'It is for the jury to say whether a man who was taking other people's money as a trustee would not desire first . . . to make a record of the account of which he was accountable.'

SALTER, J. It is a case of a very able businessman who has received very important sums of money from people who trusted him, a man who appreciates as well as any businessman in the City of London the importance of correct accounts. Any kind of accounts . . . would have rendered it impossible for the defendant to have appropriated, honestly or dishonestly, these great sums of money without immediate detection.

Mr Justice Salter summarized the indictment as follows: Bottomley was charged with having fraudulently appropriated £17,500 from the War Stock Combination scheme; £90,000 from the Victory Bond Club; and £61,000 from the Thrift Prize Bond Club. . . . The total alleged defalcations were £170,000.

SALTER, J. . . . I should certainly suggest to the jury that when they come to consider their verdict they should . . . arrive at a general conclusion, and then go through the counts and give their verdict on each. The defence generally is that the defendant had already paid to or for the benefit of depositors more than he had withdrawn, and therefore he was not acting dishonestly, although he might have been acting irregularly.

The judge commented on Bottomley's action in withdrawing £25,000 from the Victory Bond Club account and placing it in his own account on the excuse that he did it to prevent the money being taken under the Lottery Act. But the important point was that he had spent the money on himself.

'Considerable public responsibility rests on the defendant. This case is of great public importance from the point of view of commercial morality,' Mr Justice Salter declared. 'If the mere assertions of the defendant are to be accepted as sufficient in a case of this kind in this City of London, it is difficult to see how any trust funds can be protected. . . . Look at the whole matter with cool common sense and let me know your verdict.'

Bottomley was taken 'down below' while the jury considered their verdict. He was thoroughly searched to make sure that he was not carrying a revolver or any poison on his person because the authorities did not want to risk a repetition of the Whitaker

Wright case; when Whitaker Wright was found guilty of fraud at the Old Bailey in 1903 he had taken cyanide in the dock.

The jury returned after twenty-eight minutes and Bottomley was brought back into the dock. He stood up as the jury were asked, 'Is the prisoner Guilty or Not Guilty?' The foreman of the jury replied that Bottomley was Guilty on all counts except Count Seven.

Horatio Bottomley appeared unmoved by the verdict, except that his face went slightly flushed.

SALTER, J. [*turning to Bottomley*] Horatio Bottomley, you have been rightly convicted by the jury of this long series of heartless frauds. These poor people trusted you, and you robbed them of £150,000 in ten months. The crime is aggravated by your high position, by the number and poverty of your victims, by the trust which they reposed in you and which you abused. It is aggravated by the magnitude of your frauds, and by the callous effrontery with which your frauds were committed and sought to be defended. I can see no mitigation whatsoever. The sentence of the court upon you is that you be kept in penal servitude for seven years.

Bottomley nodded his head; his face was noticeably more flushed. He asked if he could consult his solicitor with a view to giving notice of appeal.

SALTER, J. You will be allowed to consult your solicitor.

BOTTOMLEY I was under the impression, my Lord, that it was sometimes put to an accused person, 'Have you anything to say before sentence is passed on you?'

SALTER, J. It is not customary in questions of misdemeanour.

BOTTOMLEY Had it been so, my Lord, I should have had something rather offensive to say about your summing-up.

Horatio had managed to get the last word, but it was a feeble attempt to create an impression in the public mind that he had been unjustly condemned. His arms were held tightly by the Governor of Brixton Prison and a warder as they took him down to the cells.

Travers Humphreys, who had scored such a notable success by his conduct of the prosecution, had first encountered Bottomley in 1914 in connection with a *John Bull* lottery prosecution. Years later, he compared the Bottomley of 1914 to the man he sent down in 1922.*

> Bottomley behaved properly from beginning to end [1914], and as his beaten opponent I take this opportunity of saying so. . . . The fact is that in those days he was a brilliant advocate and a clever lawyer, though completely unscrupulous in his methods. . . . In truth it was not I who floored Bottomley, it was Drink. The man I met in 1922 was a drink-sodden creature whose brain would only be got to work by repeated doses of champagne.

As Horatio was driven away to prison from the back entrance of the Old Bailey the crowd outside failed to recognize their former idol. A solicitor telephoned Jimmy Hare at The Dicker to tell him that Bottomley had been given seven years. Jimmy Hare broke the tragic news to Eliza Bottomley and her daughter, Florence Cohn. By then there were hardly any staff left at The Dicker, his country mansion, because there was no money to pay their wages. It was the end of an era that had lasted for over a quarter of a century.

* Sir Travers Humphreys, *Criminal Memories* (Hodder & Stoughton, 1945).

21 Man of Yesterday

If Bottomley had been caught young and his character had been moulded to match his brains, there is no height he might not have reached in business, the law or politics.
SIR HARRY PRESTON, *Leaves from my Unwritten Diary*

The main feeling of the public will not be sympathy, but perhaps a regret that a man endowed with such abilities should not have used them for the attainment of the honourable ends of good citizenship rather than for the plunder of the humble and ignorant whom his plausibility beguiled into confidence and enthusiastic support. *The Times*, leader, July 1922

Horatio Bottomley began his prison sentence when he was sixty-two, an age when most men are on their way to retirement; long years of high living, and in particular his enormous consumption of champagne, had wrecked his constitution and he was quite unfit to face the rigours of the British prison system. When he arrived at Wormwood Scrubs in the evening they emptied his pockets and only found thirty-five pounds and two tickets for the Epsom Spring Meeting, the second item indicating that he had expected to be acquitted at the Old Bailey. He weighed seventeen stone and it was impossible to find a regulation uniform to fit this short and extremely stout man who had suddenly been toppled from his 'pinnacle'. A doctor advised him to go to bed early and he was put in a hospital cell.

A warder brought him four slices of thick bread and margarine and a repulsive-looking light brown mixture in a cup. Horatio could not bear to touch any of it. Two hours later a warder came into his cell and asked if he would like to go to bed.

'I'll wait for supper,' Bottomley said.

'*That's* your supper,' said the warder, pointing to the bread and 'cocoa'. And so Bottomley went to bed on an empty stomach on his first night at the Scrubs.

'I am a particularly gregarious beast,' Bottomley wrote later in a newspaper article.* 'I can never describe the horrors of those early days and nights in the cell—ten feet by eight, bare boards, bare walls, barred windows so high up that you could see nothing.'

Eliza Bottomley and Florence came to visit him during his first fortnight in prison. Eliza had been bowled over when she heard of his sentence and could give him little comfort. He could hardly eat any food, suffered from insomnia, and was thoroughly depressed.

Henry Houston, who was trying to raise funds for Bottomley's appeal, was finding it hard going. The man in the street had lost faith in Bottomley and felt that he richly deserved his punishment. Houston was so shattered by the downfall of his old chief that he dreaded having to see him again.

'Tell Houston I quite appreciate the spirit which prompts him to keep away, but I must see him,' Horatio told his family.

Henry Houston visited him at Wormwood Scrubs in June—only three weeks after his conviction—and was shocked at the change in Bottomley. 'He had gone completely grey, his face was ashen, his eyes heavy and lustreless. He had not been shaved for the best part of a week and even then the operation had been performed not with a razor, but with a clipper.'† He was wearing regulation trousers at least six inches too long for him, coarse prison boots, and a little forage cap. Houston, remembering how 'H.B.' always prided himself on his hand-made boots, found it pitiful to see him reduced to this state.

> The sudden change in his method of life and the absence of champagne had started their work on his physical and mental powers. . . . He was passing through the really

* *Weekly Dispatch*, 7 August 1927. † Houston.

serious period that always follows a change from heavy drinking to total abstinence.

We would probably describe Horatio today as an alcoholic who was 'drying out', but he could not possibly obtain the same sympathetic treatment at the Scrubs that he used to receive when he took the cure at Carlsbad in his heyday. On account of his huge bulk Bottomley had to rely on the warders to dress and undress him; they called him 'sir' and he called them 'my friend here'.

Houston visited him again in June to discuss final details of his appeal against the Old Bailey sentence. Houston had only managed to collect £1,700 for this purpose, but it sufficed to brief four counsel to present his case. Bottomley, deluding himself that he was going to win his appeal, told Houston to make sure that Eliza and Florence got special seats in court so that they could hear every word that was spoken on this auspicious occasion.

Meanwhile The Dicker had become a house of mourning; there was hardly one servant left, all the blinds were drawn, visitors no longer called and the place was all closed up. Jimmy Hare, who had no cash left to pay the grooms, stablemen and stable-boys, hurried up to town and called at a bank and managed to tide over the wage bill into June; but at the end of the month he had to sack all the racing staff. The little village of Upper Dicker seemed dead and deserted, and the populace grieved for the loss of its 'king'.

In June Bottomley's condition deteriorated so badly that he was sent to the prison hospital. Ernest Terah Hooley was also at Wormwood Scrubs, serving a three-year sentence for the Jubilee Cotton Mill fraud. He saw Bottomley in the exercise yard in July looking very miserable; it was his first day up.

'Buck up, B!' shouted Hooley, who was pushing round a can of some liquid.

'Buck up? Don't talk rot! What have you got there?'

'Nothing that's any good to you—it's only oatmeal water for these fellows.'

Bottomley's appeal was presented to the Court of Appeal on 5 July, and this leader appeared in *The Times*:

The main feeling of the public will not be sympathy, but

> perhaps a regret that a man endowed with such abilities should not have used them for the attainment of the honourable ends of good citizenship rather than for the plunder of the humble and ignorant whom his plausibility beguiled into confidence and enthusiastic support.

After a three-day hearing his appeal against his sentence was dismissed. The court decided that there had neither been non-direction nor misdirection by Mr Justice Salter at the Old Bailey trial. Therefore Bottomley's conviction was to stand; and having regard to the number of offences of which he had been convicted, their Lordships decided there was no reason to alter the sentence passed. This verdict left Horatio stunned; he was a broken man.

'I am very tired—very tired,' he said afterwards. 'I am glad it's all over so soon. The ordeal of silence was something terrible. There were times when I felt I must get up and speak to the judges myself.'

As a result of the verdict he was obliged to resign from the House of Commons. His letter was read out to members in silence, then Austen Chamberlain, Leader of the House, moved his expulsion. Bottomley's letter to the House had a ring of sincerity:

> I desire, first of all, to express my deep sorrow for having brought this slur on the House of Commons, which I have loved as I have loved my King and country, and to be a member of which was the dream of my youth. . . .
>
> My expulsion from the House of Commons is a punishment greater and more enduring than any sentence of any Court of Law. . . . But I have myself to blame, and all I can do is to ask members of the House to judge me as they know me . . . it is entirely due to my own fault, that I am the victim of an appalling error of justice.

Only one man had the courage to put in a good word for the people's fallen idol. Colonel John Ward, an Independent Labour M.P., said, 'I cannot allow him to be expelled from the House without expressing my personal regret at the necessity.'

He went bankrupt for the third time in March 1923 and his creditors were headed by Reuben Bigland, owed £500 for the costs of the defence at his two trials. Other creditors included the Inland Revenue and Jefferson Cohn, his ex-son-in-law. He had to sell the rest of his racehorses and it galled him to learn that they fetched less than £2,000. At the examination at Carey Street Bottomley showed some of his old spirit and energy although his right arm, afflicted with neuritis, was in a sling.

'I am not going to leave the box until I have proved that these clubs cost me £90,000 and, *if that is true, I have no right to be here*, and if it is not true, I ought to be in prison for life,' he said pugnaciously.

But when he had finished speaking he had exhausted his store of energy and sank back into a chair, a tired-looking old man with the face of an invalid.

He was recognized at Wormwood Scrubs by a convict who had been a prisoner of war in Germany and received parcels from *John Bull*. He gave Bottomley a hearty welcome and introduced him to a number of P.O.W.s who were serving sentences; Horatio soon became a popular figure in the prison. He was talking quite innocently to a Borstal boy, whose father he had known, when an old warder rebuked him.

'Bottomley, don't let me find you speaking to that boy again! Don't you know that I could get the sack if I was caught allowing a *convict* to speak to a *Borstal boy*?'

The warder's attitude upset Horatio very much, particularly as he found Borstal boys at the Scrubs more vicious than the ordinary convicts. Fortunately, he managed to retain his sense of humour. He was sewing mail-bags in his cell when the padre looked in.

'Ah, Bottomley, sewing?'

'No, padre, reaping!'

Bottomley was commissioned to write his life story for *Lloyds Sunday News*. The manuscript was smuggled out of Wormwood Scrubs by an ingenious device, and caused a great rumpus at the prison. How could it possibly have got out? Suspicion fell on the warders and two of them were dismissed.

Jimmy Hare, his trainer, came to visit him.

'Well, Guvnor, this is a nice thing you've done for us,' he said.

Bottomley's eyes twinkled for a moment. 'Ah, Jimmy, you never thought to see me in khaki, did you? Better late than never!'

He was moved from Wormwood Scrubs to Maidstone Gaol

in July 1923. Two warders escorted him across London and travelled down with him from Victoria Station; it upset his vanity that nobody recognized him at the station. And yet it was perfectly understandable: ten months of prison had made an old man of him and people did not give him a second glance.

Conditions at Maidstone were very much harder than at the Scrubs. At first he had to spend twenty-three hours of the day in his cell, with only an hour for exercise. The food was appalling; there were no knives and forks during his first year and he had to tear the meat to pieces and eat it with a section of blunt tin. This régime caused him to have terrible nightmares; it was a great relief when he was detailed to start work on book-binding in the prison workshop, although he was shocked to discover that all his workmates were criminal types; amongst them were four murderers and a man convicted of incest. Horatio was amused to hear that one man had killed his wife and then his mother-in-law.

When Bottomley retired from *John Bull* in 1921, the circulation fell from over a million to 300,000, but Julius Elias decided not to kill the paper. He changed the format and made it into a more serious and responsible weekly, commissioning articles by leading writers and politicians like Arnold Bennett and Asquith. Elias showed good judgement: by the middle of 1922 *John Bull* had climbed back to a circulation of a million. He did not visit Bottomley at Maidstone, but sent him money anonymously while he was in prison. Bottomley had regular visits from his family, and Houston and some of his friends and associates came to see him. Peggy Primrose came to see him as often as the authorities would let her.

Houston was writing a book about Bottomley. 'Be just and you will be known to history as Bottomley's Boswell,' said Horatio.

After spending a year at Maidstone Bottomley became established as a very superior person. He had gone up in the estimation of his fellow convicts after they read his life-story in a Sunday paper and, as his health improved, he began to assert what remained of his magnetic personality. He was called 'Sir' or 'Guv'nor' and did light work in the printing-shop and acquired a number of special privileges. The prison barber was a ray of sunshine to the inmates because he was so unfailingly cheerful. When Horatio went for his hair-cut in January 1924 he told the barber he was afraid he would have to serve his full seven years because the authorities had a down on him.

'I shouldn't give up hope,' said the barber. 'There's a new Home Secretary who's just reprieved a double murderer, so there's a chance for you.'

'I wonder!' sighed Bottomley.

'Give them another year and by then they'll have forgotten your case and may let you out. But anyhow, buck up—*in eleven months it's Christmas Day again!*'

When Captain Gerald Clayton became Governor of Maidstone Gaol later in the year he found that Bottomley had established himself as 'king' of the prisoners and had the warders eating out of his hand. He had been given the softest job in the prison: reading proofs in the printing shop. Clayton, believing that it would be fatal for morale to let Bottomley get away with this, deliberately changed his routine and tightened up on his discipline.

The prison barber's optimistic forecast came true. In 1927 Sir William Joynson Hicks, the Home Secretary, decided to release Bottomley from Maidstone two years early in view of his good conduct. Horatio's spirits soared as he contemplated the prospect of being released some time in August. Convinced that there had really been 'an appalling error of justice' in his conviction, he had a burning desire to put himself in the right and started to make plans for a big public demonstration on the day of his release. Tommy Cox had died soon after his trial at the Old Bailey; Horatio missed him and felt that he would have organized the whole show.

A *Daily Sketch* reporter went down to Upper Dicker on 4 July to find out how the village was reacting to Bottomley's forthcoming release.

'Bottomley was Dicker, and Dicker without him has been a sad place,' said Mrs Prevett, the stationmaster's daughter. 'Dicker has gone to pieces since Bottomley went away.'

Years ago he had built all the red cottages for the work people in the village and rented them out very reasonably. The villagers talked of decking Upper Dicker with banners and engaging the Hailsham Prize Band to welcome him home. Some of the men declared they would go to Berwick station and drag his car home in triumph.

At Maidstone Bottomley was nicknamed 'John' because of his association with *John Bull*. When the long term prisoners heard that he would soon be released, they crowded round him and said, 'Do your best for us, John.' They relied on him to use his influence in the great world outside to see that prison conditions were improved.

On 28 July Captain Clayton, the Governor, had a phone call from the Home Secretary telling him to release Bottomley the following day. The authorities considered that his early release would avoid the possibility of a public demonstration if he came out in August. Clayton, therefore, told nobody at Maidstone except his wife and asked her to cook an early breakfast for two. Next morning he called Horatio in his cell at five o'clock, and told him that his release had been put forward to this date and he would be driven straight home to The Dicker.

'I refuse to go. I am not due for release yet,' said Horatio angrily.

After an argument Clayton persuaded him to get dressed and took him along to his office. There Bottomley was handed back his 1922 set of clothes and his belongings: his black vicuna jacket and striped trousers, silk shirt, grey tie and pearl pin, silk hat, black boots and gold watch and chain. He stood before a crackling fire in his long woollen pants and vest and clapped his silk hat on his head at a rakish angle:

'I refuse to leave!' he declared. 'You have no right to send me out now. I will not dress!'*

He looked so comic standing there in his long pants and top hat that the Governor could not help smiling. Ignoring Horatio's outburst, he poured out coffee and took the covers off two plates of succulent ham and eggs. There was fresh bread and butter on the table and several kinds of jam. Horatio sniffed the marvellous aroma of his first square meal for five years—and the battle was lost. Forgetting his resolutions, he put on his clothes and tucked in to the glorious breakfast.

'All right, I'll go,' he said, 'but in every town we pass through I'll stick my head out of the car and shout to the people.'

'I don't think you will,' said Clayton. 'I'm sending my chief clerk with you'—a muscular young man who had just appeared—'and every time you try to put your head out of the window I've given him orders to hit it.'

Bottomley was driven off from Maidstone Gaol in the afternoon, accompanied by the Governor's muscular clerk, and to the best of our knowledge he never once put his head out of the car. Eliza Bottomley and Florence Cohn had no idea that he

* Gerald Clayton, *The Wall is Strong* (John Long, 1958).

was being released until the Governor phoned them to expect him for dinner.

Horatio was sixty-seven, but looked much older. It was a great joy for him to be back with his family at The Dicker, although he was upset to find Florence seriously ill. Much to his relief she recovered; there was a tremendous bond between Bottomley and his daughter and, whatever his faults, he was a most charming man in his family circle.

He had signed a contract to write a series of articles for the *Weekly Dispatch* for a fee of £12,000; his early release entailed a great rush to get the first one out for Sunday's paper. Bottomley had nothing ready except some doggerel verses called 'Songs of the Cell'. Bernard Falk, editor of the *Dispatch*, read them and turned them down.

'I want something real about your life in prison. What were you thinking about all the time you were there?' he asked.

'Thinking about! My God, all I could think about was my innocence!' said Horatio indignantly.

However, he managed to write an article in time for Sunday's paper and called it 'I have Paid, But——'. Its first paragraph explains why he chose this title; it was obvious that the old leopard had not changed his spots in five years:

> A preliminary word with the Great British Public, of a section of whom I was for so many years privileged to be the trusted mouthpiece, whose confidence it is my all-absorbing ambition to regain. . . .
>
> Whatever may have been my faults, I have *paid*—but I must assert here and now, even though they were the last words that should pass my lips—*I never owed the debt.*
>
> Two days spent in the peaceful surroundings of my country home have helped to bring me back to a sense of reality. . . . I find myself a more convinced fatalist than ever before: and I speak the solemn truth when I say that all that has happened 'was to be'.
>
> Let no man prate of human affairs until he has seen humanity in all its phases. And no man can possibly know his fellow creatures until he has been initiated into the mysteries of that walled-in world in which I have been hidden for the past five years.

Later in the article he quoted a new music-hall song about himself:

Then welcome home to Bottomley,
Deny it if you can,
He played his part; he's right at heart—
And every inch a man.

'That chorus will do very well for my epitaph.'

In the articles that followed he managed to work in some of the verses from his 'Songs of the Cell'. 'Convict 13' began as follows:

13 upon his cap and coat
The Man identifies
(A number now—and once a name!)
At work or exercise.

A First Offender (legal slang)
His coat and cap are starred,
His finger prints and photograph
Are filed at Scotland Yard.

In convicts' cell! in felon's garb,
His sentence seven years,
Perchance a sigh, but ne'er a sob,
The wound's too deep for tears.

These lines will suffice to show that it was feeble stuff, even as doggerel. His articles for the *Dispatch* revolved round his experiences in prison and he wrote quite seriously on 'What Is Wrong With British Prisons'. But they were of inferior quality and it is no wonder that the series petered out after two months. Horatio seemed to have no idea that the world had moved on fast since 1922 and that by 1927 the Great War, in which he had played his big role, was half-forgotten by many ordinary people, absorbed with the effort of trying to grapple with post-war problems. He imagined that everybody would welcome him with open arms after his period of 'martyrdom'; it took him a long time to brace himself to stand the shock when former friends and associates cut him dead.

He had made certain arrangements through his friend Sir Harry Preston for Peggy Primrose to receive a small income while he was away in prison. When he came out she cheered him up through his attacks of depression; he was never happier than when in her company at her flat in Bedford Court Mansions. Peggy once said that Bottomley's trouble was 'he fancied he was walking on a red carpet that stretched into infinity', and she knew him better than anybody else.

Dr Percy Vosper became the family doctor on Bottomley's release from Maidstone; he had already attended Eliza and Florence. The doctor's daughter, Margery, was a bonny, buxom schoolgirl of fifteen when she attended a tennis-party at The Dicker. Horatio took her by the hand and introduced her to his guests: 'Allow me to present Miss Betty Nuthall.'

As Betty Nuthall was the tennis prodigy of the twenties poor Margery Vosper was expected to beat all comers, and her tennis was not of a very high standard. After she had lost the first set her partner asked, 'Are you going to the South of France this summer?' The Vospers were lucky if they even got to Margate for their holidays, and Margery blurted out that she was not Betty Nuthall—Mr Bottomley had been pulling their legs. Horatio, very angry at being exposed, called her a spoilsport.

Bottomley could hardly ever resist dropping a name. When Dr Vosper had to hurry away from lunch one afternoon to visit his patient Sir Douglas Hogg at Hailsham, Horatio shouted after him, 'Give my love to Douglas!' The doctor rather naïvely passed on the message to Sir Douglas (later to become Lord Hailsham), who was furious. 'How dare that scoundrel send me a message?' he demanded.

Margery became a frequent visitor to The Dicker. Eliza always made her welcome but Margery Vosper noted that she had a limited mentality and seemed out of things, usually burying herself in a cheap Ethel M. Dell novel. Her daughter, Florence Cohn, was then in her forties: dark, amiable and extremely stout she was the wreck of a beautiful woman. Like her father, she unfortunately drank too much. However, it must have been a great handicap for any girl to be brought up in the happy-go-lucky atmosphere of The Dicker while her mother was away in France. Margery Vosper never saw Florence standing up: she was always either resting in her bedroom or reclining on a sofa.

The family had enormous appetites. As well as breakfast, lunch, dinner and tea they indulged in lobster sandwiches at eleven o'clock; as he passed them through the hatch into the dining-room Louis Flower would say, 'Goodbye—Greedy Guts has got you.'

Mrs Beyfus, the cook-housekeeper, rather despised her 'nouveaux riches' employers, but Louis Flower was genuinely fond of the family and never minded if he had to wait a long time for his wages. Sometimes Bottomley would even ask the butler to lend him a fiver for pressing household bills. Once when playing billiards with Dr Vosper he said casually, 'You haven't got a hundred pounds on the loose, Percy?' But the simple country doctor was not quite as simple as that.

Margery Vosper remembers Peggy Primrose coming to The Dicker for a week-end—the first time she had ever seen Bottomley's 'light of love'. 'She was a kind, sweet little woman, not at all actressy. I took an instant liking to her, and couldn't help wondering how such a charming little person could have fallen for an old reprobate like Bottomley. In fact, I never could understand what had been so magical about this fat old charlatan.'*

There is something pathetic about the last phase of Horatio Bottomley's life and one should not prolong the agony. He had remained a super-optimist and refused to admit that his day was over. He planned to start another newspaper and nobody could convince him that the old format of *John Bull* was as dead as the dodo. He persuaded a few of his old friends, including Tanqueray Todd, to back it. Many of its features were taken from *John Bull* and, to underline this, he called the paper *John Blunt*. Peggy Primrose and most of his friends begged him to abandon the new project, but he was determined to show the public that he could make a come-back.

He rented expensive offices in Grosvenor Gardens and engaged W. G. Pilley, who had been editing the new *John Bull*, and several of his former staff. *John Blunt* first appeared on 16 June 1928; a slavish copy of the old *John Bull*, it had even retained 'The World, the Flesh and the Devil', which Bottomley had originated in the *Sun* in 1902. It proclaimed itself 'the Tribune of the Man in the Street' and 'the Champion of the Under Dog', titles to which Horatio no longer had any claim. Besides being an anachronism *John Blunt* was also extremely dull. Fleet Street gasped at Bottomley's nerve in daring to try and foist such an inferior paper on the public, and he had great difficulty in getting any advertising because people felt it would never last.

Henry Houston's book about his old chief, *The Real Horatio Bottomley*, has already been mentioned. In one chapter Houston described how Bottomley made a practice of attacking big firms in *John Bull* in order to force them to advertise in the

* Margery Vosper, conversations with author.

paper; one of them was J. Lyons of the famous tea-shops. In 1929 Bottomley suddenly became vindictive towards Houston and sued him for libel on the grounds that he implied that Bottomley had blackmailed firms to advertise in *John Bull*. Bottomley won the case and was awarded damages of £1,500, but it was a hollow victory. Houston had no money and could not pay the damages and the case, instead of whitewashing Horatio's reputation, only stirred up a lot of mud.

Bottomley announced in September that he was leaving England to go on a grand lecture tour of the British Empire. The readers of *John Blunt* were informed that since he would be away for a long time the paper would only be published monthly till his return. It was a feeble attempt to save his face; *John Blunt* closed down in October, having lost money steadily all the time.

His grand lecture tour began in South Africa—and ended there. At his opening lecture in Cape Town Bottomley had the bitter experience of failing to hold the attention of an audience. South Africans were not in the least interested in listening to an old man reminiscing about his palmy days in the Great War and the Edwardian period; it was the same story when he lectured at Johannesburg. The lecture tour, therefore, had to be abandoned and Horatio returned home a disappointed man.

Eliza Bottomley died at The Dicker on 7 February 1930; Horatio and Florence were at her bedside at the end. His daughter had become secretly engaged to Gilbert Moreland, a South African planter who had been staying at The Dicker. Moreland was younger than Florence and she found him much easier to get on with than her first husband, Jefferson Cohn, who had remarried in 1921. Florence and Moreland were married at Eastbourne Register Office a week after her mother's death. Horatio was not present at the event, probably because he felt they ought not to have got married so soon; it was typical of him to have these strange twists of respectability.

Perhaps it was just as well that Eliza had died and that Florence went off to make a new life in South Africa, for there was no future in England for Bottomley. The failure of *John Blunt* and a fresh crop of debts forced him to go bankrupt for the fourth time. When he was examined at Carey Street he still managed to put up a front, but who could believe him as he harked back to the money he ought to have made from his grand lecture tour of the Empire? He said he had been offered 'an extensive lecture tour of the U.S. and the British Dominions with £100,000 assured for his creditors', but the harsh immigration laws had wrecked his chances of giving lectures in Canada and the States. At the end of his long, self-pitying speech he admitted the brutal truth:

'Ever since my return home . . . I have had to suffer a cruel boycott . . . and the result is that, at the age of seventy, I have to start practically all over again.'

As a result of his bankruptcy he lost The Dicker for ever. It went to Jefferson Cohn, his ex-son-in-law, in settlement of many outstanding debts. Fortunately, Peggy Primrose remained loyal to him and took him to live at her flat. He had had several thromboses since being released from Maidstone and she had nursed him through them. He had lost weight and become a husk of his old self, but he had to try and do something. He applied for bookings for lectures in the big towns in the provinces, and was upset to hear that most of the town halls in Britain had banned him. He made regular calls on Fleet Street editors to try and persuade them to commission a series of articles, but they had lost interest in Bottomley and only published an occasional article by him. What a humiliation for the man who had once been the highest-paid journalist in Britain!

Peggy Primrose felt it was important for his morale to get some kind of job and thought of the music halls. Through a mutual friend she got Bottomley an introduction to the Windmill Theatre and Vivian Van Damm decided to engage him. He appeared there in September 1932; this melancholy notice appeared in the *Daily News*:

> The strangest turn in the new non-stop variety programme at the Windmill Theatre last night was the appearance of an old man in a dinner suit who walked slowly to the middle of the stage and cast a sad and patient eye upon a puzzled audience. He was billed as 'Revuedeville in Excelsis: Horatio Bottomley'.
>
> In a quiet manner that compelled attention he told a little string of anecdotes from his Parliamentary, journalistic, racing and legal experiences. As it went on, it became apparent that some of his old magnetism remained. . . . But the occasion had a curiously disconcerting air of pathos.

The hard-boiled audience had only come to ogle the Windmill girls in their semi-nudity and to hear some risqué jokes.

Then a broken old man in a seedy dinner suit stumbled on to the stage and began telling stories about himself, boasting of the part he had played on the home front during the war. Soon there were titters from the audience and a few people walked out, but he still droned on with his stale anecdotes. It seemed incredible that this pathetic specimen of humanity could once have been Horatio Bottomley, the great spellbinder.

Peggy Primrose realized that she had made an awful mistake in getting him the engagement at the Windmill. She read in a paper that 'Mr Bottomley spoke as well as ever, but there was no return from St Helena', and burst into tears. She was wondering if it would be possible for him to break his contract at the Windmill when he collapsed on the stage one night and was rushed to the Middlesex Hospital. It was a heart attack. Peggy Primrose stayed at his bedside day and night; to everybody's surprise he recovered. She took him home to her flat, and for a few months he kept busy entertaining the children at Masonic functions.

In April 1933 the Press reported that Bottomley had applied for an old-age pension on the grounds that he had earned it for his war services. It was a humiliating thing to have to do, but the tired old man had come to the end of his resources. Unfortunately, the authorities turned down his application, which was a bitter blow to his pride.

Reuben Bigland read about his plight and wrote and offered him £1 a week for life and a little cottage at Stratford-on-Avon. Horatio replied to his old enemy, suggesting they should meet and discuss the matter; then at the last moment he changed his mind.

'I could not with self-respect entertain the idea,' he told a friend. 'One can be the guest of the State without loss of self-esteem, but to become the protégé of Mr Bigland is a different proposition.'

He collapsed again in May and was taken to the Middlesex Hospital and put in the Prince Francis Ward, suffering from cerebral thrombosis caused by arteriosclerosis. Peggy Primrose stayed with him at the hospital, although there was little hope of his recovery. He survived an operation, then had a sudden stroke; after being unconscious for many hours he died at eleven o'clock at night.

His last words, spoken to Peggy Primrose before he lost consciousness were: 'Good-bye and God bless you. I'll see you again tomorrow.'

When the news of Bottomley's death was announced the public suddenly remembered their fallen idol. Many people attended his funeral at Golders Green Crematorium; some of the mourners were his friends, yet a surprising number were men and women who had never met Bottomley but had acquired an affection for him after hearing him speak. The service was conducted by an old friend, the Rev. Basil Bourchier, rector of St Annes, Soho, who had always overlooked Horatio's faults and held a high opinion of him.

'I hope that no one here today will forget what Mr Bottomley did to revive the spirits of our men at the Front,' said Bourchier.

Many women were in tears at the end of his address. Peggy Primrose, who had paid for the funeral, sent a circlet of red roses with the message: *Rest, beloved. I am so happy you have worked out the Karma. Gini.* She was so overcome with grief that she broke down as the coffin was borne away.

The obituary in the *Daily Mail* next day probably reflected the feelings of the man in the street:

> What opportunities he had, but how sadly they were wasted! His gifts were brilliant. He had personal magnetism, eloquence, enthusiasm, and the power to convince.
>
> He might have been a leader at the Bar, a captain of industry, a great journalist. He might have been almost anything, but for one fatal defect, known for want of a better word as a 'kink', which misdirected his efforts.

The 'kink' was his self-centred way of life and his colossal selfishness. A clergyman preached a sermon about Bottomley and claimed that he had ruined himself by ignoring the divine teaching that 'Man was brought into the world to serve and assist his fellow men'.

Anyone who studies the career of Horatio Bottomley is bound to agree with this, but selfishness was only one of his besetting sins: vanity was another major cause of his downfall. Horatio only acknowledged this fault in himself when it was too late and he had been to prison. 'I am satisfied that vanity was the principal cause of my trouble,' he said. 'I have always liked flattery. I have revelled in holding court to an army of thirsty sycophants*—most of my respectable acquaintances were so dull!'

* A reference to the many men in Bottomley's stable who virtually lived off him.

Peggy Primrose, discussing Bottomley after his death, revealed another fault. 'He was an incurable optimist. And he was incredibly vain. These two things were his downfall.'

Of course Horatio Bottomley was selfish and vain and a fatuous optimist, and he was also greedy—so greedy that he swindled humble men and women and the ex-servicemen who trusted him with their savings and bamboozled the gullible people who invested in his companies and his lotteries. The other weakness which must be included in an assessment was his passion for champagne; during the war he came to depend on it just like a drug addict hooked on heroin and it was champagne that gradually destroyed his wonderful brain.

When one looks back on his long record as a swindler, beginning with the Hansard Union in 1890, it is astonishing that he escaped a prison sentence for so long. Horatio fully realized how lucky he had been and once told Ernest Hooley: 'I have been sitting on a keg of gunpowder for years and it might go up at any moment.'

At the outbreak of the First World War Bottomley assured Henry Houston that he had resolved to turn over a new leaf and wipe out his sordid past, but high living and his vicious circle of debts drove him to find ways of making money quickly and in a few months he forgot all about his good intentions. The war transformed Bottomley into a great demagogue through *John Bull* and his *Sunday Pictorial* articles and his patriotic lectures. He became the most successful recruiting speaker in Britain and played a great part in keeping up the morale of the people. If only he could have gone straight after 1914, and had had the self-discipline to stop gambling on horses and live within his huge income, the authorities might have overlooked his disreputable past. He might have remained a popular idol and even have died solvent.

It is worth speculating on what might have happened to Horatio Bottomley if he had never been sent away to Mason's orphange at the age of nine, but had been brought up as one of the family by the Holyoakes. And what would have happened if he had not married Eliza when he was only twenty? I think it might have made all the difference to his life. Those five years at the orphanage at Erdington almost crushed the spirit of Horatio, and by the time he left he had evolved a private world of fantasy from which he never escaped. His tendency to lie and try to wriggle his way out of every awkward predicament probably originated there too. When he suddenly became a rich man in the nineties, after years of hard times, success went to his head and he started spending money like a drunken sailor and could never break the habit. The Holyoakes refused to be responsible for him after he impulsively got married without telling them. The only person who might have brought him to his senses was his wife, Eliza; it was a great misfortune that she was a silly woman who had less influence on him than his favourite collie dog.

There is a sad little epilogue to his story. A clause in his will stated that he wished his ashes 'to be scattered on the gallops of Alfriston on the Sussex Downs', and it was left to Peggy Primrose to carry out this final request. But in 1937, four years after his death, a newspaper reported that his ashes still remained at Tarbuk's, the undertakers. Mr Tarbuk had not heard from Peggy Primrose for two years and Florence, Bottomley's invalid daughter, was living abroad. Tarbuk therefore got in touch with his nephew, Bertie Dollman. When Bertie Dollman arrived at the undertakers in Clerkenwell to collect the urn containing Bottomley's ashes there was an urgent message to ring Peggy Primrose. He phoned up and Peggy entreated him to bring the urn to her flat.

She was living in genteel poverty in a top floor flat in Henry Street, St John's Wood. Bertie Dollman found her looking ill; she would have passed for a woman in her sixties.

'Bertie, don't go today. I must come with you!' she said pleadingly. 'I have been very ill since he died and other things have happened to me.'

Peggy Primrose, the only woman Horatio had really loved, was too proud to admit how desperately poor she had been since he died. He had lavished expensive presents and jewellery on her in his heyday, but everything had gone; she was not fit to work and there was nobody she could call on to help her.

Bertie Dollman, unlike the rest of the family, thought a great deal of Peggy Primrose and appreciated the delicacy of her position. He left the urn at her flat and departed.

A few weeks later they drove down to Alfriston together and scattered Bottomley's ashes on the gallops on the Sussex Downs, just as he had requested.

Bibliography

Books about Bottomley

BIGLAND, REUBEN. *Horatio Bottomley*. Farwood, 1922.

BLATHWAYS, RAYMOND. *Horatio Bottomley: the man as he is today*. Odhams, 1916.

BOTTOMLEY, HORATIO. *Bottomley's Book*. Odhams, 1909.

FELSTEAD, THEODORE. *Horatio Bottomley*. Hutchinson, 1936.

HOUSTON, HENRY. *The Real Horatio Bottomley*. Hurst & Blackett, 1923.

SYMONS, JULIAN. *Horatio Bottomley*. Cressett Press, 1955.

'TENAX'. *The Gentle Art of Exploiting Gullibility*. David Weir, 1923.

Other Sources

BIRKENHEAD, LORD. *Frederick Edwin, Earl of Birkenhead*. Thornton Butterworth, 1933.

BIRON, SIR CHARTRES. *Without Prejudice*. Faber, 1936.

BRADLAUGH BONNER, HYPATIA and ROBERTSON, J. M. *Charles Bradlaugh*. T. Fisher Unwin, 1894.

BUNCE, J. T. *Josiah Mason*. Birmingham, 1882.

CHURCHILL, RANDOLPH. *Lord Derby*. Heinemann, 1959.

CLAYTON, GERALD. *The Wall is Strong*. John Long, 1958.

COCHRAN, SIR CHARLES. *The Secrets of a Showman*. Heinemann, 1925.

DEGHY, GUY. *Paradise in the Strand*. Richards Press, 1958.

GILBERT, MARTIN. *The Roots of Appeasement*. Weidenfeld, 1966.

HARRIS, FRANK. *My Life and Loves*. Obelisk Press, Paris, 1934.

HUMPHREYS, SIR TRAVERS. *Criminal Days*. Hodder, 1946.

JACKSON, STANLEY. *The Great Barnato*. Heinemann, 1970.

JENKINS, ROY. *Asquith*. Collins, 1964.
MACCABE, JOSEPH. *George Jacob Holyoake*. London, 1922.
MARWICK, ARTHUR. *The Deluge*. Bodley Head, 1965.
MINNEY, R. J. *Viscount Southwood*. Odhams, 1954.
NICHOLS, BEVERLEY. *25*. Cape, 1926.
PANKHURST, SYLVIA. *The Home Front*. Hutchinson, 1934.
POUND, REGINALD and HARMSWORTH, A. G. *Northcliffe*. Cassell, 1959.
PRESTON, SIR HARRY. *Leaves from my Unwritten Diary*. Hutchinson, 1935.
TAYLOR, A. J. *Politics in Wartime*. Hamish Hamilton, 1964.
TRIBE, DAVID. *President Charles Bradlaugh*. Elek, 1971.

Times Law Reports

Hansard Union trial (30 January to 26 April 1893)
Joint Stock Trust trial (1 December 1908 to 13 March 1909)
Reuben Bigland's trials:
  Bow Street (8 October 1921)
  Old Bailey (23 January 1922)
  Shropshire Assizes (18 February 1922)
Horatio Bottomley's trial (19 May 1922)

Index